Making Your
Data Center
Energy Efficient

*How to Save Big on
Data Center Energy Costs*

Making Your Data Center Energy Efficient

*How to Save Big on
Data Center Energy Costs*

Gilbert Held

CRC Press
Taylor & Francis Group
Boca Raton London New York

CRC Press is an imprint of the
Taylor & Francis Group, an **informa** business
AN AUERBACH BOOK

CRC Press
Taylor & Francis Group
6000 Broken Sound Parkway NW, Suite 300
Boca Raton, FL 33487-2742

Printed in the United States of America on acid-free paper
Version Date: 20110728

International Standard Book Number: 978-1-4398-5553-9 (Paperback)

Visit the Taylor & Francis Web site at
http://www.taylorandfrancis.com

and the CRC Press Web site at
http://www.crcpress.com

Teaching graduate school courses in various aspects of data communications and HTML coding over the past decade has been a two-way street with respect to the transfer of knowledge. Thus, it is with a considerable sense of gratitude for their inquisitive minds that I dedicate this book to the students at Georgia College and State University.

Contents

PREFACE   xiii

ACKNOWLEDGMENTS   xvii

CHAPTER 1   RATIONALE FOR ENERGY CONSERVATION AND
ITS FINANCIAL IMPLICATIONS   1

The Cost of Energy   2

    Energy and Power   2

    Units of Power   2

    BTUs and Horsepower   3

Comparing Energy   5

    Oil, Gas, and Electric Costs   5

      The Cost of Oil   5

      The Cost of Natural Gas   8

      The Cost of Electricity   9

Financial Metrics   10

    The Return on Investment (ROI)   10

      ROI Analysis   12

    What Is Time Value?   14

      Future Value Basics   14

    Future Value Interest Factors   16

    Present Value Basics   17

Annuities   19

    Payment Frequency   20

    Types of Annuities   20

    Determining the Future Value of an Ordinary Annuity   20

Present Value of an Annuity   22
Considering Monthly Cash Flows   23
Annuity Due   25
Annuity Notations   26
Payback Period   26
Discounted Cash Flow   27
Weighted Average Cost of Capital   27
Internal Rate of Return   30
Computing the IRR   31
Using Excel   33
NPV Functions in Excel   34
ROI Functions in Excel   35
IRR Summary   36
Summary   37

CHAPTER 2   UNDERSTANDING ELECTRICAL TERMS   39
Understanding Electricity   40
Atoms and Electrons   40
Electric Generators   40
Turbines   42
Circuit Measurements   42
Circuits   43
Electrical Power   44
Direct Current versus Alternating Current   46
Direct Current (DC)   47
The Power Supply   48
Power Supply Types   48
Operation   49
Phase   49
Power Rating   50
Meters to Consider   51
AC Measurements to Consider   51
RMS   51
Power Factor (PF)   53
Importance of the Power Factor   53
Ground   54
Electricity Distribution   57
The Power Plant   57
Transformers   57
Types of Transformers   60
Transformer Wiring   60
Service Methods   60
Single Phase versus Three Phase   62
The Service Panel   64
Types of Service Panels   65
Operation   66

Inside the Service Panel 68
Building Service Panel 68
Circuits 69
Types of Circuits 70
Individual Circuits 71
Plugs and Sockets 71
Office Plugs and Sockets 72
UPS 74
Standby Generators 76
Selecting a Generator 78

CHAPTER 3 GENERAL HEATING AND COOLING
CONSIDERATIONS 79
Climate Control Systems 80
Ventilation 81
Heating Systems 82
Forced-Air Systems 82
Boilers 83
Rating/Capacity 83
Radiant Heating Systems 84
Heat Pumps 85
SEER and HSPF Ratings 86
Types of Heat Pumps 87
Hybrid Heat Pump 89
Solar-Assisted Heat Pump 89
Dual Fuel Heat Pump 90
Air-Source Heat Pump 92
Geothermal Heat Pumps 92
Electric Resistance Heating 95
Types of Electric Resistance Heaters 95
Radiators 97
Steam Heating 97
Hot Water Radiators 98
Hot Water Heaters 99
Types of Water Heaters 99
Conventional Tank Storage Water Heaters 100
Tankless Water Heaters 101
Indirect Water Heaters 102
Cooling Systems 103
Central Air Conditioners 103
Types of Central Air Conditioners 104
Sizing 105
Cost Comparison 105
Other Features to Consider 106
Heat Pump Cooling 107

Chillers   107
    Use in Air-Conditioning   108
    Types of Chillers   108
    Classification   110
  Factors to Consider   112
    Rapid Restart Capability   112
    Operating Multiple Chillers   112
    Checking the Refrigerant Line   113
    Optimize Cooling during Cold Weather   113
    Examine Ductworks   114
    Examining Air Filters   114
    Heating and Cooling Items to Consider   115
  Considering the Long Term   115

CHAPTER 4   READING AND UNDERSTANDING YOUR
            ELECTRIC, GAS, AND WATER METERS   119
  The Electric Meter   119
    Electric Meter Categories   119
    Examining the Electric Meter   120
  Reading an Electric Meter   125
    Load Meters   126
    Recording Data   127
      Operation   128
    Digital "Smart" Meters   128
  Smart Meters and the Smart Grid   129
    Reading the Smart Meter Display   130
    Smart Meter Problems   132
    Standards   133
    Possible Causes of Billing Inaccuracies   134
    Why Rates Matter   137
  The Natural Gas Meter   138
    Types of Gas Meters   138
    Meter Reading   139
    Estimating the Monthly Gas Bill   141
  The Water Meter   143
    Locate Your Meter   143
    Water Bills   145
    Abnormalities in the Water Bill   147
    Smart Water Meters   149

CHAPTER 5   DATA CENTER EQUIPMENT ENERGY
            CONSUMPTION   151
  Operational Modes to Consider   152
    Power Loads   152
  Commonsense Items to Consider   154
    Obtain Smart Power Strips   154
    Check Cell Phone Charger Ratings   154
    Unplug Rarely Used Devices   155

Ensure Monitors Are Turned Off When Not Used   155
Turn Off or Place Computers in a Standby Mode   156
Favor Energy Star Equipment   157
General Cost Computations   158
Device Consumption   159
Varying the Cost per kWh   161
Servers   162
Computer Memory   163
Rack Pack Considerations   165
Communications Equipment   165
Cisco 3750 Series   167
Cisco StackPower and EnergyWise Technology   168
Other Techniques to Reduce Energy Consumption   171
Fan Speed Considerations   171
Rack Placement and Cooling Considerations   171
Available Calculators   176

CHAPTER 6   MINIMIZING COMPUTER ENERGY CONSUMPTION   179
Sleep Mode Considerations   179
Power Options   180
Accessing Power Options   180
Editing a Power Plan   183
CPU States   185
Advanced Settings   186
Processor Power Management   189
Display   191
Multimedia Settings   191
Computer Power Efficiency   192
Accessing the Command Prompt   192
Examining an Energy Report   200
Wake-on-LAN   207
Enabling Wake-on-LAN in Windows   207
Wake-on-LAN Capabilities   208
Limitations   209
Wireless Network Use   209
Delivery Confirmation   210
Security Issues   210
Specific Computer Linkage
                                                      210

CHAPTER 7   MAKING YOUR DATA CENTER ENERGY
             EFFICIENT   213
Techniques to Consider   213
Finding Energy Loss   213
Replacing Monitors   214
Waiting Area Display   215
Upgrading the Operating System   216
Purchase Energy Star Compliant Products   217

Consolidation and Virtualization   217
Telework   219
Consider Cloud Computing   219
Consider Desktop and Server Power Management
Products   220
Consider Processor Efficiency   221
Consider Data Storage Consolidation   223
Examine IT Hardware Utilization   223
Consider Higher Voltage Power Distribution   224
Utilize Wireless Humidity and Temperature
Transmitters   224
Minimize Phantom Energy Loss   226
Use Energy-Efficient Motors   227
Examine Airflow   228
Reduce Air Handler Operations When Not Necessary   228
Controlling the Power Factor   228
Use Caulking and Weather-Stripping to Block
Air Leaks   229
Consider a Chargeback Policy That Includes
Energy Cost   230
Consider Increases in Electricity Cost   230
Water Considerations   231
Examine Water Heater Settings   231
Examine Water Usage   231
Replacing Lighting   232
Lumens   233
Watts as a Measurement Tool   233
Lumens per Watt and Lux   234
Determining Watt Dissipation   235
Luminous Energy   236
Illuminance   236
Lighting Efficiency   236
Color Temperature   237
Representative Lighting Color Temperature   238
Comparing Lighting   238
Building Management Areas to Consider   244
Consider Adding Insulation   244
How Insulation Works   245
Types of Insulation   245
Rating Insulation   246
Changing the Building Roof Color   246
Use Reusable Filters   247
Consider Electric Vehicles   247

INDEX   249

Preface

The goal of this book is to inform building managers, IT personnel, and networking specialists of methods to reduce the cost associated with operating a data center. Unlike books that look at a data center from the point of sizing electrical requirements to operate equipment, by examining both equipment and building facilities this book focuses on minimizing the costs associated with the energy required to properly manage all aspects of the energy consumed in operating the data center. In addition, for readers not well versed in either financial or energy terms, the first two chapters in this book provide a detailed discussion of how to compute the return on your investment associated with minimizing the consumption of energy and the terms associated with different types of energy.

The development of the World Wide Web resulted in a considerable effect not only upon how we purchase items and review financial information from the comfort of our homes and offices as well as by the manner in which we perform numerous work-related activities but, in addition, the near-exponential growth in so-called server farms. Today it is common for many organizations to have data centers filled to the brim with a variety of different servers, ranging from mainframes and dedicated Web servers to a variety of blade servers. What these data centers have in common is a tremendous appetite for energy. In fact, many trade publications now recognize the importance of energy-saving initiatives and devote either a column or a section of their publication to this topic, and other publications periodically publish a special issue focused upon one or more energy topics.

Although few organizations were concerned with the cost of operating a data center a decade ago, due to the skyrocketing cost of energy the operational cost of data centers is now a common consideration. In this book we examine a variety of techniques that can be used to reduce this cost. Some techniques examine lighting and when possible, insulation, whereas other techniques focus attention upon equipment. All techniques can have a considerable effect upon the cost of operating a data center, especially because reducing heat generated by equipment can have a dual effect during the cooling season. That is, in summer months when cooling requires air conditioners to run for extended periods of time the reduction in heat generated by equipment and even lighting has a dual effect: less heat in a data center requires a lower amount of air conditioning. Simply said, reducing heat generation not only directly saves energy but can indirectly save on the cost of heat removal.

In this book I first carefully review the rationale for conserving energy. In addition to political correctness, we learn how conservation and careful equipment selection can affect the corporate bottom line. Because readers will have a mixture of background and work experience, I carefully review a variety of terms to ensure we have a common understanding of their meaning and use. Next, I devote a chapter to one of the least-understood topics that most people are vaguely familiar with, general heating and cooling considerations. The reader may not have direct control over the selection of a furnace or hot water heater; however, it's important to be able to recognize the efficiency and inefficiency of different types of devices so that if the occasion arises you may be able to have a degree of input into the decision-making process.

In another chapter I examine the techniques required to effectively monitor different types of meters. Most attention today is focused upon so-called smart meters that have two-way communication capability; however, there are tens of millions of "dumb meters" that when properly read can provide you with an insight to the consumption of energy and methods you can consider to reduce your energy consumption.

Because products from different vendors commonly perform similar functionality but consume different amounts of electricity, we turn our attention to this topic in another chapter. Once this is accomplished we devote a chapter to considering how to minimize the energy consumption of different devices. Within the past few years the Apple iPhone, Blackberry Storm2, and other smart cell phones incorporating browser software now allow these activities to be performed while on the go. In addition, a new generation of small WiFi devices ranging in size from mini-notebooks that weigh a few pounds to devices that can fit in your shirt pocket enable these activities to be performed from coffee shops, sandwich shops, airports, and hotel rooms and lobbies without incurring the cost of monthly data plans. Although these gadgets certainly improve employee performance, one little-known fact is that when charging such devices they may consume collectively a substantial amount of "phantom energy," which some utilities refer to as "vampire voltage" and which can substantially elevate an organization's electrical bill. Thus, this author would be remiss if he did not cover this topic. Thus, in addition to devoting an entire chapter to methods that you can use to make your data center more efficient I also discuss phantom energy as well as methods that can be used to minimize its cost to the organization.

In Chapter 5 readers will encounter Tables 5.2 and 5.3 of the monthly expense associated with operating equipment. These tables convert many problems into a simple table lookup process, inasmuch as the cost of operating equipment is based upon the number of hours used per day and the operating cost of electricity. Concerning the latter, because the cost of electricity can vary considerably from one location to another, this author produced the tables in Chapter 5 using a kilowatt hour (kWh) cost varying from 5 cents to 25 cents, which includes the most efficient and least costly billing found to the most expensive billing encountered.

As a professional author who writes on technology-related topics I am interested in and with which I experiment, I highly value reader feedback. You can either write me via my publisher whose mailing address is in this book or you can send an e-mail to me directly at gil_held@yahoo.com. Let me know if I spent too much or too little effort covering a particular topic, if I should have included another aspect of data center energy efficiency in this book, or any other comments you wish to share with me. Because I frequently travel I may not be able to respond to you overnight, but I will make every effort to respond to your comments within a reasonable period of time. Because many previous comments and suggestions concerning other books I wrote made their way into subsequent editions, it's quite possible that your comments will have a role in shaping the scope of coverage of a future edition of this book.

Gilbert Held
Macon, Georgia

Acknowledgments

The creation of the book you are reading represents a team effort even though there is only the name of this author on its binding and cover. From the acceptance of a proposal to the creation of a manuscript, from the proofing of the manuscript to the printing of proofs, and from the correction of page proof typos and errors to the creation of cover art and the printing of this book many individuals contributed a considerable amount of time and effort. Thus, I would be remiss if I did not acknowledge the effort of several persons as well as the CRC Press publication team that resulted in the book you are reading.

Once again, I am indebted to Rich O'Hanley, publisher at CRC Press, Taylor & Francis Group, for agreeing to back another one of my research and writing projects.

Due to a considerable amount of travel, I realized many years ago that it was easier to write a book the old-fashioned way using pen and paper than to attempt to use a laptop or notebook when faced with circular, rectangular, square, and other odd-ball electrical receptacles that could vary from one side of a city to another. Once again, I am indebted to my wife Beverly for her fine effort in converting my handwritten chapters into a professional manuscript.

In concluding this series of acknowledgments I would like to take the opportunity to thank all of the "behind the scenes" workers at CRC Press. From the creation of page proofs to the finished book I truly appreciate all of your efforts.

1

RATIONALE FOR ENERGY CONSERVATION AND ITS FINANCIAL IMPLICATIONS

The purpose of this chapter is to develop a firm understanding of conserving energy. As we probe into this topic we show that although it is important to save money, the conservation of energy also represents a mechanism to extend the life of equipment as well as provide additional savings by reducing cooling necessary to keep the temperature in a data center at a relatively low level. Because many times during the decision-making process it's important to evaluate different equipment, we need to be aware of the time value of money. Doing so provides us with a mechanism to compare the lease versus purchase of equipment as well as different types of contracts. Thus, we examine such financial terms as interest, interest on interest, the compound value interest factor (CVIF), the present value interest factor (PVIF), and how to compute the return on investment (ROI) by expending funds to conserve energy. As a friend once said, "You need to spend money to make money," but by computing the ROI, payback period, and the internal rate of return (IRR) you can determine if expending funds is a financially viable method. As we note later in this chapter, there are several financial metrics we can compute, with each having a variety of strengths and weaknesses. Because our focus is upon conserving energy, we need to have a viable understanding of the role different metrics play in our economic analysis and we do so in this chapter. Now that we know where we are going, it's time to grab a can of soda or a bottle of water and your favorite munchies while we begin to explore the rationale for conserving energy.

The Cost of Energy

In this section we turn our attention to the cost of energy. Because it is important that all readers have a common background, we first briefly describe what the term means as well as several other energy-related terms, such as joules, British thermal units (BTUs), and horsepower; the latter probably very familiar to those who work with automobiles. Although we probe much deeper into energy-related terms and especially electricity which powers just about every data center, for now we focus our attention upon obtaining a common background in energy-related terms.

Energy and Power

The word "energy" is derived from the Greek word *energeia* and represents a scalar physical quantity that can be assigned to objects and particles. There are different types of energy, such as thermal energy, sound energy, light energy, and electromagnetic energy. This last one is probably familiar to readers who sat through a high school physics class and used their right hand to determine the direction of the magnetic field when current flowed in a direction where they raised their fist so that their thumb was the current and the curved fingers represented the electromagnetic field. In the International System of Units, energy is measured in joules, however, most persons are familiar with energy represented by kilowatt hours (kWh) on their monthly electric bill. In actuality, the term kWh on your electric bill represents the power your home or office consumed. We probe considerably deeper into technology in Chapter 2, but for now it's important to understand that from a technical perspective, power is the rate at which work is done. Thus, power can be considered as a work per unit of time ratio. Mathematically, it is computed using the following equation.

$$Power = Work/Time$$

Units of Power

The standard metric unit of power is the watt (W). As is implied by the preceding equation for power, a unit of power is equivalent to a unit of work divided by a unit of time. Thus, a watt is equivalent to a

Table 1.1   Common Watt-Hour (Wh) Multiples

VALUE	SYMBOL	NAME
1,000	kWh	kilowatt-hour
1,000,000	mWh	megawatt-hour
1,000,000,000	gWh	gigawatt-hour
1,000,000,000,000	pWh	petrawatt-hour

joule/second. Because these metrics describe small amounts of energy and power, its more common to deal in larger units, such as kilowatt hours which represent a unit of energy equal to 1,000 watt hours or 3.6 megajoules. Simply stated, energy in watt hours is the multiplication of power in watts times the duration in hours. The kilowatt hour is most commonly known as a billing unit for energy delivered to consumers by electric utilities. However, in large data centers and industrial complexes that use a significant amount of electricity, larger metrics, such as megawatt hours (mWh) in which a megawatt represents 1,000,000 watt hours and even gigawatt hours (gWh) where one gigawatt represents 1,000,000,000 watt hours, are periodically used. Table 1.1 provides a list of common watt hour multiples. Note that the term petrawatt-hour (pWh) represents a billion kilowatt hours or a trillion watt hours (Wh).

BTUs and Horsepower

The British thermal unit represents a unit of energy equal to about 1.06 kilojoules. It also represents the amount of energy needed to heat 1 pound (0.454 kg) of water 1°F (0.556°C). The latter should be familiar to anyone who sat through a basic chemistry class, especially when this author's professor attempted to heat a pound of water and instead ignited his tie.

Without considering the effect of tie immolation, the term "BTU" is commonly used to describe the power of heating and cooling systems, such as furnaces, stoves, and air conditioners as well as the heat value or energy content of fuels. When used as a unit of power, BTU *per hour* (BTU/h) is the correct unit, although this is often abbreviated as simply "BTU."

A word of caution is warranted when describing the unit MBTU. Although you might think of this metric as describing a million BTUs, it is defined as one thousand BTUs. This definition probably dates to Roman times, where "M" stands for one thousand (1,000). This can be easily confused with the International System of Units mega prefix "M," which results in the multiplication of BTUs by a factor of one million. To minimize confusion many companies and engineers use the term MMBTU to represent one million BTU. Alternatively, it's common to encounter the use of the word *therm*, where a therm represents 100,000 BTU. A *therm* is approximately equal to the energy equivalent of burning 100 cubic feet (ccf) of natural gas. Because gas meters measure volume and not energy content, a therm factor is used by gas companies to convert the volume of gas used to its heat equivalent, enabling them to calculate the actual energy used. The therm factor is usually represented in units of therms/ccf and will vary with the mix of hydrocarbons in gas. Natural gas with a higher than average concentration of ethane, propane, or similar chemicals will have a higher therm factor, whereas impurities, such as nitrogen, will give it a lower therm factor.

Another term we become familiar with in this chapter is horsepower. Originally, the term dates to the development of the steam engine, which provided a reason to compare the output of draft horses with that of the engines that could replace them. The term horsepower was over a period of time widely adopted to measure the output of piston engines, turbines, electric motors, and other machinery. The definition of the unit evolved to represent several measurements of power, however, today the watt is the preferred measurement of power. This is probably due to the fact that the definition of the horsepower varies between different applications. For example, mechanical horsepower, which is also known as imperial horsepower is exactly 550 foot-pounds per second, and is approximately equivalent to 745.7 watts. In comparison, the metric horsepower of 75 kilogram force-meter per second (kgf-m per second) is approximately equivalent to 735.499 watts. To add to potential confusion, boiler horsepower is used for rating steam boilers and is equivalent to 34.5 pounds of water evaporated per hour at 212°F, or 9809.5 watts, whereas one horsepower for rating electric motors is equal to 746 watts. Fortunately, most data centers do not use steam boilers, but if you do you may need to know the applicable conversion to watts.

Table 1.2 BTU Content of Common Energy Units

2 barrels (42 gallons) of crude oil = 5,800,000 BTU
1 gallon of gasoline = 124,238 BTU
1 gallon of diesel fuel = 138,690 BTU
1 gallon of heating oil = 138,690 BTU
1 barrel of residual fuel oil = 6,287,000 BTU
1 cubic foot of natural gas = 1,027 BTU
1 gallon of propane = 91,033 BTU
1 short ton of coal = 19,977,000 BTU
1 kilowatt hour of electricity = 3,412 BTU

Comparing Energy

The BTU is the most commonly used unit for comparing fuels. Because energy used in different countries is highly likely to originate from different places, the BTU content of fuels varies slightly from country to country. Table 1.2 provides a comparison of the BTU content of nine common energy units in the United States.

Oil, Gas, and Electric Costs

Because a data center can be located literally just about anyplace, it's possible that power can be in the form of a variety of fuels. Although the possibilities are mind-boggling, we can limit our consideration of the variety of fuels to the three most common ones used to power buildings and equipment in such buildings. Thus, in this section we examine the cost of oil, gas, and electricity.

The Cost of Oil Most readers are familiar with the terms "crude oil" and "barrels of oil" due to the 2010 BP oil spill in the Gulf of Mexico, but in reality they do not represent a direct cost associated with data center operations. However, the cost of a barrel of oil can indirectly affect such costs. The effect can be major or minor based upon the location of the data center and the utility firms that provide power to the data center.

If the data center is located in an area where the electric utility burns a considerable amount of oil, then an increase in crude oil prices will eventually result in an increase in the cost of electricity required to operate the data center. If the data center is located in the northeast

United States or certain parts of Europe and Asia where heating oil is used to heat many buildings during the winter, then an increase in crude oil prices will eventually result in higher heating bills during the winter for some organizations. This is because at refineries, crude oil is separated into different fuels including gasoline, kerosene, heating oil, diesel, and even jet fuel. Heating oil and diesel fuel are closely related products and are referred to as distillates. The main difference between the two fuels is that heating oil is allowed to contain more sulfur than diesel fuel. Approximately 11 gallons of distillate are refined from each 42-gallon barrel of crude oil, of which less than two gallons are heating oil and the remaining nine gallons are diesel fuel. However, because diesel fuel requires additional processing to remove sulfur, it is more costly to produce than heating oil. Thus, although the price of a barrel of crude will affect the price of heating oil it will also affect the price of electricity in some locations where electric utilities depend upon its use to generate electricity.

When you analyze the major refinery components of a barrel of oil, it explains why gasoline is usually less expensive than diesel fuel and why diesel fuel is less costly per gallon than home heating oil. That is, approximately 26 or more gallons of gasoline are refined from a barrel of oil, whereas diesel fuel and home heating oil account for 11 and 2 gallons, respectively. If you add up the number of gallons you will not obtain 42, as the numbers of gallons of gasoline depend upon the viscosity of crude as well as the type of refinery run, with the latter indicating if certain by-products of oil, such as plastics, are to be produced.

When this book was written the cost of a barrel of crude oil varied between $70 and $77, but when this book was published, the price had increased to between $105 and $108. The price of a barrel of crude could change daily from a few pennies per barrel to a few dollars. However, just a few years ago the price of crude oil peaked at $150 per barrel, and just 10 years ago its price hovered in the low $20 per barrel range. What this means is that the price of oil has been highly variable over the past decade and can continue to fluctuate considerably. This means that a data center where heating the building might depend upon heating oil or a location where the electric utility depends upon the use of oil to generate electricity can result in significant swings in the variable cost associated with operating the center. As indicated in Table 1.3, there is a wide range of sources used to generate electricity, from the use of

Table 1.3   Electricity/Heat in United States in 2007

	ELECTRICITY (GWh)	HEAT (TJ)
Production from		
Coal	2118455	100382
Oil	78136	37339
Gas	915196	366297
Biomass	49543	33445
Waste	22110	14232
Nuclear	836634	0
Hydro[a]	275545	—
Geothermal	16798	0
Solar PV	16	—
Solar thermal	673	0
Wind	34603	0
Tide	0	0
Other sources	1147	0
Total Production	**4348856**	**551695**
Imports	51396	0
Exports	−20143	0
Domestic Supply	**4380109**	**551695**
Statistical Differences	−7	0
Total Transformation[b]	**0**	**0**
Electricity Plants	0	0
Heat Plants	0	—
Energy Sector[c]	**288248**	**184029**
Distribution Losses	267043	66203
Total Final Consumption	**3824811**	**301463**
Industry	928828	238201
Transport	8173	0
Residential	1392241	0
Commercial and Public Services	1336315	63262
Agriculture/Forestry	0	0
Fishing	0	0
Other Nonspecified	159254	0

Source: Table reproduced courtesy of the International Energy Agency (IEA).

[a] Includes production from pumped storage plants.

[b] Transformation sector includes electricity used by heat pumps and electricity used by electric boilers.

[c] Energy sector also includes own use by plant and electricity used for pumped storage.

coal and oil, to gas, nuclear, geothermal, and solar panels. The latest available compilation was provided by the International Energy Agency (IEA) for the referenced table showing production sources from 2007, even the doubling of wind and solar energy each year since then which today accounts for a very small fraction of electric production.

The use of hedging might be warranted as a mechanism to smooth out possible cost variances of oil, however, it should be mentioned that hedging commodities requires a significant degree of financial experience and may not be suitable for data center managers. Instead, you may wish to consider the cost associated with the conversion of heating to a more economical source of energy if your organization owns the building. If you have a lease you might consider asking the owner about alternative heating, especially if your organization pays for utilities and your organization has a short-term lease. In addition, if the state where your data center resides allows alternative power sources you can consider obtaining bids from other electric utilities. The end result should be to minimize your organization's cost while maintaining an applicable level of utility usage.

The Cost of Natural Gas   Once considered as a useless by-product of crude oil production until the second half of the twentieth century, natural gas was almost always flared into the atmosphere. In fact, if you view several older movies from the 1960s and 1970s involving the state of Texas you might encounter one or more scenes where, when drilling for oil, natural gas was encountered and burned at the source. Today natural gas is recognized as the cleanest-burning conventional fuel, producing lower levels of greenhouse gas emissions than do heavier hydrocarbon fuels, such as coal and oil. Natural gas now provides 23% of all energy consumed in the world and is commonly used to generate electricity, heat buildings, power vans and some light trucks and other vehicles, and is used as a raw material in many consumer products, such as those made of traditional plastics. In fact, the International Energy Agency predicts that the demand for natural gas will grow by more than 67% through 2030.

Figure 1.1 illustrates the monthly price of natural gas sold to commercial customers in the United States. The graph can be viewed at http://tonto.eia.doe.gov/dnav/ng/hist/n3020us3m.htm and indicates that after peaking between 2005 and 2009 the cost per thousand

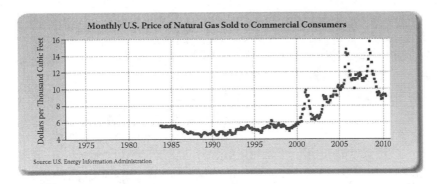

Figure 1.1   Monthly U.S. price of natural gas sold to commercial consumers.

cubic feet are in decline. If you read the *Wall Street Journal* or another financial publication you are probably aware of the significant increase in the reserves of natural gas discovered in the United States over the past few years due to a new type of drilling. This increase in reserves resulted in a steep decline in the price of natural gas and has resulted in many utilities converting generating facilities to its use. In addition, from watching television or reading the local newspaper you're probably aware of the fact that under the leadership of Mr. T. Boone Pickens a major effort is underway to attempt to convert vehicles to use natural gas as a fuel. In addition to reducing demand for oil and having a considerable positive effect upon the balance of payments of the United States this movement relies on the fact that a vast quantity of natural gas has been discovered, by some calculations providing a 30-year supply for current discoveries. This means that with additional drilling natural gas should be readily available as a fuel source for both heating and the generation of electricity, two areas of key importance to many data centers.

The Cost of Electricity   Like the weather, the cost of electricity is variable, currently based in most places upon the type of fuel used to generate electricity. In the Pacific Northwest of the United States a considerable amount of electricity is generated by water, referred to as hydroelectricity. Unless a drought is occurring, large-scale consumers in the Seattle area were paying approximately 6 cents per kWh, whereas consumers in many areas of California were paying approximately 15 cents per kWh as most of their electric generation was from oil, which is more expensive than hydro. In fact, if your data center is located in some areas of the world you may face a bill of 25 cents or more per kWh. A good source for comparing electric rates by states in the United States can be found at http://www.eia.doe.gov/cneaf/electricity/epm/table5_6_a.html. At that location the United States Energy Administration has a table entitled, "Average Retail Price of Electricity to Ultimate Customers by End-Use Sector, by State, May 2010 and 2009," which indicates the price in cents per kilowatt hour. At the EIA website you can also access information on the generation of electricity by state for different renewable energy sources, such as biomass, wind, geothermal, and solar.

Financial Metrics

Now that we have a general indication of the cost and variability of oil and natural gas, let's turn our attention to examining a few financial metrics. This mechanism evaluates certain energy-related projects to determine if they are economically viable. Thus, in concluding this chapter let's discuss what is referred to as the return on investment (ROI), payback period, discounted cash flow, and internal rate of return. To do so we need to obtain knowledge of the present and future value of funds as well as to obtain some experience with both understanding and computing the value of different types of annuities. Because any investment in equipment or our building should result in a lowering of utility expenses, we can use those lower expenditures as similar to a cash flow. Thus, as we turn our attention to financial methods that can be used to rank projects we are a bit unconventional and assume that instead of investing in machinery designed to manufacture widgets where the monthly flow of raw material is converted into some product that provides our organization with cash, we lower our utility bills. Then, the stream of lower utility bills can be viewed as a stream of payments, which in effect is cash flow.

The Return on Investment (ROI)

The return on investment represents a commonly used financial metric for evaluating and comparing different types of business investments. The ROI is often used alongside other financial metrics for projecting potential cash flow results, such as net present value (NPV), payback period, and internal rate of return. Each of these metrics can be used to determine information about the overall pattern of cash inflows and outflows, but each carries a different meaning as we shortly note. The popularity of the use of ROI can be judged by an advertisement in the August 2–August 8, 2010 issue of *Bloomberg Businessweek*. In that issue SAS Business Analytics Software had a full-page advertisement in which the firm specified that organizations could see up to a 400% ROI through the use of its business analytics software. In addition to this magazine issue, other magazines periodically contain advertisements from other vendors that denote potential ROIs from the use of a variety of products.

An ROI analysis is one of several approaches to evaluating and comparing investments. With ROI, the decision maker will evaluate an investment by comparing the magnitude and timing of expected gains to the magnitude and timing of investment costs. A good ROI means that investment returns compare favorably to investment costs. In the last few decades, the ROI approach has been applied to a wide range of asset purchase decisions, such as factory machinery and computer systems, as well as single vehicle and fleet purchases.

As we perform an ROI note that it compares investment returns and costs by constructing a ratio, or percentage. When performing an ROI a ratio greater than 0.00 (or a percentage greater than 0%) means the investment returns more than its cost. Although this is usually a good decision criterion to fund a project, in the real world there are numerous projects that compete for funds. Thus, after the ROI is computed for a number of projects they are more than likely ranked by such factors as their necessity, cost, and obviously their ROI, with the higher ROI considered the better choice by itself, all other criteria being equal.

One problem associated with using ROI as the sole basis for decision making is that by itself it tells us nothing about the likelihood that expected returns and costs will be as predicted. The ROI in effect does not inform us about the risk of an investment. ROI simply shows how returns compare to costs, which may or may not be true. However, the lack of predictability is also true of other financial metrics, such as net present value and internal rate of return. For this reason you may wish to consider measuring the probabilities of different ROI outcomes to include both the magnitude of computed ROIs and the risks that go with it.

ROI Analysis   A return on investment analysis begins with a cash flow stream, a series of net cash flow figures expected to occur from an investment. That investment can be the lease or purchase of a building, the acquisition of machinery, or the savings you expect from an investment in more efficient equipment that reduces your energy expense. To perform an ROI you need to consider both the inflows and outflows of expenses over a period of time. That time period, although theoretically extending in certain cases for a rather long time, is actually limited either by corporate policy or such practical events as the expected life of equipment. For example, purchasing a more efficient redundant array of inexpensive disks (RAID) system that consumes less energy could theoretically result in a perpetual reduced level of electricity consumption. However, from a practical standpoint the RAID system might have an expected life of three to five years. In addition, due to taxes, certain governments allow what is referred to as depreciation, a noncash expense that reduces the value of an asset due to wear and tear, age, and obsolescence. Because depreciation is a noncash expense it lowers an organization's earnings while increasing its cash flow.

Concerning inflows and outflows, if you purchase a RAID system you would immediately have an outflow that represents your payment for the disk system. However, you would then save on your organization's electric bill each month, because we assume you purchased a more efficient RAID system. In our example we assume that the useful life of the RAID system is three years.

Suppose the cost of a more efficient and larger capacity RAID system is $1,000. Let's assume that its installation results in the savings of 400 watts/hour. Let's also assume the utility bills your organization 10 cents per kWh. Assuming the RAID is powered on 24 hours/day, your organization can be expected to save 9.6 kWh per day (400 watts × 24 hours/day/1,000), or 288 kWh per 30-day month. This savings translates into a reduction of $28.80 per month, which represents the monthly return on your investment.

Table 1.4 illustrates in a very simplistic manner the inflows and outflow of cash on a monthly basis for the hypothetical RAID system. Note that there is only one outflow, which represents the payment for the RAID system. In comparison, there are 36 monthly inflows, each fixed at $28.80 and representing the cost associated

Table 1.4 Cash Inflows and Outflows for a RAID System

MONTH	INFLOW	OUTFLOW	NET CASH FLOW
1	28.80	1000.00	−971.20
2	28.80		28.80
3	28.80		28.80
—	—	—	—
36	28.80		28.80
Total	1036.80	1000.00	36.80

with saving on electricity. For this simple analysis we assume that maintenance is included in the purchase price, which may not be applicable for certain types of equipment nor for a three-year period. Thus, if our organization were required to pay maintenance we would then adjust the cash flows to indicate when and what payments were due.

In examining the entries in Table 1.4, the negative cash inflow at the outset and the positive cash flow in later months illustrate the fact that most investments initially have costs exceeding incoming benefits, but if things go as planned, incoming benefits should eventually outweigh costs. In the above example (which is highly simplified), we note that over a three-year period the cost of a new RAID system essentially pays for itself by a reduction in the cost of energy consumption over that period of time. The ROI is frequently derived as the "return" from an action divided by the cost of that action. This type of ROI is referred to as a "simple ROI," as it does not take into consideration the time value of money. For our RAID example, a simple or simplified ROI is computed as follows:

$$\text{Simple ROI} = \frac{\text{Gains or Energy Savings} - \text{Investment Cost}}{\text{Investment Cost}}$$

$$= \frac{1,036.80 - 1,000}{1,000} = 0.0368$$

For our RAID example the ROI is 3.68%. This return appears to be rather small, however, it does not consider the fact that when purchasing new equipment you receive a new warranty, newer technology, and, in the case of disk drives, more than likely additional capacity. Thus, the ROI previously computed is only based upon the accrual of energy savings, which could increase if the rates charged by the utility increase. In addition, we have not considered the time value of money. Concerning the latter, simply put, which is worth more: a dollar today or a dollar at a future date in time? Of course, the answer is that a rational person would prefer to receive the dollar today. However, under certain circumstances, such as the archaic tax system in the United States, it may pay to defer income. Because we are talking about rational people, our answer will stand that all things being equal, it is better to receive a dollar today than tomorrow. To fully understand the time value of money we first discuss some basics associated with the future value of money and how it is computed. Using this information as a base we then turn our attention to the present value of money (or savings) received in the future.

What Is Time Value?

Again, if you're like most people, you would choose to receive the $1 today rather than some day in the future. OK, $1 may not be much, so let's make it $10, or even $100 or perhaps a rather nice round amount of $1,000. Now unless your name is Buffet or Gates, taking a payment now is just plain instinctive. And again, at a basic level, the time value of money demonstrates that, all things being equal, it is better to have money now rather than at a later date. But why is this? Ten $100 bills have the same value as ten $100 bills one year from now, don't they? Actually, although the bills are the same, you can do more with the money if you have it now because over time you can earn interest on your money. For example, by receiving funds today, you can increase the future value of your money by earning interest on the money over a period of time.

Future Value Basics   Assume you receive $1,000 today and invest the money at a simple annual rate of 4%. During 2010, interest rates on relatively short terms of up to a year were near zero, however, this situation more than likely will change over the next few years. In fact, if the past is any guide to the future, short-term rates may increase to 4% or more over the next few years. Returning to our example, the future value of your investment at the end of the first year is $1,040, which of course is calculated by multiplying the principal amount of

$1,000 by the interest rate of 4% and then adding the interest gained to the principal amount. Thus, our computation is as follows:

Future value of $1,000 at end of year = $1,000 + 1,000 × .04
= $1,040

We can rewrite the preceding equation by factoring the $1,000 as follows:

Future value of $1,000 at end of year = $1,000(1 + .04)

Now let's assume similar to craps at a Las Vegas casino, but perhaps with a safer CD, you let your investment ride another year. Let's assume you can obtain a 4% rate of interest for another year. To compute the amount you would have at the end of year two, you would take the $1,040 and multiply it again by 1.04 (0.04 + 1). At the end of two years, you would have $1,081.60 computed as follows:

Future value of investment at end of second year
$= \$10,040 \times (1+.04) = \$1,081.60$

The preceding computation is equivalent to the following equation:

Future value of $1,000 at end of second year
$= \$1,000 \times (1+.04) \times (1+.04)$

If we remember the rule of exponents, which states that the multiplication of like terms is equivalent to adding their exponents, the preceding equation can be represented as follows:

Future value of $1,000 at end of second year
$= \$1,000 \times (1+.04)^2 = \$1,081.60$

Based upon the preceding, guess what the value of our investment at the end of year three would be? And year four? To compute the value of our investment at the end of year three we would use the following equation:

Future value of $1,000 at end of third year = $1,000 \times (1 + .04)^3$

Similarly, the future value of $1,000 at the end of the fourth year becomes $1,000 \times (1+.04)^4$ Now, let's assume you "let it ride" for 10 years. Yes, the value of your $1,000 becomes $1,000 \times (1 + .04)^{10}$.

Now we should see a pattern emerging. If we know how many years we would like to hold a present amount of money in an investment, the future value of that amount is calculated by the following equation:

$$\text{Future value} = \text{Original amount} \times (1 + \text{interest rate period})^{\text{Number of periods}}$$

Using interest terminology where *FV* is shorthand for "future value" we can rewrite our equation using *P* for principal and *n* for the number of periods as follows:

$$FV = P \times (1 + i)^n$$

Future Value Interest Factors

Because rational people do not like to compute equations that have been computed literally tens of thousands of times previously we can simplify life through the use of tables of future value interest factors (FVIFs) that appear in many financial publications as well as at numerous sites on the Internet. The key unknowns in determining the future value of an investment are the number of periods (*n*) and the interest rate (*i*), therefore most tables of FVIFs use a row/column approach similar to Table 1.5. In Table 1.5 the interest rate ranges from 1 to 10% in increments of 1% horizontally by column. The period (*n*) ranges from 1 to 10 vertically by row. To illustrate the use of Table 1.5 we return to our prior example where we invest $1,000 for two years at an interest rate of 4%. If we turn our attention to the

Table 1.5 Future Value Interest Factors

n/I	1%	2%	3%	4%	5%	6%	7%	8%	9%	10%
1	1.010	1.020	1.030	1.040	1.050	1.060	1.070	1.080	1.090	1.100
2	1.020	1.040	1.061	1.082	1.103	1.124	1.145	1.166	1.188	1.210
3	1.030	1.061	1.093	1.125	1.158	1.191	1.225	1.260	1.295	1.331
4	1.041	1.082	1.126	1.170	1.216	1.262	1.311	1.360	1.412	1.464
5	1.051	1.104	1.159	1.217	1.276	1.338	1.403	1.469	1.539	1.611
6	1.062	1.126	1.194	1.265	1.340	1.419	1.501	1.587	1.677	1.772
7	1.072	1.149	1.230	1.316	1.407	1.504	1.606	1.714	1.828	1.949
8	1.083	1.172	1.267	1.369	1.477	1.594	1.718	1.851	1.993	2.144
9	1.094	1.195	1.305	1.423	1.551	1.689	1.838	1.999	2.172	2.358
10	1.105	1.219	1.344	1.480	1.629	1.791	1.967	2.159	2.367	2.594

4% column and second row in Table 1.5, we note the FVIF as 1.082. Thus, if we multiply our $1,000 investment by the FVIF of 1.082 we obtain $1,082. Wait a second, we previously computed the value as $1,081.60, so why the 40 cent discrepancy? The reason is due to rounding, which commonly occurs in financial tables. In the example shown in Table 1.5 note that there are only three decimal positions, so we can make an educated guess that rounding occurs in the third decimal position. This also indicates that not all tables are equal and if we have a significant investment we may prefer to use financial tables that are accurate to five or more decimal positions.

Now that we have an understanding of the value of interest upon interest through compounding in computing FVIFs we can turn our attention to the present value of funds to be received in the future. Referred to as the present value of income, we note shortly that similar to the use of tables to assist in computing future values there are tables we can use to simplify the computation of present values.

Present Value Basics

If you could receive $1,000 right now, the present value would be $1,000 because present value is what your investment gives you today. If you were going to receive $1,000 in a year, the present value of the amount would not be $1,000 because you do not presently have the funds. To determine the present value of $1,000 to be received in a year, you need to determine the amount that you need to invest today that will result in a value of $1,000 at the end of one year. Simply put, you need to determine how much you need to invest today at a given rate of interest to receive $1,000 one or more periods into the future.

Previously we noted that the future value of an investment is equal to the principal (*P*) times $(1 + i)^n$ or,

$$FV = P \times (1 + i)^n$$

where *i* is the interest rate and *n* is the number of periods.

To calculate the present value, which represents the amount you would have to invest today to obtain a future value, you need to subtract the accumulated interest from $1,000. To accomplish this, you need to discount the future payment amount by the interest rate for the period. In essence, you are simply rearranging the future value equation so that you may solve for P. The future value equation can be rewritten by replacing the principal or P variable by the present value (PV) and dividing both sides of the equation by $(1 + i)^n$, obtaining:

$$PV = FV/(1 + i)^n$$

where PV = present value, FV = future value, i = interest rate, and n = number of periods.

Based upon the preceding we can compute the present value of a future payment. For example, let's compute the present value of $1,000 to be received in two years. To do so we use the preceding formula, recognizing that $1/(1 + i)^n$ can be represented by $(1 + i)^{-n}$ because due to the properties of exponents, 1 divided by a value raised to an exponent is equal to the value raised to a negative exponent. Thus, the present value of a future payment at a rate of 4% interest two years from now becomes:

$$PV = \$1,000 \times 1/(1+.04)^2 = \$1,000 \times (1+.04)^{-2}$$
$$= \$1,000 \times .925 = \$925$$

Based upon our computation we should be indifferent with respect to receiving $1,000 today or $925 in two years, assuming an interest rate of 4%.

Inasmuch as PVIFs are similar to FVIFs in that the computations have occurred numerous times, as you might expect, there are tables of PVIFs we can use to facilitate our computations. Table 1.6 provides an example of a table of PVIFs where they are listed for $1 in future payments to three digits of accuracy for integer interest rates ranging from 1 to 10% compounded for up to 10 periods of time.

As an engineer, one of the most common mistakes I find many people make is failing to see if the data actually make sense. Thus, let's digress a bit and quickly review the data presented in Tables 1.5 and 1.6 to determine if they are logical. First, let's examine Table 1.5 which is a table of future value interest factors. If we deposit a dollar today, then adding interest should increase the value by time. In addition, as interest increases, the value of our investment plus interest increases. Thus, FVIFs should rise based upon the number of periods

Table 1.6   Present Value Interest Factors

n/I	1%	2%	3%	4%	5%	6%	8%	10%
1	0.990	0.980	0.971	0.962	0.952	0.943	0.926	0.909
2	0.980	0.961	0.943	0.925	0.907	0.890	0.857	0.826
3	0.971	0.942	0.915	0.889	0.864	0.840	0.794	0.751
4	0.961	0.924	0.888	0.855	0.823	0.792	0.735	0.683
5	0.951	0.906	0.863	0.822	0.784	0.747	0.681	0.621
6	0.942	0.888	0.837	0.790	0.746	0.705	0.630	0.564
7	0.933	0.871	0.813	0.760	0.711	0.665	0.583	0.513
8	0.923	0.853	0.789	0.731	0.677	0.627	0.540	0.467
9	0.914	0.837	0.766	0.703	0.645	0.592	0.500	0.424
10	0.905	0.820	0.744	0.676	0.614	0.558	0.463	0.386

and interest rate, which the table indicates, so it passes the logical test. Now let's examine Table 1.6, which contains a table of present value interest factors. Simply stated, a dollar in the future is worth less than a dollar received today. Thus, the entries in the table of PVIFs should decrease in value as the period and interest rate increases. Because they do, the table also passes the logical test. Now that we know the tables are logical let's move on to discussing how saving a fixed amount of energy per month can be considered as being similar to an annuity. Thus, we discuss annuities and how they can be considered to represent a method to determine the effect of energy savings over a period of time.

Annuities

An annuity represents a series of fixed payments that you will either pay or receive. As you get closer to retirement you may be bombarded by sales personnel trying to sell you various types of annuities, such as equity-indexed, deferred variable, and similar types of products. Although such annuities may be worthwhile to consider, the focus of this book is upon saving energy and as such we can expect to lower various monthly utility bills if successful. The savings resemble a string of payments, therefore the use of simple types of annuities can be used to project the potential savings. In this chapter we discuss two basic types of annuities because we are focused on determining the effect of reducing the cost of energy on the corporate bottom line and not on retirement, a completely different topic.

Payment Frequency

An annuity has a payment frequency that can vary considerably, from monthly payments to quarterly, semiannually, and even annually. If the annuity pays semiannually, it then resembles a common bond, which typically pays the holder every six months and the face value of the bond at maturity.

Types of Annuities

There are two basic types of annuities referred to as ordinary income and annuity due. An ordinary income annuity requires payments to be made at the end of each period, similar to a conventional bond or certificate of deposit (CD) that pays annually, semiannually, quarterly, or even monthly. The second type of common annuity is referred to as an annuity due. Here payments occur at the beginning of each period, similar to a monthly rent payment.

We can think of a bond or CD as representing an ordinary annuity. For either financial instrument we receive a series of payments and at maturity we (it is hoped) receive the principal back. In comparison, an annuity due is similar to rent, inasmuch as we would typically make payments at the beginning of the month on a rental property. Now that we have a basic understanding of the two basic types of annuities let's perform a few calculations. In doing so we first determine the future value of an annuity because we can use that value to easily determine the present value of the annuity.

Determining the Future Value of an Ordinary Annuity

To compute the future value of an annuity we need to determine the future value of each payment received at the end of each period of time. For example, consider Figure 1.2, which illustrates how the replacement of a more energy-efficient device in our data center could result in saving $1,000 per month on our organization's electric bill. Although we still receive the monthly electric bill, the effect of lowering its cost by $1,000 per month can be considered to represent payments of $1,000 per month over the life of the device. Note that for now we are not discussing the details of the device, only specifying

Payment (cost saving) at the end of each period

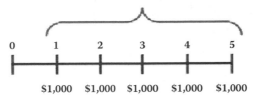

Figure 1.2   Series of payments received at the end of each period.

that a new device reduces our organization's electric bill by $1,000 per month. Later in this book we become more specific, but for now we are simply becoming familiar with the mathematics associated with determining the present value of a series of future savings.

Using Figure 1.2 and assuming an interest rate of 4% we determine how much we will have at the end of year 5. At the end of year 1 we would have $1,000 \times (1 + .04)^0$ or $1,000. At the end of the second period of time we would receive $1,000 \times (1 + .04)^1$. At the end of the third period we would receive $1,000 \times (1 + .04)^2$, and at the end of the fourth year we would receive $1,000 \times (1 + .04)^3$ and the payment at the end of the fifth year would be $1,000 \times (1 + .04)^4$. Thus, if FVA represents the future value of the annuity, we obtain:

$$FVA = \$1,000 \times (1+.04)^0 + \$1,000 \times (1+.04)^1 + \$1,000 \times (1+.04)^2 \\ + \$1,000 \times (1+.04)^3 + \$1,000 \times (1+.04)^4$$

Simplifying the preceding by factoring out the payments we obtain:

$$FVA = \$1,000 + \$1,000 \times (1+.04)^1 + \$1,000 \times (1+.04)^2 \\ + \$1,000 \times (1+.04)^3 + \$1,000 \times (1+.04)^4$$

Using the values from Table 1.5 we obtain:

$$FVA = \$1,000 + \$1,040 + \$1,082 + \$1,125 + \$1,170 \text{ or } \$5,417$$

Note that if n represents the number of payments and Pmt represents the payment received each period, we can define the general equation for the future value of an ordinary annuity as follows:

$$FVA = Pmt + Pmt \times (1+i) + Pmt \times (1+i)^2 + Pmt \times (1+i)^3 \\ + \cdots + Pmt \times (1+i)^{n-1}$$

or,

$$FVA = \frac{Pmt \times (1+i)^{n-1}}{i}$$

Present Value of an Annuity

Now that we computed the future value of an annuity let's turn our attention to its present value. Remember, the present value of a future series of payments will be discounted because we cannot earn interest on the payments until they are received. Thus, each payment needs to be discounted by the interest rate we could earn if we received the payment today and could put the cash to work.

Returning to Figure 1.2, the first reduction in our utility bill of $1,000 occurs at the end of period 1. If we could earn 4% on our funds, then the present value of the first reduction in our utility bill becomes $1,000/(1 + .04)^1$. For the next payment, which can be considered as the second reduction in our utility bill, the present value becomes $1,000/(1 + .04)^2$. Similarly, the present values for the third, fourth, and fifth utility reductions are $1,000/(1 + .04)^3$, $1,000/((1 + .04)^4$, and $1,000/(1 + .04)^5$.

If *Pmt* represents the payment or utility bill decrease per period, i represents the interest rate per period, and n represents the number of periods, the present value of the annuity (PVA) becomes:

$$PVA = \frac{Pmt}{1+I} + \frac{Pmt}{(1+i)^2} + \cdots + \frac{Pmt}{(1+i)^n} = \frac{Pmt}{1+i}$$

$$\times \left(\frac{1+1}{1+i} + \frac{1}{(1+i)^2} + \cdots + \frac{1}{(1+i)^{n-1}} \right)$$

Note that the second factor in the above equation represents a geometric progression with a scale factor of 1 and a common ratio of $1/(1 + i)$. Thus, we can define the present value of an ordinary annuity as:

$$PVA = \frac{Pmt}{1+I} \times \frac{1 - \dfrac{1}{(1+i)^n}}{1 - \dfrac{1}{1+i}}$$

We can simplify the above equation to obtain:

$$PVA = \frac{Pmt}{i} \times \left(1 - \frac{1}{(i+1)^n}\right)$$

Considering Monthly Cash Flows

Because utilities normally bill on a monthly basis, we should consider the effect of receiving a monthly stream of reduced bills instead of receiving a yearly reduced bill. To do so we simply need to replace the interest rate by the yearly rate divided by the number of periods per year. In addition, we need to change the number of periods (n) to the number of years (y) multiplied by the number of periods per year (m). Doing so, we obtain:

$$PVA = \frac{Pmt \times m}{I} \times \left(1 - \frac{\frac{1}{(1+i)^{ym}}}{m}\right)$$

Note that as the number of periods approaches infinity the present value of the annuity will approach the payment per period divided by the interest rate. This means that we can obtain a relatively decent approximation of the present value of future savings over a long period of time using the following formula:

$$PVA_{\text{Limit } n \to \infty} = \frac{Pmt}{i}$$

Thus, even an infinite series of payments with a nonzero interest rate will have a finite present value. In fact, due to the life of some light emitting diode (LED) bulbs beginning to be marketed that exceed 50,000 to 100,000 hours of operation, purchasing such devices can result in the electrical savings extending out for 10 to 30 or more years. In actuality, even if powered on most of the time for 10 or more years, an LED more than likely will not fail. Instead, it will reach its half-life in terms of brightness and will still be "lighting up" similar to the Energizer Bunny® that keeps on going.

With utility bills on a monthly basis, the previous computation would require a y value between 10 and 30 whereas the value of m would be 12, representing the number of billing periods in the year. I'm not sure how readers like to use tables or compute the value of an interest rate plus 1 to a large power, but because an infinite series of finite payments with a nonzero interest rate has a finite value we can approximate the present value of a future stream of monthly savings. For example, consider an LED bulb this author recently saw at Lowes, the home improvement store. Priced at \$39 plus tax, its cost was considerably higher than incandescent and compact fluorescent lights (CFL). However, the LED bulb consumed 6 watts of energy in comparison to 75 watts for an incandescent costing 85 cents and 14 watts for the CFL. Using a cost of 10 cents per kWh and an expected life of 10 years, which is actually conservative, we can easily compute the present value of energy consumption for each of the three types of lights as follows:

$$PV_{incandescent} = \frac{30 \text{ days} \times 24 \text{ hours/day} \times 75 \text{ watts} \times 10 \text{ cents/kWh}}{.06}$$
$$= \$90.00$$

$$PV_{CFL} = \frac{30 \text{ days} \times 24 \text{ hours/day} \times 14 \text{ watts} \times 10 \text{ cents/kWh}}{.06}$$
$$= \$16.80$$

$$PV_{LED} = \frac{30 \text{ days} \times 24 \text{ hours/day} \times 6 \text{ watts} \times 10 \text{ cents/kWh}}{.06}$$
$$= \$7.20$$

The previous computations illustrate the present value of future energy cost for three types of lights. However, the computations do not consider the cost of each light nor the fact that the replacements of incandescent bulbs will occur approximately every three months, whereas the CFL can last approximately a year. In addition, the labor involved in swapping out incandescent and CFL bulbs is also ignored at the present time.

Based upon simply considering the cost of energy, the use of CFL lights to replace incandescent is fairly obvious. A more difficult consideration is whether to purchase LED lights to replace CFL lighting. Then you would need to consider the tangible fact that every 8,760 or so hours you would need to replace the CFL inasmuch as they typically can be powered on for approximately one year. There is also some labor involved in replacing the bulb, so you might run a new analysis and come to a different conclusion, especially if the light fixture required a considerable amount of effort to reach.

Annuity Due

The second type of basic annuity is known as an annuity due. This type of annuity assumes payments are made at the beginning of each period, similar to the manner by which rent is usually due on the first of the month. Because each payment is made one period sooner, we need to reduce each of the previously developed formulas by one period. Thus, without going through a rigorous development we can simply note that the future value and present value of an annuity due is as follows:

$$FVA \ due = Pmt \times \frac{[(1+i)^n - 1]}{i}$$

$$PVA \ due = Pmt \times \frac{[1-(1+i)^{-n}]}{i} \times (1+i)$$

Here Pmt represents for our purposes the monthly cost reduction obtained by making an investment in a more energy-efficient device or product, such as a building's insulation. In comparison, n represents the number of periods and i represents the interest rate per period. Note that the interest per period is often expressed in terms of the annual percentage rate (APR) r, and the number of interest periods per year p. Thus, the interest per period is equal to the annual percentage rate divided by the number of interest periods per year,

$$i = r/p$$

Based upon the fact that interest can be specified on a periodic basis as well as by an APR rate, we need to carefully consider the value of i that we use in our computations. For example, if we assume an interest rate of 6% compounded monthly then the rate per period becomes 6/12 or 0.5 because there are 12 periods in a year.

Annuity Notations

Readers should note that there is a series of mathematical notations for annuities. The basic symbol for the present value of an annuity is α. A variety of notations can be added, such as the payment frequency, age of a person when an annuity commences, the number of periods covered by the annuity as well as other data. The focus of this book is upon energy conservation in the data center therefore we do not discuss annuity notations other than to denote they are employed by life insurance agents and actuaries.

Payback Period

Although determining the return on investment allows us to rank projects for the finite resources of our organization, there are other methods that may be used to determine if a project is financially viable. Among those methods are the payback period and the internal rate of return.

The payback period is a rather simple computation that is used to determine length of time required to recover the cost of an investment. It is computed by dividing the cost of a project by either the annual or monthly cash flows to determine the annual or monthly payback period. Thus, the payback period (PBP) is computed as follows:

$$PBP = \frac{\text{Cost of project}}{\text{Annual or monthly cash flows}}$$

All other things being equal, the better investment is the one with the shorter payback period. For example, if an energy-efficiency investment is estimated to have a cost of $100,000 and you anticipate a decrease in your organization's utility bills of $20,000 annually, then the payback period will be $100,000/$20,000, or five years.

Although the payback period can be used as a mechanism to rank investments it suffers from several drawbacks. First, it ignores any benefits that occur after the payback period. Thus, it ignores continuing reductions that could occur due to enhancing your data center. Second, it ignores the time value of money as well as any increase in utility rates that would enhance an investment. Due to these limitations it is common for organizations to consider the use of other methods of budgeting, such as the previously discussed return on investment as well as the use of discounted cash flow and the computation of the internal rate of return or discounted.

Discounted Cash Flow

Another financial tool used as a decision criterion to determine the viability of a project as well as a method to rank projects is referred to as the discounted cash flow (DCF) method.

DCF represents a valuation method used to estimate the attractiveness of an investment opportunity. To perform a DCF analysis we first estimate the future cash flows from a project and then discount them to arrive at a present value, which is used to determine the potential for investment. Typically, the weighted average cost of capital for an organization is used to discount future cash flows to their present value.

Weighted Average Cost of Capital

Although the weighted average cost of capital (WACC) appears to represent a simplistic term, in actuality it can take some research to compute unless you can simply pick up the phone and dial someone in finance who has done the computation. This is because the weighted average cost of capital represents the determination of an organization's cost of capital in which each category of capital is proportionately weighted. Every source of capital, such as common stock, preferred stock, bank loans, and bonds are included in a WACC computation.

The theory behind the use of WACC is the fact that a commercial company should be willing to invest in a project as long as it increases the wealth of shareholders who are the owners of the company (in theory) as well as generate a reasonable return above the cost of obtaining capital. What that return should be, however, depends upon many factors including the economic environment, the current Federal Reserve Bank discount rate, and many others.

Although it's impossible to predict with significant precision future cash flows as the length of a project increases, we need a method of analysis to enable managers to make a decision. By considering utility savings in effect to represent future cash flows we can examine a series of past utility bills to denote potential savings in the future if we decide to undertake a project, such as replacing the heating system in the building, purchasing a new chilled water system, or any one of literally hundreds of potential energy-saving methods one can consider to reduce the cost of operating a data center. Thus, it becomes possible to calculate future cash flows with some degree of precision. However, although it's possible to compute future cash flows, we need to consider the duration of those flows. We know when we will make the investment, but how long will we receive a stream of lower utility bills? The answer might be literally "forever" if we were replacing insulation, however, for most situations there is a defined period that we need to consider. For example, the life of a RAID system might be three to five years, whereas the life of a new high-voltage air conditioner (HVAC) system might be between 7 and 12 years, depending upon the brand selected and the data center's location inasmuch as a location on the Gulf of Mexico, many cities in the United Kingdom, or either the East or West Coast of the United States that is exposed to salt water has a corrosion effect. In addition, as we noted several times previously in this chapter, a dollar received today is worth more than a dollar received later in the year. Thus, we need to discount future cash flows.

Based upon the preceding, it's clear that you cannot simply add up all the predicted future cash inflows and subtract the sum from your initial investment as a criterion to determine a potential investment's viability. Thus, the future cash flows resulting from potential utility bill savings that will occur at a different point in time must be discounted back to when you make your investment.

Most public companies have at least two methods by which they can finance the capital required for a new project: debt and equity. Most companies use a mixture of debt and equity to fund new projects. Thus, we need a mechanism to determine the weights of debt and equity to calculate the WACC. That mechanism occurs by determining the market value of debt and equity, dividing each by the total market value of the firm. Then we can compute the WACC by multiplying the cost of debt by the interest rate paid to debt holders and the cost of equity is multiplied by the cost of equity, adding the two computations together. However, because the cost of debt is tax deductible, we need to adjust the cost of debt by multiplying its value by $(1 - t_{cr})$ where t_{cr} represents the corporate tax rate. Thus, WACC is computed as follows:

$$WACC = [\{C_{d} \times (1 - t_{cr}) \times D/V\} + \{Ce \times E/V\}]$$

where:

D = Market value of debt.

E = Market value of equity.

V = Total value of firm (Market value of debt + Market value of equity).

t_{cr} = Corporate tax rate percent.

C_{d} = Cost of debt (interest rate paid to debt holders).

Cost of equity = Expected rate of return required by stockholders.

For nonfinancial majors the term *cost of equity* deserves a few words of explanation. In finance the cost of equity represents the return that stockholders require for a company. The formula used to determine the cost of equity (COE) is shown below.

$$COE = \frac{\text{Dividends per share}}{\text{Market value of stock}} + \text{Growth rate of dividends}$$

As an example of the cost of equity, assume a stock pays $1.00 per share in dividends and currently has a price of $20 per share. Let's also assume that the company has in the past grown its dividends by 4% per year and we expect that growth rate to continue. Then, the cost of equity becomes:

$$COE = \frac{1}{20} + .04 = .09$$

Based upon the preceding, the cost of equity can be viewed as representing the return the market demands in exchange for owning an asset to include the risk of ownership.

Returning to our WACC example, let's assume the market value of our organization includes $400 million in equity and $600 million in debt, with an average interest cost of 5%. Let's also assume our corporate tax rate is 25%. Then, the WACC becomes:

$$WACC = [\{.05 \times (1 - .25) \times 600,000,000/1,000,000,000\}$$
$$+ \{.09 \times 400,000,000/1,000,000,000\}]$$

Thus, the weighted average cost of capital in this example is 5.85%, of which 2.25% is contributed by debt and 3.6% by equity. Note that in general many companies can lower their overall cost of capital if the company increases the debt component of its capital structure. This results from the fact that in the United States interest is a tax-deductible expense whereas a dividend is not. The net result is that an increase in debt will involve more interest expenses that represent an allowable deduction against income, saving the company taxes as long as there is sufficient income. However, it should be noted that debt has to be repaid according to the indenture associated with bonds, whereas a dividend can be cut or eliminated. Thus, companies usually have a mixture of debt and equity that will be structured to promote the overall financial health of the organization.

Remember, in the above example the WACC was computed assuming that our organization only has debt and equity. In some organizations the capital structure can be more complex to include preferred equity, convertible debt, warrants, and a variety of options, and in some situations government loans. The important thing to realize is that the WACC represents the minimum return that a company must earn on an existing asset base to satisfy its owners and creditors. Thus, the higher the present value of energy savings over the WACC the better the project will rank for resources. Although you may never actually have to compute the WACC because you should be able to pick up the telephone and make a call to the finance department, knowing how it's computed represents an additional tool of knowledge. As we conclude our exposure to finance we turn our attention to another popular method used to decide if an investment should go forward, referred to as the internal rate of return.

Internal Rate of Return

The fourth method we discuss that can be used to rank projects in financial terms is referred to as the internal rate of return method. The IRR represents the discount rate that generates a zero present value for a series of future cash flows. Thus, it is also referred to as the discounted cash flow rate of return. Because we determine an interest rate such that the sum of future cash flows has a present value of zero, the IRR is also referred to as the effective interest rate. In addition, the term *internal* is used to denote that the computation of the IRR does not include any external factors, such as inflation, competition, government regulations, and so on. That "so on" can include environmental factors, such as how to dispose of CFL lights that contain mercury. Thus, sometimes you really need to think about many parameters beyond energy savings, especially when considering the fact that the disposal of burned-out CFL lighting is becoming regulated by many municipalities.

If we represent a series of cash flows at periods 0 through n as CF_0, CF_1, ... , CF_n, then we can compute the internal rate of return by solving the following formula for the interest rate i that results in the discounted cash flows equaling zero:

$$CF_0 + \frac{CF_1}{(1+i)^1} + \frac{CF_2}{(1+i)^2} + \frac{CF_n}{(1+i)^n} = 0$$

If you're familiar with mathematics you will note that solving for the interest rate represents a trial-and-error method. That is, you would first select a value to use for i and assuming you do not get a perfect match, adjust the value as you close the gap toward zero. Once you determine the IRR you can use it as a decision criterion. For example, if the computed internal rate of return exceeds the organization's cost of capital the project would be considered to go forward. Conversely, if the internal rate of return is less than the cost of capital the project would probably be rejected. This author uses the term "probably" because sometimes politics gets in the way of coherent financial decision making. For example, in the past this author managed a communications network that terminated at a large data center. Near the end of some fiscal years this author was asked to spend funds that from an economic perspective would not otherwise have been financially viable but because the funds (if unspent) would be lost, he patiently followed orders and bought equipment.

Computing the IRR

When using the IRR method for energy-related projects we can consider the potential savings in our utility bills to result in cash flows. For example, let's assume we were considering replacing one device in our data center with another due to the potential electrical savings touted by the manufacturer of the new device. Let's further assume

Table 1.7   Hypothetical Cash Flows

YEAR	CASH FLOW
0	−37800
1	8000
2	8250
3	8500
4	8750
5	9000

that you put pencil to paper and determined that to spend \$37,800 on the new equipment your cash flows from reduced electrical consumption would be as listed in Table 1.7, where the initial cash outflow denotes the up-front cost of the equipment. In this example, for simplicity we consider the annual savings in electricity as initially being \$8,000 and that the yearly savings will increase by approximately 3.125%, or \$250 per year, each year over the life of the equipment due to an increase in electric rates.

Based upon the previous assumptions the internal rate of return is computed as follows:

$$-37,800 + \frac{8,000}{(1+i)^1} + \frac{8,250}{(1+i)^2} + \frac{8,500}{(1+i)^3} + \frac{8,750}{(1+i)^4} + \frac{9,000}{(1+i)^5} = 0$$

Because computing the internal rate of return is a trial-and-error process, let's begin by trying a 5% rate. In our computation we want to see if the following equation is equal or close to zero. We say close to zero as usually we are only precise to a few decimal digits of accuracy. Thus, this author added a question mark to the end of the following equation in which i was replaced by .05.

$$-37,800 + \frac{8,000}{(1+.05)^1} + \frac{8,250}{(1+.05)^2} + \frac{8,500}{(1+.05)^3} + \frac{8,750}{(1+.05)^4}$$
$$+ \frac{9,000}{(1+.05)^5} = 0?$$

Working out the mathematics, we obtain:

−37800 + 7619.04 + 7482.99 + 7342.62 + 7198.68 + 7051.74 = (1104.93)

Note that in the above solution a pair of parentheses was used to indicate a negative result. Because an interest rate of 5% results in a negative sum this tells us that an IRR of 5% is too high. Thus, let's continue our trial-and-error approach and use an interest rate of 4%. Then, we want to determine if the following equation is closer to zero:

$$-4,000 + \frac{8,000}{(1+.04)^1} + \frac{8,250}{(1+.04)^2} + \frac{8,500}{(1+.04)^3} + \frac{8,750}{(1+.04)^4}$$
$$+ \frac{9,000}{(1+.04)^5} = 0?$$

Once again we work out the mathematics, obtaining −37800 + 7692.31 + 7627.59 + 7556.47 + 7479.54 + 7397.34, which equals −46.75. Although we are closer to zero, our result is still negative so let's reduce the interest rate a bit to 3.9% and try our computation again. Doing so we obtain:

$$-37,800 + \frac{8,000}{(1+.039)^1} + \frac{8,250}{(1+.039)^2} + \frac{8,500}{(1+.039)^3} + \frac{8,750}{(1+.039)^4}$$
$$+ \frac{9,000}{(1+.039)^5} = 0?$$

Again we work out the mathematics, obtaining −37800 + 7699.71 + 7642.28 + 7578.31 + 7508.37 + 7433.01, which equals 61.68. So now we have swung slightly positive, indicating that the divisor factors in the equation for which we are attempting to solve for i is too small. This means that we should increase the value of i and try again.

Using Excel

To save some time we can consider the use of a spreadsheet program to easily compute various values of i to determine one that provides a near zero result for the number of decimal points we are comfortable with determining. Table 1.8 depicts an extract from an Excel spreadsheet used by this author to compute several values of the potential IRR given the assumptions concerning the cost of the investment and the

Table 1.8 Computing a Possible IRR Using an Excel Spreadsheet

CASH FLOW	n	i = .05	i = .04	i = .039	i = .0395	i = .0396
−37800	0	−37800.00	−37800.00	−37800.00	−37800.00	−37800.00
8000	1	7619.05	7692.31	7699.71	7696.01	7695.27
8250	2	7482.99	7627.59	7642.28	7634.93	7633.46
8500	3	7342.62	7556.47	7578.31	7567.38	7565.19
8750	4	7198.65	7479.54	7508.37	7493.94	7491.05
9000	5	7051.74	7397.34	7433.01	7415.15	7411.59
SUM OF DISCOUNTED CASH FLOWS						
		−1104.96	−46.75	61.68	7.40	−3.44

stream of yearly cash flows resulting from a reduction in the cost of electricity from the new equipment.

In examining the entries in Table 1.8 there are a few items that warrant a bit of elaboration. First, if you focus your attention upon using an interest rate of .05 or 5%, the spreadsheet produces a sum of −1104.95 whereas our earlier computation produced a result of −1104.93. The reason for the slight variance in results is due to the fact that at first this author used a calculator for the computation and being the sort of person who likes to use computers for a tedious job, turned to the use of a spreadsheet to compute how close a series of interest rates are to obtaining the IRR for the problem at hand. Second, and just as important, Microsoft's Excel, as do other spreadsheets, includes many built-in functions that make it relatively easy to compute net present values and internal rate of return. Although Table 1.8 required this author to code his own equations, let's digress for a moment and discuss four important financial functions built into Excel and other spreadsheets.

NPV Functions in Excel   There are two NPV functions included in Excel, one used for determining the NPV based upon cash flows occurring at regular intervals and the second used for cash flows occurring at irregular intervals. The NPV function built into Microsoft's Excel for regular cash flows is of the form NPV(rate, value$_1$, value$_2$, … , value$_n$) where the rate represents the interest rate and the values represent the series of cash flows. For example, using =*NPV*(.05,500,500,500,600,700) returns a value of $2,403.71 when using Excel. The second NPV function, which is used to determine the net cash value when cash flows occur at irregular intervals is the

XNPV function. Its format is XNPV(rate, value$_1$, value$_2$, … ,value$_n$). Although you can use values in both functions, you can also reference cells.

ROI Functions in Excel   A second financial function included in Excel and other worksheets can be used to determine the internal rate of return using cash flows that occur at regular or irregular intervals. To determine the IRR based upon cash flows that occur at regular intervals is the IRR function, whose format is IRR(values,[guess]). Here the values should be specified as a range of cells, such as D1…D12 if there are 12 periods of cash flows. You can also place your initial guess in a cell, however, note that you would enter 5% as .05 in the cell. The use of the IRR function results in an iterative search procedure that begins with your guess and then repeatedly varies that value until a correct IRR is reached. Note that the guess argument is optional and if not included Excel will use 10% as the default value. To illustrate the use of the built-in IRR function let us return to the prior example where we pay $37,800 for new equipment that will reduce the cost of electricity by varying amounts, from $8,000 at the end of period 1 and increasing by $250 per period, until a savings of $9,000 is achieved in period 5.

Figure 1.3 illustrates the use of the IRR function with an initial guess of .1 or 10%, which is the default value. It should be noted that the function returns a value of 4%, which if you need precision you might be better off using a trial-and-error approach in Excel than depending upon the returned value through the use of the IRR function. In fact, this author tried formatting the cell to three digits of precision and still was provided with .040 whereas a trial-and-error approach indicated that the IRR was approximately 3.96%.

A word of caution is in order concerning the IRR. Mathematically, IRRs are just the roots of a NPV function. Sometimes there are multiple roots for a NPV and determining which one, if any, to use can require some logic. What is required is for you to look at the cash flows to see if a result or one of multiple results is a meaningful IRR. By summing up the cash flows you can tell immediately if they are positive or negative, in effect using a discount rate of zero to do so. If the cash flows are negative it's impossible to lose money and still have

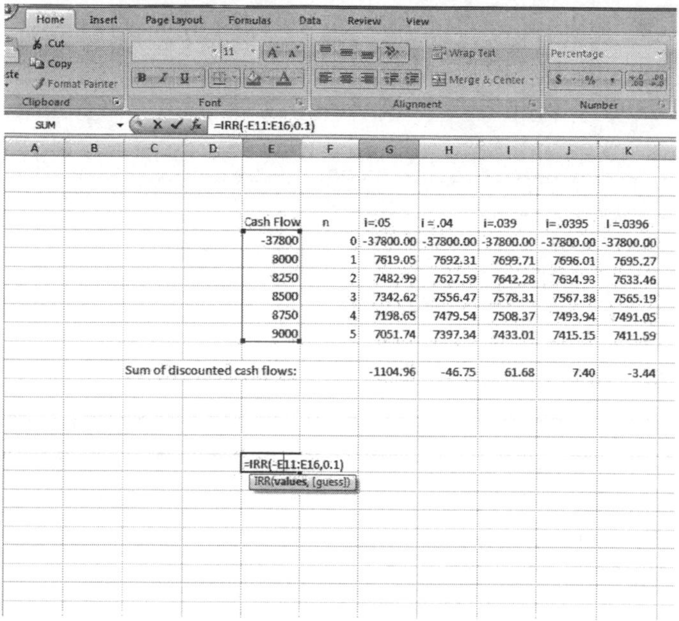

		Cash Flow	n	i=.05	i =.04	i=.039	i= .0395	I =.0396
		-37800	0	-37800.00	-37800.00	-37800.00	-37800.00	-37800.00
		8000	1	7619.05	7692.31	7699.71	7696.01	7695.27
		8250	2	7482.99	7627.59	7642.28	7634.93	7633.46
		8500	3	7342.62	7556.47	7578.31	7567.38	7565.19
		8750	4	7198.65	7479.54	7508.37	7493.94	7491.05
		9000	5	7051.74	7397.34	7433.01	7415.15	7411.59
Sum of discounted cash flows:				-1104.96	-46.75	61.68	7.40	-3.44

=IRR(-E11:E16,0.1)
IRR(values, [guess])

Figure 1.3   Using the IRR function in Excel.

a positive rate of return, so right away you can discard a result based upon logical thinking.

The second IRR function available in Excel is used to determine the internal rate of return using cash flows that occur at irregular intervals. In Excel this function is XIRR and its format differs slightly from the IRR function as you need to specify dates for the cash flow values. Thus, the format for the XIRR function is XIRR(values,dates,guess).

IRR Summary

The IRR represents a financial investment decision tool. As such, the computed IRR should be used as a decision criterion as to whether a specific project is worth the initial investment. Often, managers mistakenly use it as a mechanism to rate mutually exclusive projects. If the projects are mutually exclusive then their utility value to the organization differs and a comparison of IRRs may not be meaningful. For example, a manager may have a budget that allocates $100,000 for building improvements during the year. If the chiller is on its last legs whereas the installation of insulation between the ceiling tile and roof trusses is a nice to-do event, computing and comparing the IRR of each is not meaningful.

Summary

In this introductory chapter we learned that there are a number of valid reasons to conserve energy, of which its effect upon the bottom line of our organization might be just one of several factors we need to consider. In general, reducing energy consumption results in a lower level of heat dissipation. This in turn usually allows the life of equipment to increase as well as reduces the need to remove heat from our facility. Next, we examined four key financial-related metrics that can be used to evaluate the merits of a project. In doing so we realized that we can use repetitive energy savings that accrue due to the replacement or enhancement of buildings and equipment as equivalents to a stream of cash referred to as cash flow. This allows us to consider the use of the return on investment, payback period, discounted cash flow, or internal rate of return as mechanisms for red- or green-lighting a project.

As a graduate school teacher, this author noted a preference for the use of NPV resulting in the discounted cash flow method being preferred when comparing projects. However, in the commercial environment where this author also worked for many years, he noted a preference for the use of the IRR method over a discounted cash flow method. Apparently, some managers find it easier to compare investments of different sizes in terms of percentage rates of return than by dollars, particularly in the investment banking area where "sharks" swim, looking to literally gulp down companies. In general, the use of the net present value method provides a better reflection of the value of a project whereas the use of the IRR provides a better insight into whether the investment exceeds the cost of capital. Then, the higher a project's IRR, the more desirable it becomes to undertake the project. ROI works well when both the gains and the costs of an investment are easily known and where they clearly result from the action to be performed.

In a complex business environment it may not always be easy to determine specific returns from replacing a device with a more modern product other than its energy savings and even those savings projected out into years may have a large degree of variability associated with them, which can result in the ROI method becoming less trustworthy as a guide for decision support. However, as you extend predictions of future events farther into the future you will also sacrifice the trustworthiness of the other financial methods noted in this chapter. Thus, if you need to consider the cost of capital you may wish to consider the discounted cash flow method as a mechanism to rank projects. Similarly, because the IRR method does not consider the cost of capital in certain situations you can eliminate its use. Or, if you're looking for a very simple approach you might consider the payback method. Regardless of the method used, the important thing is to consider carefully the potential cash flows resulting from a product or device. We can usually determine not too far in the future energy savings, however, what is harder to project are the intangible benefits and their economic value to our organization. For example, focusing again on the replacement of CFL bulbs by LED lighting, how can you assign a value to replacing a bulb every year? It's not just the cost of the bulb you need to consider but its physical ordering, receiving, stocking, and perhaps having janitorial services grab a ladder and take 10 minutes to actually perform the work. Although you will be computing the cost of these events over multiple departments, the end result is you will be examining potential cash flows for your entire organization.

2

UNDERSTANDING
ELECTRICAL TERMS

In the first chapter in this book readers were briefly exposed to the rationale for conserving energy and a variety of financial methods that can be used to determine the viability of replacing or acquiring equipment based upon the potential reduction in energy consumption. In this chapter we turn our attention to understanding a number of electrical terms that provide us with the ability to compare and contrast products from the same or different vendors based upon their energy-related specifications. Thus, this chapter can be considered as similar to the first in that it builds up a base of knowledge for readers.

In this chapter, to mimic a popular song from the 1960s, we literally "begin at the beginning" by examining how electricity in the form of current and voltage is generated and distributed. To accomplish this we initially focus our attention upon understanding basic electricity, examining how circuits operate, the difference between alternating current (AC) and direct current (DC), the significance of the volt (V), ampere (A), ohm, and watt (W), as well as the manner by which electricity reaches the home or office. Because almost every device found in a data center operates using electrical power, we also discuss such key topics as the power factor of AC devices to include its significance. Using this information as a base we then discuss why you should consider the use of uninterruptible power supplies (UPS) even if your organization has a backup generator. In concluding this chapter we discuss how we compute the life-cycle cost of electricity. In doing so, we note that for many devices that operate on a 24/7 basis, such as web servers and mainframes as well as most types of data communications equipment, the operating cost can significantly exceed the acquisition cost of devices.

One of the most basic errors an author can make is to assume readers are familiar with the underlying technology associated with the topic of the book. After making this mistake a few times when this author was literally "wet behind his pen," I vowed not to make this mistake again. Thus, some readers who are very familiar with the generation and distribution of electricity might be inclined to skim this chapter. Because this author spent a considerable amount of time attempting to bring all readers to a similar level of knowledge, I believe that even the most experienced reader will gain knowledge from the coverage of topics in this chapter. Thus, I believe that even readers with a vast knowledge of electricity may wish to examine the contents of this chapter carefully.

Understanding Electricity

In this section we focus our attention upon obtaining an appreciation of electricity. Commencing with a review of atoms and their electrons, we discuss conductors, how current flows in a wire, the manner by which electricity is generated, basic circuit measurements, and the major difference between alternating current and direct current.

Atoms and Electrons

Electricity represents a form of energy that occurs due to the flow of electrons. Every atom, which represents a microscopic structure found in all matter, contains one or more electrons that have a negative charge. In some materials, such as rubber, plastic, glass, and even air, electrons are tightly bound to the atoms. Because the electrons in effect do not move, they cannot conduct electricity and are referred to as electrical insulators. In comparison, most metals have electrons that can be easily detached from their atoms. Such electrons are referred to as free electrons and provide the ability for electricity to flow through different types of material. Copper, gold, silver, aluminum, and other metals having electrons that can be easily detached from their atoms are known as electrical conductors because they conduct electricity. Although electricity requires a conductor to move, it also requires something to make it flow through the conductor. That "something" is an electric generator.

Electric Generators

An electric generator converts mechanical energy into electrical energy based upon the relationship between magnetism and electricity. In

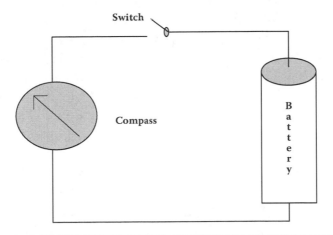

Figure 2.1   The relationship between electricity and magnetism can be observed by closing the switch and viewing the change in the direction of the needle of the compass.

the physics class you may have attended your instructor probably had a small experiment during which a wire was moved across an electric field, resulting in the flow of an electrical current in the wire. A similar but reverse experiment sometimes used by a physics instructor is to move electrons through a wire and observe how their flow results in the creation of a magnetic field around the wire. An example of the latter is illustrated in Figure 2.1 where a battery is used to generate the flow of electrons when the switch is closed. At that time the compass needle will move due to the magnetic field created by the flow of electrons. As we shortly note, the relationship between magnetism and the flow of electricity paved the way for the construction of power plant generators which, to paraphrase another old tune, will in effect "light up our lives."

If we return our attention to Figure 2.1 we can use that illustration as a mechanism to state the well-known right-hand law discussed in many physics classes. That is, if you take your right hand and clasp your four fingers together and move them inward toward your palm while extending your thumb upright, you can use your hand to view the relationship between the flow of current and the induced electromagnetic field. Here the thumb indicates the direction of the flow of electricity and the position of the four fingers indicates the direction of the electromagnetic force. For example, if the thumb is pointing upward then the electromagnetic force flows counterclockwise. In comparison, if the thumb points down to indicate a reversal of polarity that causes current to flow in the opposite direction then the electromagnetic force flows in the clockwise direction. Now that we have an appreciation for the relationship between an electromagnetic force and the flow of current let's turn our attention to how generators operate.

The large generators used by an electric utility have a stationary conductor formed in a ring shape. A magnet attached to the end of a rotating shaft is located inside the stationary conducting ring, with the conducting ring wrapped with wire. As the magnet rotates it induces a small electric current as it passes each section of wire. Cumulatively, the series of electric currents result in one current of considerable size. The shaft positioned within the stationary conducting ring is driven by a turbine whose blades are commonly turned by water or steam. Thus, let's discuss the role of the turbine in the electric generator process.

Turbines

The most basic type of turbine is a water-powered device, with water from a dam falling over its edge, causing the blades of a turbine to spin. A second type of turbine is a fossil-fueled steam turbine, in which natural gas, oil, coal, or nuclear power is used to heat water in a boiler to produce steam. The resulting steam is pressurized and flows through the turbine, resulting in its blades spinning, which in turn spins the shaft that generates electricity. Because the turbine and generator are closely related, many manufacturers, such as General Electric, produce what is referred to as a turbine generator.

Circuit Measurements

The magnitude of the generated current resulting from the flow of electrons is referred to as amperage, which is measured in amps and denoted by the symbol I. In comparison, the pressure used to push electrons is referred to as voltage, which is measured in volts and denoted by the symbol V.

As electrons flow in a conductor they encounter resistance. Resistance represents the ratio of voltage to current and is measured in ohms, where 1 ohm is defined as the resistance when 1 volt is applied to a material and the current is 1 amp. Resistance is denoted by the symbol R. The relationship between voltage, current, and resistance is referred to as Ohm's law, where:

$$R \text{ (ohms)} = \text{voltage/current} = \text{volts/amps} = V/I$$

Based upon Ohm's law we only need to know two of three measurements to compute the third. For example, assume we measure the current in a circuit to be 5 amps when 120 volts is applied. From Ohm's law

$$R = V/I = 120 \ V/5 \ I = .24 \text{ ohms}$$

Similarly, if we know the resistance of a circuit is 24 ohms and measure the current flowing through the circuit we can compute the voltage. That is, again from Ohm's law we have:

$$R = V/I \text{ or } V = I \times R$$

Then,

$$V = 5 \text{ amps} \times 24 \text{ ohms} = 120 \text{ volts}$$

Circuits

Although electrical circuits can become quite complex we can obtain an appreciation for how they operate by focusing our attention upon their common components, using a simple series circuit as shown in Figure 2.2 as a frame of reference. Regardless of the type of electrical circuit each circuit has several factors in common. First, the source of electricity, which is shown as a battery in Figure 2.2, has two terminals, a positive terminal and a negative terminal. Second, the source

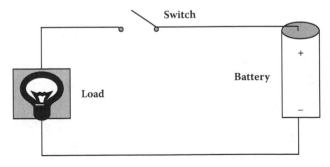

Figure 2.2   All circuits have a source of electricity, a load, and two wires used to transport electricity between the source and the load.

of electricity, shown as a battery but which can result from a generator located hundreds of miles away, pushes electrons out at a certain
voltage. In the example shown in Figure 2.2 a typical AA battery will
push electrons out at 1.5 volts. As electrons flow from the negative terminal to the positive terminal through the conductor the path forms
a circuit. The load can be a lightbulb, computer, television, stereo, or
a motor, and it will be powered by the electricity flowing through the
circuit. The key difference between the circuit shown in Figure 2.2
and the ones used to power our lights, computers, and most motors is
due to their oscillations or lack of oscillations. In Figure 2.2 a battery
is used to provide constant power and the circuit thus has direct current. In comparison, the typical home or office uses alternating current in which both current and voltage oscillate. Later in this chapter
we discuss in considerable detail both AC and DC.

Electrical Power

Power can be considered to represent the rate of doing work. In an
electrical circuit power is the rate of using energy and is measured in
watts, denoted by the symbol W.

Power is also the product of volts and current in a circuit, such that:

Power(watts) = voltage × current = volts × amps = V × I

In North America, the power outlets in the walls of homes and
offices are configured so that they deliver 120 volts. If you locate a
portable space heater and view its label you might note that it operates at 120 volts and draws 10 amps. This means that its power in
watts is:

Power(watts) = 120 volts × 10 amps = 1200

If instead of a space heater let's assume you locate a 60-watt lightbulb and plug it into a lamp which in turn is connected to a 120-volt
receptacle. You can use the preceding equation to compute the current
that flows in the circuit that illuminates the lightbulb. Because $P = V \times I$, then:

$$I = \frac{P}{V} = \frac{60}{120} = .5 \text{ amp}$$

Thus, a 60-watt lightbulb placed in a 120-volt socket draws .5 amp when illuminated.

Because electricity is consumed over time a power company measures consumption in terms of power used over a period of time. For example, a 60-watt bulb lit for a period of 8 hours results in the use of 480 watt-hours (Wh). Because the watt represents a relatively small amount of power, electric utilities bill customers based upon the number of kilowatt-hours of electricity consumed, where the kilowatt-hour (kWh) represents 1,000 watt-hours. One exception to the preceding are factories and other large consumers of electrical power. Such consumers may receive their monthly utility bills indicating consumption in terms of megawatt-hours (MWh), where the megawatt-hour represents 1,000 kWh or 1,000,000 Wh.

Electric rates in the United States commonly vary from approximately 5 cents per kWh to 25 cents per kWh. Typically, the kWh cost is lower in locations where electricity is generated through the use of water flowing across different types of barriers, referred to as hydroelectric generation. Of course, when an area that depends upon hydroelectric generation experiences a drought the utility is forced to import more expensive fossil-fuel or nuclear-generated electricity.

If we use an average cost of 12 cents per kWh for electricity we can note the bargain it provides in comparison to the functions it allows. For example, a 100-watt bulb left on during an 8-hour day consumes 100 watts × 8 hours or .8 kilowatt-hours of electricity. At a cost of 12 cents per kWh it costs slightly under a dime to light up our desk throughout the workday. Although the use of electricity can be a bargain, if you grew up with your parents telling you to "turn off the lights" when you left your room their words rang especially true when you consider the typical organization that employs 50 to 100 or more employees. If those employees do not turn off the lights when they leave for the day your organization winds up consuming power for, say, 100 unnecessary lights for 16 hours each day. Then, a hundred 100-watt bulbs left on for an additional 16 hours each day burns up $2.40 of electricity per day or $72 per month at 12 cents/kWh not counting the fact that the bulbs will burn out faster and need to be replaced. Unfortunately, if your organization is so lax that employees leave the lights on, they more than likely leave their personal computers on which can significantly increase unnecessary expenses.

For a second example of the cost of electricity, consider the 25-cubic-foot refrigerator installed in most homes and many offices. A modern 25-cubic-foot refrigerator will consume approximately 575 kWh of power during its full year of operation. At a cost of 12 cents per kWh this works out to a cost of $69 to operate the refrigerator throughout the year. In comparison, some older refrigerators consume well over 1,200 kWh of power per year. At a cost of 12 cents per kWh, the operation of a refrigerator that consumes 1,200 KWh of electricity works out to an annual expenditure of $144, or $75 more than a more efficient device. If your organization is located in a higher-cost area and pays 20 cents per kWh the savings can be more dramatic. For the preceding example the yearly operating cost difference would increase to $125 per year. Thus, if your organization has an older refrigerator in the break-room you might want to examine its operating cost.

Direct Current versus Alternating Current

Batteries, solar panels, and fuel cells generate current that always flows in the same direction between their terminals. Thus, these types of power generators produce direct current.

Because power plants generate electricity by moving a shaft that turns a magnet inside a stationary conducting ring, the direction of current periodically reverses, or alternates, resulting in such power referred to as alternating current. In North America current reverses direction 60 times per second, whereas in Europe generators produce power that alternates the direction of current 50 times per second. This explains why we refer to current in North America being produced at 60 cycles per second (CPS), and current in Europe is produced at 50 CPS. An alternate term used to refer to CPS is hertz, abbreviated Hz, named in honor of the German physicist Heinrich Hertz who in 1883 detected electromagnetic waves.

The major advantage of alternating current is the fact that it's very easy to change the voltage of the power produced by a generating plant. As we note later in this chapter, a transformer can be used to increase or decrease voltage. The key reason for the use of AC in homes and offices is one of economics. It's more economical for a power plant generating several million watts (MW) of power to transmit a high voltage with low amperage instead of a low voltage with high amperage. For example, a power plant capable of generating 1 million watts of power could transmit 1 megavolt (MV) at 1 amp. Sending 1 amp only requires a thin wire. In comparison, transmitting 1 M amp at 1 volt would require a very large diameter wire and would result in a considerable loss of power due to the heat associated with moving a million amps through a large conductor. Thus, it's more economical to transmit power at high voltage and relatively low amperage.

Power plants use transformers to convert lower voltage generated alternating current to very high voltages for transmission. Because high voltage can literally fry both humans and equipment a series of transformers is used to reduce the voltage that flows from main feeder lines onto branch lines, and other transformers reduce the voltage on branch lines down to the 120 volts that typically enters the home or office. Although the first commercial electrical power transmission (developed by Thomas Edison in the late nineteenth century) used direct current, Nikola Tesla (whose name is used by Tesla Motors, a manufacturer of all-electric vehicles) pioneered the development of commercial alternating current that supplanted Edison's method of DC transmission. However, in the mid-1950s, high voltage DC (HVDC) transmission was developed, which is now gaining acceptance as an alternative to high voltage alternating current transmission systems.

Direct Current (DC)   As previously mentioned, DC is produced by batteries, fuel cells, and solar panels. Direct current represents the unidirectional flow of electricity and is used in nearly all electronic systems as the power supply, including computer systems. In addition, both the older analog-based telephone still common in homes and offices as well as the more modern cell phone operate through the use of DC. Concerning the former, it is actually a DC and AC device. That is, the old telephone most of us still have operates via a 48-volt battery located in the telephone company central office. Although it operates via DC, during the ring cycle, an AC voltage is transmitted. Thus, when someone calls you, an AC signal is sent; once you pick up the phone, it runs by DC; or when there is no ring signal being sent it is operating as a DC device. A 48V voltage was selected because it was sufficient when telephone networks were established to transmit through kilometers of thin telephone wire and still be of a low enough voltage to be safe. In addition, 48V are easy to generate from lead acid batteries, which were required in telephone company central offices to ensure continuity of operation if the primary voltage was lost. In comparison, the modern cell phone commonly uses a lithium battery and operates as a DC device, obtaining a recharge through the use of a power supply, which in the wonderful world of cell phone technology is referred to as a charger.

In actuality, there is a variety of ways used to charge cell phones, ranging from DC to DC, through a universal serial bus (USB) port attachment cable to using an AC adapter, cigarette lighter adapter, and even wireless charging with the introduction of several products since 2009 that can charge a cell phone without a connection. Of course, the wireless charger needs to be plugged into an AC source, but the charging is performed without wires. One unfortunate result of the use of chargers or power supplies is the fact that energy is lost when the charger is plugged in but the device being charged is either fully charged or removed. This situation is referred to as a phantom load or vampire load and results in a small cost that cumulatively can add up to become significant. Later in this book we discuss this topic in more detail.

The Power Supply

Although referred to as a charger in the mobile phone world, the component that supplies power to the other components in a computer is the power supply. The power supply is normally designed to convert AC (commonly 115 to 127 volts alternating current (VAC) in North America, parts of South America, Japan, and Taiwan; and 220–240 VAC in most other locations) to usable low-voltage DC power for use by the internal components of a computer or other type of electronic device. Some power supplies have a switch to change between voltages. Other models include automatic sensors that switch input voltage automatically.

Power Supply Types

The power supply for electronic devices can be subdivided into linear and switching power supplies. The linear power supply is considered to represent a relatively simple device with circuitry that reduces voltage by dissipating it, making its efficiency low. In addition, its bulk and weight become a burden when used to support high-current equipment due to the need for large transformers and the use of heat-sinked electronic regulation circuitry. In comparison, a switched-mode power supply that has the same rating as a linear supply will be smaller and commonly is more efficient, however, it will be more complex and thus more costly. The modern computer power supply is designed to convert 110–240-VAC power to several output DC voltages in the range +12 V, –12 V, +5 V, +5 V, and +3.3 V. The 3.3 and 5 volts are typically used by digital circuits, and the 12 volt is used to run motors in disk drives and fans. The main specification of a power supply is in watts. The first generation of computer power supplies were linear devices, but as cost became a driving factor, and weight became important, switched mode supplies are today almost universally manufactured.

Operation

There are DC to DC power supplies, but the most common power supply is one that converts AC to DC. To do so, the power supply includes a transformer to convert voltage from a wall outlet to a lower voltage and a rectifier functioning as a converter, converting alternating voltage to a pulsating direct voltage. Depending upon the quality of the power supply there is a variety of other components in the device, including a filter, resistors, and capacitors that are used to smooth the resulting DC pulses. The quality of the power supply results in a varying degree of what is referred to as the ripple factor, where ripple represents the small amount of unwanted residual periodic variation of the DC output of a power supply, which results from an AC input. Ripple results from the incomplete suppression of the alternating waveform within the power supply. Although some degree of ripple is superimposed on direct output voltage, for charging batteries this is not a problem. However, in larger power supplies the amount of ripple can be equated to "you get what you pay for."

Phase

One key difference between AC and DC is the fact that both voltage and current on the former oscillate or vary by time. As mentioned

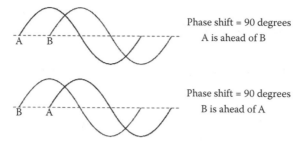

Phase shift = 90 degrees
A is ahead of B

Phase shift = 90 degrees
B is ahead of A

Figure 2.3   Example of phase shifts between two waves.

earlier, the oscillation rate is 60 times per second in the United States and 50 cycles per second in many other countries around the world. When capacitors or inductors are in an AC circuit the current and voltage will not flow so they peak at the same time. To ensure we have a good understanding of how current and voltage oscillation can be referenced let's review the operation of a standard sine wave that is illustrated at the top of Figure 2.3 labeled A. If we just examine the sine wave there we note that it begins at zero (0), rises to 1 at 90 degrees, recrosses zero at 180 degrees, falls to –1 at 180 degrees, and returns to zero at 360 degrees. If we compare waves we can have numerous results when they are out of phase with one another. For example, in the top portion of Figure 2.3 we see a phase shift of 90 degrees, with signal A ahead of B or referred to as "A leading B." In the lower portion of Figure 2.3 the reverse has occurred, with signal B now leading A with the same phase shift of 90 degrees. This situation is referred to as B leading A. In the real world A and B represent AC voltage and AC current, with the phase angle varying from 0 (only resistance on a circuit and voltage and current in phase) to various phase shifts.

Power Rating

The rating of a computer power supply is based upon its maximum output power in watts. Common power ranges from approximately 200 watts to more than 500 watts for what are regarded as small form factor systems intended for use in a personal computer. In comparison, higher-end power supplies commonly range from 750 watts to 2,000 watts for servers and mainframe computers and up to 4,000 watts for supercomputers.

Meters to Consider

There are two types of meters you need to consider to analyze circuitry, both of which in effect are measuring tools. The first type of meter should be analyzed by a trained and licensed electrical technician and is used to measure the current, voltage, or resistance in a circuit. The second measures the power consumed by your home, office, or building and is usually available for use by lay personnel, assuming they read the directions provided with the meter. In this chapter we focus our attention on the first type of meter and the next chapter focuses on the second type.

A key device used to measure the current in a circuit is the ammeter. As its name implies, it is used to measure the amperage in a circuit. An ammeter is usually combined with a voltmeter and an ohmmeter in a multipurpose instrument. When used to measure current the device commonly has several potential settings, with one selected by turning a dial, which in turn varies the resistance to perform a measurement. Some ammeters are designed for AC circuits, whereas other ammeters are used for DC circuits. Similarly, a voltmeter employed to measure the electrical potential difference between two points in an electric circuit can be obtained to operate on AC or DC circuits. In addition to being designed to operate on different types of electricity the meter can be analog or digital. Although analog meters were the first to be developed, digital meters date back to the 1950s. Regardless of the type of meter used, the device represents a measuring tool that a trained technician will commonly employ when troubleshooting what appears to be an electrical-related problem.

AC Measurements to Consider

There are two terms that are both important and frequently misunderstood so let's turn our attention to them in this section. Those terms are the root mean square (RMS) and power factor (PF).

RMS

Because AC measurements are often referred to in terms of DC power equivalence, the fact that AC is sinusoidal means we must consider the variations of alternating current. If you're familiar with mathematics, you know that the root mean square represents a measure of the magnitude of a varying quantity. In a DC circuit the power (P) is easy to compute from Ohm's law because the current (I) equals the voltage (V) divided by the resistance (R) or:

$$I = \frac{V}{R}$$

Then, because the power represents volts times amperes, we obtain:

$$P = V \times I$$

Thus, in terms of current and resistance the power in a DC circuit becomes:

$$P = I^2 \times R$$

Although the preceding formula is valid for DC circuits, suppose the current varies by time as in the case of AC. Then, the formula must be modified to reflect that. To determine the average AC power dissipated over time we would need to determine the RMS value. To do so we would perform the following three mathematical functions:

1. Determine the square of the waveform function (usually a sine wave).
2. Average the function resulting from the first step over time.
3. Compute the square root of the function resulting from the second step.

For a sine wave, the RMS value is 0.707 times the peak value, or 0.354 times the peak-to-peak value. Thus, the power on an AC circuit is actually noted as:

$$Power_{avg} = (I_{RMS})^2 \times R$$

Because AC has both alternating current and voltage the average power expressed in terms of current and voltage becomes:

$$Power_{avg} = I_{RMS} \times V_{RMS}$$

Note that most utility voltages are expressed in RMS terms. Thus, a common 120-volt AC circuit actually carries about 170 (120/0.707) peak volts (pk), or 338 (120/0.354) volts peak-to-peak (pk–pk).

Power Factor (PF)

A second potentially misunderstood term you need to become acquainted with is the power factor. The power factor also arises when we discuss alternating current and is defined as the ratio of real power to apparent power. The power ratio is a dimensionless number between 0 and 1 and is often expressed as a percentage, such as a 70% PF, which is equal to .7 PF. To understand the power factor we need to make a distinction between real power and apparent power. Real power represents the capacity of a circuit, whereas apparent power represents the product of current and voltage of a circuit. Thus, real power will be less than or equal to apparent power.

If θ is used to represent the phase angle between current and voltage then the power factor can be expressed as follows:

$$PF = \cos\theta \times V \times I$$

Importance of the Power Factor   In a purely resistive AC circuit the voltage and current waveform are in phase with each other. This means that they change polarity at the exact same time in each cycle. When the circuit has reactive loads, such as during the operation of an electric motor, the energy stored in device capacitors or inductors results in a time difference occurring between voltage and current waveforms.

This means that during each cycle of AC voltage some additional energy beyond that used directly by the device will be stored, resulting in an increase in the current in the line that is essentially wasted as it is not used directly by a device. Thus, a circuit with a low power factor will require a higher current to transport a quantity of real power in comparison to a circuit with a higher power factor. Thus, the goal of an electric utility is to have a PF of unity because a lesser value means that they will have to supply more current to the user for a given amount of power use. In addition, when a power factor decreases this means that the utility will require larger capacity equipment in place than would otherwise be necessary. Due to this, many utilities will penalize a large electric consumer if its power factor is much different from unity.

In an office environment you do not have to be concerned about the PF of circuits that contain purely resistive heating elements, such as heaters. This is because purely resistive heating elements have a PF of unity. However, from an electrical use viewpoint, you might become concerned about the use of heaters in July to remove the chill from an office when a simple temperature adjustment at the thermostat might eliminate their use. In comparison, circuits that contain capacitive or inductive elements, such as electric motors where the windings act as inductors and lamp ballasts have a power factor below unity.

If your organization uses a large number of motors and the utility is assessing your organization for its PF you can consider several options. First, you should ascertain the monthly charge to determine if an effort to raise your organization's PF is worth the cost. Next, you might consider having a technician or electrician use a power factor monitor to determine the source of the reason or reasons your organization is being penalized. If you can isolate the variance in the PF to equipment that is old or obsolete, you might consider its replacement. In addition, because capacitors have the opposite effect of inductors they may be able to be used as a mechanism to compensate for inductive motor windings. In fact, some industrial sites have installed large banks of capacitors strictly for the purpose of correcting the power factor back toward one to save on utility company charges. Now that we have an appreciation of AC measurement to include the root mean square and power factor, let's conclude our basic review of electricity with a few words about ground.

Ground

Ground, as the term implies, refers to a connection to the earth. A ground acts similarly to a reservoir of charge and functions as a mechanism to prevent shock. On a transmission line you can see electric poles where a bare wire is connected from the upper portion of the pole to a coil placed in the base of the pole. The coil is in direct contact with the earth, which provides a ground. If you carefully look at a series of electric poles in your neighborhood you can see the ground wire running between poles as well as attached to the coil at the base of each pole. There are three conductor systems we need some knowledge of when referencing AC power, which is commonly referred to as "mains electricity" and represents the general-purpose (AC) electric power supply.

First is the good old earth. Although a reasonably good conductor is an earth conductor, referred to as an "earthing conductor," it is primarily used to limit the voltage imposed by lightning and AC line surges. If you have a coaxial cable entering your home and look at its connection you might notice a wire that branches off into the ground that represents a typical earthing conductor. The recommended minimum sizes of earthing conductors for both copper and aluminum are specified in a standards publication such as the National Electric Code (NEC) and AS/NZS 3000:2007 Electrical installations (known as the Australian/New Zealand Wiring Rules). Equipment earthing conductors are normally used as bonding conductors, representing a second type of ground. A bonding conductor is what gives us the safety path for fault current, which is similar to regular current and like all current, is seeking its source and not the earth. Thus, bonding ground is designed to provide protection against fault current, such as one resulting from a frayed or damaged conductor. When this happens a short circuit will occur. This in turn will result in a current protection device, such as a circuit breaker or older fuse to activate and disconnect the faulty circuit. Thus, bonding, a term used to refer to the interconnection of all exposed noncurrent-carrying metal objects together will result in each object remaining near the same potential level, reducing the potential for shock or even the occurrence of death. Note that in many organizations the equipment bonding conductor is usually also used as the equipment earthing conductor.

You should also ground data communication and data processing equipment to the electrical service, however, simply grounding equipment to structural steel may be insufficient. This is because the sensitivity of most electronic equipment is such that they need to prevent loops or transients that can damage the equipment. Thus, you should carefully read the specifications and installation manuals of equipment to determine the appropriate method required to both ground and bond them.

A third type of grounding used is referred to as a grounding electrode conductor (GEC). A grounding electrode conductor is a conductor that connects one part of an electrical system, commonly at the electric service panel, to one or more earth electrodes. The GEC is required to be copper, aluminum, or copper-clad aluminum. Another term used for grounding electrode conductor is "system grounding" and most electrical systems are required to be grounded. The rationale for the GEC is to limit the voltage to earth imposed by lightning events and contact with higher voltage lines as well as to stabilize the voltage to earth during normal operation.

The US NEC 100-A and the UK BS 7671 as well as other publications list systems that are required to be grounded. The grounding electrode conductor is usually but not always connected to the leg of the electrical system, which is referred to as the "neutral wire." The sizing of the GEC is based upon the size of service feeders. In the United States sizing values are listed in Table 250-66 of the NEC.

The grounding electrode conductor is commonly bonded to a metal water pipe at the outside of a building, however, the introduction and growing acceptance of the use of PVC types of plastic pipes resulted in some countries banning the grounding to water pipes. As an alternative, the GEC can be connected to a concrete-encased electrode or structural steel in some structures. Different size conductors are specified by the NEC based upon the type of conductor and its rating in amps. Now that we have an appreciation for the manner by which electricity flows into our home and office and the general grounding of equipment let's turn our attention to how electricity flows to our home or facility. As we do so, we discuss the operation of the transformer that is used both by utilities as well as within many organizational facilities and is usually unnoticed but extremely important.

Proper grounding is extremely important. This importance is due to providing protection from shock hazards and in the extreme, cardiac arrest, severe burning, and even death. Although many types of electronic devices are battery powered and operate at low voltages that are not considered a shock hazard, the chargers for such devices are plugged into an AC outlet where the current and voltage can be a hazard if the outlet or the main power becomes a hazard. Table 2.1 provides an indication of the potential effect of electrical current upon a person. This table represents a general guide as the weight, condition

Table 2.1   General Effect of Current upon a Person

CURRENT	POTENTIAL EFFECT
≤ 1 mA	Possible slight tingle
1–5 mA	Slight to moderate shock
6–30 mA	Painful shock, loss of muscular control, and inability to let go of device person is touching
31–150 mA	Extreme pain, severe muscular contractions, possibility of death

of the person, and other factors contribute to his or her reaction to various currents.

Electricity Distribution

Although most homeowners and office workers take electricity for granted, unless a storm knocks out our power lines we really do not place much emphasis on how power is distributed to our location. In this section we do not wait for a sudden storm or the crash of an automobile or truck into a power company facility to impede the flow of electricity to appreciate how it arrives at our door. Instead, we turn our attention to the manner by which electricity travels into our home or office.

The Power Plant

Electricity begins its travel to our home or office at a power plant. That plant uses water, coal, natural gas, or nuclear fuel to generate steam, which is used to make a turbine spin. The spinning of the turbine in turn generates electricity. In the case where water is used, typically a dam is constructed to gather water into a narrow channel. As water flows into the channel it moves toward locks that can be raised or lowered and control the flow of water across the dam. As water flows through the locks its pressure is used to spin the blades of a turbine. In effect the force of gravity and the motion of the water cause the turbine to spin. When a nonrenewable fuel, such as coal or natural gas is used, combustion is employed to heat water into steam. Similarly, when nuclear fuel is used, uranium control rods are inserted into a reactor to generate heat via a controlled nuclear fusion process that is used to turn water into steam. For both nuclear- and nonnuclear-generated steam, the result is similar, with the steam pressurized and used to turn the blades of turbines connected to a shaft placed in a magnetic field that generates electricity.

Transformers

Electricity is generated by a turbine installed at a power plant that is normally located at a distance from the majority of the plant's

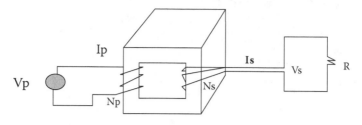

Figure 2.4   A transformer can be used to increase or decrease voltage.

customers. For example, a large power plant located at Four Corners, where Arizona, Utah, Nevada, and New Mexico are joined to one another is located hundreds of miles from major population centers. To facilitate the flow of electricity over long distances the power plant will use transformers to increase voltage so that electricity can flow on high-voltage lines with a minimal loss.

A transformer makes use of Faraday's law and the ferromagnetic properties of an iron core to either raise or lower alternate current voltage. As a refresher for some readers who may have skipped a physics class or the first section of this chapter that discussed magnetic properties, Faraday's law states that any change in the magnetic environment of a coil of wire will cause a voltage to be induced in a coil. By adjusting the area of an iron core and the number of turns of a wire on each side of the core we can either raise or lower a secondary or output voltage with respect to the primary or input voltage.

To illustrate the operation of a transformer consider Figure 2.4. In this example the primary voltage is produced by the power plant generator. The output or secondary voltage is then transported via a high-voltage power line to a metropolitan area.

From Faraday's law:

$$\frac{V_s}{V_p} = \frac{N_s}{N_p}$$

where:
V_p = primary voltage
V_s = secondary voltage
N_s = secondary number of turns
N_p = primary number of turns

Although a transformer can be used to raise or lower voltage it cannot increase or decrease power. Thus, for an ideal transformer we have:

$$P_p = V_p I_p = V_s I_s = P_s$$

where:
P_p = primary power
P_s = secondary power
V_p = primary voltage
V_s = secondary voltage
I_p = current primary
I_s = current secondary

When the voltage is raised by a transformer, the transformer is referred to as a step-up device. Because the power cannot increase, when the voltage is raised the current is proportionally lowered. Thus,

$$I_s = V_p I_p / V_s$$

In actuality, both the primary and secondary transformer circuits have resistance that affects the output of the device. Thus, the previously presented computations can be considered to represent an ideal transformer that has no resistance. Although transformers do indeed have resistance, in order to explain the flow of electricity from a power station to a home or office, in this section we assume a perfect world and an ideal transformer. Thus, for the purpose of understanding the role of transformers we need to note that the ratio of primary and secondary windings and primary voltage affects the resulting secondary voltage. If the number of primary windings (N_p) is greater than the number of secondary windings (N_s) then the secondary voltage (V_s) will be less than the primary voltage (N_p). If the number of secondary windings (N_s) is greater than the number of primary windings (N_p) then the opposite will be true. That is, the secondary voltage (V_s) will be greater than the primary voltage (V_p).

From the power plant's transformer, electricity is coupled onto high-voltage lines to enable power to flow relatively long distances. At locations where groups of customers are located the high-voltage line is coupled to a transformer located in a facility referred to as a substation.

The transformer location in the substation is a step-down device with a lesser number of secondary coils than primary coils. Thus, the substation reduces the voltage via a step-down transformer for distribution on power lines that can run either overhead or underground.

Types of Transformers   As the power lines reach a particular area where homes or offices are within close proximity the high voltage on the utility line is further reduced by the use of smaller transformers. You can usually note these transformers, which appear as circular containers mounted on utility poles or as small rectangular metal enclosures set on concrete pads. Figure 2.5 illustrates a pole-mounted transformer operated by Georgia Power in Macon, Georgia. Figure 2.6 shows a rectangular metal enclosure set on a concrete pad in the neighborhood where this author's home is located. The metal enclosure contains a transformer whose output is placed onto power lines that run underground to homes in the neighborhood. For either type of transformer they typically reduce the voltage provided by the regional transformer to 120 volts for use in the home or office.

Transformer Wiring   Because electricity flows in a circuit there must be at least two wires routed from the last transformer that produced 120-volt output into the home or office. One wire represents a hot wire, and the second represents a neutral wire. Older homes and offices that only have two wires entering the facility can only provide 120-volt current. In comparison, more modern homes and offices commonly have three wires entering the facility. Two of those wires are hot, each carrying 120 volts and the third wire is neutral. Thus, the inbound voltage permits an electrician to provide circuits in the home or office that operate at either 120 or 240 volts.

Service Methods   There are two methods used to provide electric service to homes and offices. One method is referred to as overhead service and the second method is referred to as underground service. If the home or office has overhead service, the wires emerge from a transformer and are routed as an aerial line to a weatherhead mounted on the roof or side of the facility. The weatherhead is a conduit that allows wires from the transformer to be spliced into wires that are routed to an electrical meter. The meter measures how much

Figure 2.5   A utility pole-mounted transformer.

Figure 2.6   A metal enclosure used to house a transformer whose output flows onto underground power lines.

electricity the house or office uses and provides information that affects your monthly bill. From the electric meter wires are routed into a service panel that distributes electricity throughout the home or office.

Single Phase versus Three Phase   Now that we have some knowledge concerning the operation of a transformer let's use that information to discuss the difference between single-phase and three-phase AC circuits. Although the common single-phase AC has the key advantage of the use of a single wire pair, twice every cycle it will go to zero assuming a 60 Hz rate. Thus, the standard household and small office receive single-phase power, however, for larger industrial organizations as well as the electric utility a better method of power transmission is sought. That method is referred to as three-phase AC transmission.

Three-phase electric power represents a common method of AC power transmission used by utilities due to its economics resulting from the use of a lower amount of conductive material than equivalent single- or dual-phase systems transmitting at the same voltage level. Although at one time there were several dual-phase systems and it was popular in the United States, it is this author's opinion that today they resemble the dodo bird. That is, they are an extinct species. However, as a historical note, the development of dual-phase AC can be attributed to Nikola Tesla, who in effect was the discoverer of multiphase current. However, the actual development of three-phase AC occurred in Germany and Switzerland, where it is known as "rotating current" for its property of constant power.

As you might expect, in a three-phase system three circuit conductors are used to transport three alternating currents of the same frequency. Each circuit reaches its instantaneous peak value at a different time. For example, if we take one conductor as the reference, the other two currents flowing on the two remaining circuits will be delayed in time by 120 and 240 degrees, or one-third and two-thirds of one cycle of the electrical current. The delay between phases has the effect of providing a constant power transfer over each cycle of the current, which by the way, makes it possible to produce a rotating magnetic field in an electric motor and explains why almost all larger electric motors are three-phase devices.

In North America almost every home is connected to the power grid via a single-phase system. Because it results in a considerable saving to utilities due to savings in conductor expense, most transmissions are three-phase, with the phase split out and individual loads fed from a single phase. However, some large companies with a considerable amount of machinery, such as industrial motors, more likely than not have a three-phase connection to the utility grid. Note that a three-phase system may or may not have a neutral wire. A neutral wire allows the three-phase system to use a higher voltage while still supporting lower-voltage single-phase appliances. In high-voltage distribution situations it is common not to have a neutral wire as the loads can simply be connected between phases, a technique referred to as a phase–phase connection. In North America the three wires were originally color-coded black, red, and blue, and the neutral wire, if present, colored white and the earth ground colored green. The more modern 277/480 system uses brown, orange, and yellow for the three wires, with neutral and earth ground remaining white and green. This three-phase system uses what is referred to as a Wye (Y) configuration, with each phase separated by 120 degrees from the others (0, 120, 240). The voltage from each end to the Y center is 277 V and the end-to-end voltage is 480 V, which mathematically is the square root of 3 times 277.

The Service Panel

The service panel represents the location in a home or office where electricity provided by a utility enters the facility for distribution within the facility. Many times we use the terms fusebox or circuit breaker to refer to the service panel, although those terms are not technically correct. Some more common names for the service panel include a distribution board, panelboard, and electrical panel.

Figure 2.7 illustrates the relationship among the utility line, weatherhead, utility meter, and service panel, indicating the ownership with respect to the customer and the utility. In examining Figure 2.7 note that although the service panel is shown inside the building, it can also be mounted outside, although doing so requires a weatherproof box that adds to its cost as well as makes checking the panel a bit more difficult. Also note that an overhead utility line is shown providing power to the home or the office building. If an underground power line were used, the power line would be routed from a transformer mounted on a slab underground to the edge of the home or office. At that location the power line would be routed through a conduit in the

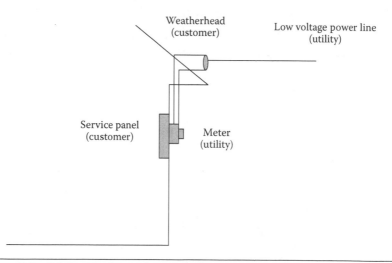

Figure 2.7   Relationship of power line, weatherhead, meter, and service panel when power is provided by an overhead line.

form of a pipe into the electric meter. Thus, the weatherhead would not be needed.

Types of Service Panels   There are two types of service panels used in homes and offices. The first type, which is primarily associated with older homes and offices, is a fused service panel. This type of service panel, which was located in the author's first home during the late 1960s, consists of a rectangular box into which an electric line from the outside meter is wired. Each of the circuits in the home is protected through the use of a circular fuse that blows when too much current flows through it, resulting from a current overload condition. Technically, the fuse has an element that will melt when the current becomes high enough to provide a sufficient amount of heat. Once blown, a fuse cannot be fixed and must be replaced. Thus, homes and offices with older fuse panels typically need a supply of fuses to be readily available as replacements when a fuse blows.

The second, and for many a more modern type of service panel, is a breaker panel. This type of panel contains a series of circuit breakers that trip when they sense heat caused by an excess amount of current flowing through the breaker to the circuit protected by the device. When the circuit breaker trips it shuts off power to the circuit and power remains off until you physically reset the breaker. Most modern breakers will display a red tab when they are blown as well as position themselves in the OFF position. Other breakers will simply move to the OFF position when they are tripped, whereas a pushbutton breaker will pop out when a trip occurs.

Although fuse panels often are less costly and simpler than a similar rated circuit breaker, when an abnormal amount of current attempts to flow the fuse will blow. Then the blown fuse must be replaced with a new device, which is less convenient than simply resetting a breaker. In addition, the use of both fuses and circuit breakers has a tendency to discourage people from investigating circuits. For example, replacing a fuse or flipping a breaker without isolating the circuit first can be dangerous if the fault is a short circuit.

In an industrial setting fuses are still used, especially due to their low cost and ability to operate at high voltage and current levels. In addition, because motors initially draw a surge of power, it's common to use a time delay fuse that only opens when an excessive amount of current flows for a predefined amount of time. In comparison to the time-delay fuse another type is referred to as a fast-acting fuse. This type of fuse is used when speed of protection is extremely important, such as for protecting electronic devices.

Both fuses and circuit breakers are used to protect equipment and personnel from the potential risk of shock and fire. In addition, they provide a mechanism to isolate circuits and systems from the main AC power. Proper selection of a fuse or circuit breaker involves considering a variety of factors. Those factors include the voltage and current rating, interruption rating, the maximum circuit fault current allowed, and usually an Underwriters Laboratory (UL) approval. Regardless of the method used to indicate a trip condition, you should first unplug any device on the circuit controlled by the fuse or breaker prior to replacing the fuse or resetting the breaker. Then, you can replace the fuse or flip the breaker to the ON position or on a pushbutton device, push it all the way in and then release it to perform a reset operation.

Operation   Figure 2.8 illustrates the breaker service panel in this author's current home. At the top of the box power enters through two hot wires. Although you cannot see them, the hot wires are commonly colored black and red, and a white wire is used for the return. At the top of the service panel is the main breaker, which when flipped or repositioned turns off power to the entire home.

Depending upon the location of a home or office, some electrical codes require the addition of a main disconnect location outside the structure whereas other codes allow the main disconnect to be placed within the home or office. For either location, shutting off the power turns off the flow of electricity to all circuits routed from the panel through the home or office.

The service panel is normally arranged in two columns, with the individual breaker positions numbered left to right along each row from top to bottom. Thus, odd-numbered breakers are located on the leftmost column and even-numbered breakers are located in the right-most column. A circuit breaker designed for three-phase can be obtained to enable users to derive 120 volts. This is because three-phase means you have three separate 120-volt supplies coming into the panel, labeled A phase, B phase, and C phase. Each one of these circuits is protected by the amp breaker per phase, somewhere approximately at or above 225 amperes. Within each individual service panel are individual circuit breakers at much lower amperage. For illustrative purposes let's assume they are 20 amp circuits. This means that if any of those individual circuits draws more than 20 amps the breaker controlling that circuit will trip. For example, if you plug in too many PCs, printers, and other devices into a common circuit at one time in your office the breaker controlling that circuit

Figure 2.8   A breaker service panel.

will trip. However, other circuits as well as the main power source will not trip.

Inside the Service Panel   Returning our attention to the service panel located in this author's current home, let's discuss the breakers shown in Figure 2.8. Note the two rows of breakers running vertically inside the panel. If you look carefully at Figure 2.8 you will note that on some rows there are two miniature breakers. Those minibreakers control low amperage circuits whereas a normal-sized breaker controls a higher amperage circuit.

If you remove the metal panel in the circuit breaker box, which by the way should be done by an experienced and licensed electrician, you will be able to see two hot wires, each carrying 120 volts, referred to as hot bus bars, routed to the main disconnect. A 120-volt breaker is attached to one wire, and a 240-volt breaker is attached to both wires. The hot wire for each circuit in this author's home is attached to each breaker, and a hot bus bar has green or bare copper ground wires attached to the bar. In addition, there is a thick ground wire attached to the neutral bus bar that represents the main ground wire. That wire is routed out of the service panel to either a cold-water pipe or rod, with the latter commonly required to be driven at least eight feet into the ground. If a cold-water pipe is used, because it leads into the ground via other pipes it can also serve as a ground. In addition to the main ground, each individual circuit must be grounded. This is commonly accomplished by the use of a green or bare copper wire attached to the neutral bar.

Building Service Panel   Although the home and office service panels are similar, there are some distinct differences. First, the home is commonly limited to one service panel whereas the office can have several. Second, in the home, electricity is single-phase with a frequency of 60 Hz in the United States and typically 50 Hz in Europe, whereas an office or industrial facility may have a single-phase, three-phase, or a combination of both single-phase and three-phase systems.

In the United States a three-phase transformer is commonly used by an electric utility to transmit a high-voltage, three-phase AC for distribution to the general public. Just about all homes operate on single-phase AC, with a step-down transformer used by the electric utility to provide the required voltage of 120 volts. When the output of the transformer is connected with the standard mains voltage (a term used to refer to the voltage from the utility to the customer, this term also refers to the general-purpose AC electric power supply) it's also possible to output 240-V three-phase as well as three different single-phase voltages, 120 V between two of the phases and the neutral, 208 V between the third phase and neutral, and 240 V between any two phases to be made available from the same supply.

As previously mentioned, the larger electric motor represents a key direct use of a three-phase load. Such motors are used in fans, blowers, compressors, pumps, and other types of motor-driven devices. One common example of the direct use of a three-phase AC is large air-conditioning equipment. Because a three-phase motor usually rated above 7.5 kW is more compact, less costly, and operates more efficiently than single-phase motors, three-phase AC is commonly encountered in data centers to provide power for the air handlers, high-efficiency heat pumps, and similar devices. It should be noted that the advantages associated with three-phase motors may make some organizations consider the use of phase converters if three-phase power is not available to their location. A phase converter as its name implies converts the phase of power. Although the 1-to-3 phase converter can be found using an Internet search, a word of caution is in order. A product designed for three-phase AC will work when powered through a converter, however, it will usually operate at a lower efficiency. Thus, if your facility does not have three-phase AC and you're considering, for example, adding a high-efficiency heat pump designed for three-phase operation, you might ask the manufacturer's technical support for efficiency information when the product was used via a phase converter. Although you know the rated seasonal energy efficiency ratio (SEER) for direct three-phase from the product's specification sheet, you want to determine its efficiency if three-phase results from the use of a phase converter.

Circuits

Prior to discussing the types of circuits found in the home and office a few words are warranted discussing the closed and open circuit as well as the short circuit. As you might assume, the closed circuit represents a complete path for current to flow. In comparison, an open circuit does not have a complete path and due to this it impedes the flow of current. Thus, an open circuit cannot provide power to a device. A third general type of circuit we should be familiar with is the short circuit. A short circuit technically represents a very low resistance path. This type of circuit usually occurs unintentionally, possibly due to the fraying of a wire pair so the individual wires touch each other or failure of a device that results in the circuit ceasing to function. Because a large amount of current will flow toward the path of least resistance that will generate heat which can start a fire, we use fuses and circuit breakers as protection devices. By automatically opening the circuit the fuse or circuit breaker creates an open circuit, stopping the flow of current.

Types of Circuits   From the service panel each breaker or fuse protects a circuit routed throughout the home or office. Those circuits are referred to as branch circuits and can be subdivided into three general categories. Those categories are general-purpose, small-appliance, and individual circuits.

General-Purpose Circuits   General-purpose circuits are used to provide electricity to several receptacles used for lighting and small electrical appliances, such as fans, personal computers, and similar devices. As we noted earlier in this chapter, a single 100-watt lightbulb draws approximately 1 ampere of current. Due to the low amperage requirement of lighting, a 120-volt general-purpose circuit that commonly uses a 15- or 20-amp circuit breaker is wired to several receptacles, allowing a group of table lamps, fans, and a personal computer and printer to use one branch circuit. Figure 2.9 illustrates the routing of wires from a circuit breaker to provide electricity for two receptacles and a switch that controls the flow of current to a light.

Small-Appliance Circuit   A second type of circuit is used to power small appliances. Because small appliances such as microwaves, toasters, and mixers can draw a lot of current when turned on, each small-appliance branch circuit is connected to only a few receptacles. Inasmuch as appliances are primarily located in a kitchen or cafeteria area, the small-appliance circuit is installed in those locations.

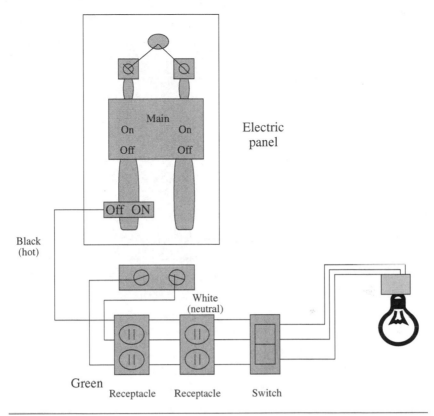

Figure 2.9   A typical 120-volt general-purpose circuit.

Individual Circuits   The purpose of an individual circuit is to provide electricity to a location where a lot of power will be consumed. Typically, individual circuits are used to provide power to a dishwasher, trash compactor, and similar appliances in the home.

When large appliances, such as washers, dryers, electric ranges, and ovens are powered by individual circuits, such circuits provide 240-volt current.

Plugs and Sockets

The first use of electricity was for lighting and resulted in the development of the familiar screw-in socket. As the use of electricity expanded to power fans, vacuum cleaners, and similar devices a mechanism was required to provide a safe method to connect devices to circuits, giving rise to a two-pin electrical plug and socket. The original electrical two-pin plug and wall socket were designed by

Harvey Hubbell and are commonly referred to the Hubbell adapters. Patented by Hubbell in 1904, this electrical connectivity mechanism was widely adapted by other manufacturers. Improvements to the Hubbell design included the grounded consumer plug that added a round grounding pin to the two-pin electrical plug and a ground hole in the outlet socket. For many years the two pins and socket slots in a wall outlet were the same height, allowing an electrical cord to be plugged into a socket either right-side or left-side up. Beginning in the 1950s sockets and plugs were polarized via the inclusion of a neutral blade and corresponding slot in the socket that is wider than the live blade slot and corresponding wall outlet slot, ensuring that an electrical plug can be inserted into the socket correctly. It's interesting to note that certain types of polarized plugs will not fit into unpolarized sockets because the unpolarized slots are too narrow to accommodate the plug. However, both unpolarized and polarized plugs will normally fit into polarized sockets as well as three-prong sockets that include a grounding pin. Wall sockets are commonly referred to as power points, power sockets, electric receptacles, or electrical outlets. Regardless of nomenclature, the socket represents female electrical connectors that have slots or holes that accept and deliver current to the prongs of inserted plugs.

There is an excellent reason to travel with a box of electrical outlet adapters. That reason results from what appears to be a wide variety of plug/socket configurations as you move around the globe. For the sake of space we do not cover the wide variety of plug and socket combinations encountered other than to provide a word of caution. That is, when you are in a foreign location it is a good idea to check first with either the hotel if you are staying there or a building manager to ascertain the parameters of a circuit prior to using an adapter. Many computers have adapter power converters that automatically switch between 120 VAC and 220 VAC, however, some do not. Similarly, other types of charges may or may not switch automatically, so it is also an excellent idea to read the label on the adapter prior to its insertion into a wall socket.

Office Plugs and Sockets   Although you can expect to encounter plugs and sockets in the office similar to those used in the home, there are also some plugs and outlets that are restricted to the office environment.

Table 2. 2   Common Pin Counts and Applications for Different Wiring Systems

AC POWER DISTRIBUTION SYSTEM	CONNECTOR PINS	COMMON APPLICATION
Single-phase w/o safety ground	2	Lamps, double insulated appliances
Single-phase w/ safety ground	3	Most type of business equipment
Three-phase w/o safety ground	3	Not common today
Three-phase w/safety ground	4	Three-phase business equipment and machinery
Single-phase center tapped w/ safety ground	4	Large residential appliances
Three-phase with neutral w/o safety ground	4	Not common today
Three-phase with neutral w/ safety ground	5	Three-phase equipment with unbalanced loads

For example, hospitals typically use an AC power connector rated at 15 amps at 125 volts, which supports wire of various diameters. In comparison, in an office environment there is a range of connectors that may be used, ranging from a snap-in panel mounted male AC connector rated at 15 amps at 250-volts AC to three-prong female and male AC connectors rated at 10 amps and 250 volts. Sometimes the hardest effort involved in designing a new equipment installation is ensuring your organization has the correct cables and connectors to mate equipment to various power sources. You can facilitate the installation of new equipment by the so called "rule of Ps," which refers to Proper Planning Prevents Problems.

Table 2.2 provides a summary of the common standardized types of AC connectors used in North America to include the number of pins and their typical application. Readers should note that there are over 150 different styles of AC conductors currently defined, to include straight-blade and twist-lock connectors. The straight blade connector is primarily used for 15-amp, 208-volt single-phase circuits and the twist-lock connector is used for both 15-amp, 208-volt single-phase and 30-amp, 125-volt three-phase connections.

The International Electrical Commission (IEC) has published standards for AC interconnection between pieces of equipment, two of the more popular standards being IEC 60320 and IEC 60309. The IEC 60320 C13/14 connector type is built into most personal computers and monitors. The use of a female connector is noted as C13, and the use of a male connector is noted as C14. The standard

Figure 2.10   The IEC 60309 and 60320 female connector receptacles.

provides a rating of 10 amps. The IEC 60320 C19/20 standard connector is frequently used by servers and UPS systems. The C19 is used to denote a female connector, and C20 denotes a male connector. This standard provides a rating for up to 16 amps. Figure 2.10 illustrates the IEC 60320 C13 and IEC 60320 C19 connectors commonly built into personal computers and servers. The top figure shows the common PC connector, and the lower portion of the figure illustrates the common server connector.

UPS

Most readers are familiar with the brown trucks with the UPS logo, however, in this book we use the mnemonic to denote an uninterruptible power supply. An uninterruptible power supply or UPS represents an electrical device that provides power through a battery to a load when the main source of power fails. UPS systems have an on-battery run-time that is relatively short, with some systems limited to just 5 or 10 minutes whereas other systems may have literally banks of batteries numbering in the hundreds to provide a few hours of power. In addition, to ensure that the user knows the system is running on battery power and should perform an orderly shutdown, the UPS system will usually generate a periodic audible beep. The typical use of UPS systems within a data center is to protect such equipment as servers,

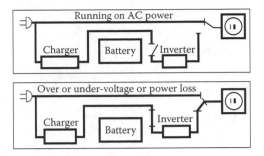

Figure 2.11   The operation of a basic UPS System. Top: The UPS provides power from AC to an outlet and charges its battery. Bottom: When power fails the UPS uses the battery and an inverter to provide power to the outlet.

personal computers, telecommunications devices, and other electrical devices from an unexpected power disruption. UPS systems range from small units with a limited battery capacity designed to provide protection for a single computer to large systems that can provide protection to an entire data center. In most situations the UPS sort of grows, with individual offices procuring systems to protect different projects and the computer systems associated with such projects.

Figure 2.11 illustrates in schematic form the general operation of a UPS system. The top portion shows that when normal power is received the UPS system provides such power to one or more outlets as well as charges a battery or series of batteries. The UPS system examines the received voltage for either an over- or undervoltage or power loss. When such a situation occurs the UPS disengages its connection to the outlet and internally connects the outlet via an inverter to the battery. This is shown in the lower portion of Figure 2.10. Here the inverter converts the DC battery power to AC.

To illustrate why some organizations have to build a separate UPS room let's visually examine the batteries and generator used at a typical large data center. Figure 2.12 shows the bank of batteries that are constantly recharging when main power is up and running. If you count the batteries you will easily be able to identify more than 100, with each battery rated at 12 volts, 400 watts. In spite of a battery count in excess of 100, when main power is lost the batteries can only provide between 30 and 40 minutes of power to the main building that houses two small data centers consisting of rack-mounted servers as well as a variety of communications equipment. When you add the cost of the batteries, which have to be replaced every few years to the

Figure 2.12   The 12-V 400-W batteries are constantly charged from the main voltage to provide 30 to 40 minutes of power if the main power should fail.

cost of a standby generator, this more than likely explains why only the first floor of the two-story building where the data centers and communications equipment are located are connected to the UPS.

Standby Generators

For most data centers that operate 24/7 a number of individual UPS systems, although nice to have, only provide a limited amount of power. Thus, many data centers will supplement individual UPS systems with standby generators. Some generators operate in a hot standby mode, consuming diesel fuel at a reduced level until they are required to provide a full load to the facility. Other generators need to be powered up and technically are not equivalent to a standby generator.

Figure 2.13 illustrates the standby generator used at the two-story data center mentioned by this author as having a separate UPS building. Although it may be difficult to determine the size of the generator due to the lack of a yardstick being held near the device, you can judge its size by the four batteries located near the ground to the right of the generator. Each of those 12-V batteries is approximately twice the size

Figure 2.13   A standby generator designed to provide power to a data center may require a separate building commonly referred to as the UPS building.

of a conventional automobile battery. In fact, although you will have to believe this author, the entire generator including the barrels at the top that hold diesel fuel are well over six feet high and extend roughly 14 feet in length to the exhaust. Thus, when you consider the bank of batteries and the size of a generator you can easily understand why some organizations require a separate building to hold this facility.

Regardless of the type of generators, the motor is operated on an alternative to electricity, such as diesel fuel, natural gas, or, for the home or small office use in some areas, propane. The standby generator uses an automatic transfer switch to monitor utility-supplied power. When the power fails, the transfer switch in theory turns on the generator or increases its operation to provide a full load while periodically checking the status of the utility power so it can switch back. This author uses the term "in theory" as in the well-known Murphy's law, when you really need something, like electrical power, a standby generator may not work correctly. From 30 years of experience with standby generators, more often than not the transfer switch has failed on five different systems over the years, resulting in a live person being required to go out to the utility shed where the standby generator was located to throw the switch. This happened even after testing at 3 a.m. on a Sunday. Although the transfer switch worked during the test, when the utility dropped power to the building a week later it failed and was replaced for a small fortune. This author's experience with standby generators has been far from great, however, it should be mentioned that they have worked successfully numerous times and need to be considered for almost every data center.

Selecting a Generator

When selecting a generator you need to consider a variety of factors. For example, do you want to provide backup power to the computer room or to the entire building or something in between? This will affect the size of the generator required as well as its cost. Similarly, you need to determine the length of time required to bring the generator online. Should it be near instantaneous or are you willing to wait a few seconds to a few minutes? This will affect whether you need a real standby generator or one that will power up and gradually take over as your UPS batteries diminish. In addition to sizing the generator you need to consider its alternate fuel. How long will the generator be required to run and what is its fuel consumption? How will you stock the fuel and where will you place it to minimize safety problems and comply with various codes? These are just some of the factors you need to consider when selecting a generator.

3

GENERAL HEATING AND COOLING CONSIDERATIONS

In this chapter we focus our attention upon two key areas associated with the expense of operating a data center that are often overlooked. Those areas are the heating and cooling systems within a building. Concerning heating systems, in addition to reviewing the operation and cost of different types of heating systems we also discuss the too often taken for granted hot water heater. When you think about the hot water heater, most of these devices are on 24/7 but the hot water they make is used infrequently. However, the cost of producing and keeping the water either warm or hot can be considerable. In some cases, hot water heaters may have been installed 20 or more years ago and are inefficient by today's standards. Thus, we include a checklist of items to consider at the end of this chapter which, when performed, may acquaint you with one or more items to place on your action list of things to do.

Although we primarily focus our attention on equipment in Chapter 5, it's difficult to separate the cooling of equipment and that of a building. Thus, when we discuss cooling in this chapter, which every data center must have, we discuss techniques used to remove general heat from the data center as well as techniques developed to reduce heat generated by data center equipment. As we turn our attention to this topic we also discuss emerging technology that combines solar panels with heat pumps that can considerably reduce the cost of keeping a data center hot or cold by generating up to a portion of the electricity needed to keep the heat pump operational.

Because both heating and cooling represent climate control we first discuss the basic components associated with this general category of devices. Using this information as a base, we then focus our attention upon heating systems to include hot water heating. Next, we turn our attention to cooling systems, examining systems ranging from heat pumps and air conditioners to chilled water and in-ground systems. According to the U.S. Department of Energy, the expenditure of energy on heating and cooling can easily represent over 50% of the overall use of energy in a typical home or office building. Although different industries use different amounts of energy, such as aluminum smelters being much more energy intensive than a machine shop, the cost of heating and cooling a data center can vary from a few thousand dollars a year for a very small series of Internet servers to over a million dollars a year in the cost of electricity for much larger data centers. Thus, it's important to become knowledgeable about heating and cooling of both space and equipment as well as to obtain an understanding of actions you can implement to reduce your organization's use of energy.

Climate Control Systems

A climate control system in effect exchanges heat, either adding it through the use of different types of energy to produce heating or removing heat, again using different types of energy. Thus, every climate-control system can be considered to have three basic components: a source of warm or chilled air that causes heating or cooling; a mechanism to distribute the air, such as a fan and ducts; and a mechanism that is used to regulate the system to ensure that the temperature stays within a certain predefined level. The latter can be a simple thermostat or a more complex device, such as a programmable thermostat.

Both heating and cooling operate on the principle that heat will always move from a warm object to a cooler one. Suppose you microwave a dish containing soup. If you heat the container for the recommended amount of time and open the microwave door you can observe heat movement in the form of steam leaving the heated soup into the cooler environment of the air around you. Although furnaces, heat pumps, and space heaters place heat into the air to make your home or office warmer they may either use the same energy (electric) or use natural gas. In addition, if you are located in the northeastern United States or some other locations where heating oil is the predominant heating fuel, you may use an oil-based furnace or a boiler to provide heating, with the latter commonly used to generate steam that flows to radiators. In comparison, cooling (which is basically the removal of heat) can occur through the use of chilled water powered by electricity, a heat pump also powered by electricity, or air conditioners powered by either natural gas or electricity. In addition, a new type of heating and cooling in which the temperature of the earth (which is near constant in many areas at 55°Fahrenheit) can be used. This type of heating and cooling is commonly referred to as a ground-source heat pump, which although powered by electricity can be more efficient than a heat pump that uses air to add or remove heat. Although heat pumps, air conditioners, and chillers are mostly powered by electricity, readers should note there are always exceptions to many statements found in print. Thus, you can obtain heating and cooling systems powered by other types of energy, although the location where your data center resides or is being built may be a limiting factor concerning the availability and potential utilization of systems powered by other types of energy.

Ventilation

Most types of climate control systems will use the same ventilation series of ducts for heating and cooling. One exception might be the use of radiator-based heaters and a central air conditioner using ducts for removing heat. Regardless of the type of climate-control system employed, the key to efficient energy use is to maintain a comfortable temperature level for both personnel and equipment. In many data centers this author has visited he could see space heaters operating in almost every office and cubicle in the summer, attempting to raise the temperature in those locations to a more comfortable level for the employees. Doing a little mathematics, because each space heater is usually a 1,500-watt device, assuming they were on for 8 hours per day and turned off when the employee left for the day, the yearly operating cost at just 10 cents per kWh assuming the employee takes a 2-week vacation becomes:

50 weeks per year × 40 hours/week × 1,500 watts/1,000 × .1 kWh

or $300 per year. Now multiply that amount by the number of space heaters in the building where your data center is located and you are beginning to note that an organization that does not adjust its heating and cooling will usually develop a significant economic problem over time that may be easy to overlook. That is, as the temperature isn't adjusted to facilitate employee comfort some workers will begin to bring space heaters into the office. Gradually additional workers will do so, with the economic result of an increase in the organization's electric bill. At first the increase is hardly noticeable inasmuch as $300 per year divided by 12 months is rather hard to discover when a data center may have a $30,000 per month or more electric bill. However, over time, the monthly electric bill will significantly rise as additional employees bring space heaters into the workplace. In addition, some employees will forget to turn off the heaters at night, and other employees may simply leave the heater "always on." Thus, although policy could prohibit their use it's much better to preclude conditions arising that would make employees consider their use in the first place.

Heating Systems

In this section we obtain an overview of the different types of heating systems that can be found in most buildings housing a data center. Starting with the more common forced-air system we also describe and discuss several other types of heating systems. Those additional types of heating systems include boilers, radiant heating, different types of heat pumps, electric furnaces, radiators, and even steam heating.

Forced-Air Systems

One of the most common heating systems is a forced-air system. A forced-air system can be powered by electricity, natural gas, or even oil. The forced-air system distributes heat produced by a furnace through a system of metal ducts or conduits leading to vents, with the air blown by an electrically powered fan, called a blower. As the warm air from the furnace flows out of vents it will either reduce the effect of cooler air or displace the colder air. The actual method will depend upon the manner by which return ducts are available in individual rooms or if a centralized return system is used. When each room has a return duct then the cooler air flows through another set of ducts, called the cold-air return system, to the furnace to be warmed or reheated. This system is adjustable: you can increase or decrease the amount of air flowing through your home or office. Note that both central air-conditioning systems as well as heat pumps use the same forced-air system to include a common fan or blower. Through the use of a common forced-air system that employs the same ducts and blower the cost of heating and cooling is reduced. Typically a furnace is sized to work with a specific type of air conditioner. Sometimes a dual fuel system is employed, where a gas or oil furnace is "mated" with a heat pump, enabling electricity to be used when the temperature is above a predefined level for heating, and the heat pump is reversed to provide cooling. When the level of outdoor temperature falls below a certain level during the heating season the furnace operates to provide heating, and when the temperature is above a predefined setting the heat pump operates to provide cooling.

Boilers

The use of a boiler results in water being heated that circulates through pipes to radiators or other types of heating panels. Water used for heating is typically found in older homes and office buildings. Commonly an oil-burning furnace is used to heat the water, although the use of wood in some isolated locations as well as natural gas can also be found.

When considering a boiler, check its annual fuel utilization efficiency (AFUE). The AFUE is the most widely used measure of a boiler's heating efficiency. In fact, it is also used to measure the efficiency of furnaces. The AFUE represents a measurement of the amount of heat actually delivered to your home or office compared to the amount of fuel that you must supply to the boiler or furnace. Thus, a boiler that has an 80% AFUE rating converts 80% of the fuel that you supply to heat, with the remaining 20% literally lost out of the chimney or flue pipe. Note that the efficiency of newer boilers is specified in terms of its AFUE. Boilers manufactured since 1992 must have an AFUE of at least 80% for use in the United States. In comparison, many old boilers have AFUE ratings of only 55–65%.

Rating/Capacity

Perhaps the oldest method used for rating boilers is by their horsepower (hp). One horsepower is defined as the ability to evaporate 34.5

lbs of water into steam at 212°F and above. Today some smaller boilers are still rated in this manner, however, larger boilers have their capacity specified in pounds of steam evaporated per hour, under specified steam conditions. Another measure used for boiler capacity is in terms of BTUs, where 33,472 BTUs equals 1 hp.

Radiant Heating Systems

One of the more interesting types of heating systems is based upon the use of radiant heating. A modern radiant heating system operates by heating the floor, walls, or the ceilings of rooms by embedding heating coils in the form of panels into those surfaces at the time the home or office is constructed or modernized. A second type of radiant heating system, which is much older than the embedded heating elements, is based upon the use of radiators. The radiators are heated and their heat is used to warm a room. Because modern radiant heating systems are based upon the use of electricity they can be costly to operate in cold climates, and therefore are primarily used where either electricity is inexpensive or the weather only requires a minimal amount of heating.

Concerning older types of radiant heating, such systems typically heat water that is distributed through a series of pipes to radiators located throughout a home or building. Typically one or more pumps are used to distribute the heated water, similar to the manner by which a blower distributes heated air in a furnace-based heating system, with the pump replacing the blower and the pipes replacing the ductwork. Because a radiant heating system's components cannot be used for cooling it is more expensive than other dual-use systems when both heating and cooling are considered as an entity. In spite of this, you can expect to encounter modern radiant heating in newly constructed homes and office buildings that are constructed on concrete slab foundations. Here a network of pipes is installed in or under the slab. As the weather becomes cooler hot water will be distributed through the pipes, heating the concrete. The concrete in turn will warm the cooler air. Because heat rises, the air throughout the home or office building will become warm. Unfortunately, this type of radiant system is prone to some potentially expensive repair bills to correct problems. First, due to mineral buildup in the pipes, they can become clogged, which explains why many such installations now require the installation of a water filter. In addition, the boiler and pump used to distribute the hot water can fail, making the system inoperative. Due to these problems the use of in-ground radiant heating is limited.

Heat Pumps

Heat pumps either by themselves or as a part of a dual fuel system provide the capability to transfer heat from one environment, such as indoors, to a second environment, usually outdoors. Because the heat pump can transfer heat in either direction it represents a bidirectional device. The key to the operation of a heat pump is a reversing valve that enables the direction of the flow of refrigerant to be changed, enabling heat to be pumped from an evaporator coil located outside to a condenser located indoors. As the evaporator coil outside gains heat from its surroundings the refrigerant is compressed and sent to the indoor coil where the heat is transferred via an air handler into the ductwork. When in a cooling mode of operation the heat pump works similarly to a conventional air conditioner, using an evaporator coil inside a building to absorb heat that is transferred via a refrigerant line outside where a fan dissipates the heat. If you carefully examine a heat pump you will notice that the outside unit is similar to an air conditioner, with copper coils surrounded by aluminum fins that assist in the heat transfer process. However, unlike an air conditioner, the heat pump can transfer heat bidirectionally, although obviously only one direction at a time.

Note that the heat pump in a heating mode uses the outdoor coil as an evaporator and the indoor coil becomes the condenser. Thus, in a cooling mode the condenser and evaporator coils are literally switched. Also note that if you heat with electricity, a heat pump can reduce the amount of electricity used for heating by approximately 25% to 35% and possibly even as much as 40%. Another advantage of a heat pump is that they dehumidify better than standard air conditioners. This can result in a reduction in energy usage as well as additional cooling comfort in hot, humid summer months. Unfortunately, when used for heating, the heat pump can be unsuitable for certain geographical areas where it can become extremely cold. For example, when the outdoor temperature falls below approximately 40°F, a less-efficient panel of electric resistance coils similar to those contained in a conventional toaster are enabled to provide indoor heating, thus explaining why heat pumps are usually not very efficient for heating in areas with cold winters. To reduce this problem many manufacturers of heat pumps now offer "dual fuel" systems that mates the heat pump to a high-efficiency gas furnace, which is discussed later in this chapter.

SEER and HSPF Ratings

As a review for some readers, SEER represents a mnemonic for seasonal energy efficiency rating, which is a rating and performance set of standards developed by the U.S. government and equipment manufacturers to produce an energy consumption rating. The resulting rating system has a universal format and compensates for varying weather conditions while being easy to understand. For example, the higher the SEER, the more efficient and usually more costly a device is. Today most heating and cooling devices have a SEER rating of 12 whereas high-efficiency heating and cooling systems have a SEER of 14 and above. Another rating that warrants a brief mention is the HSPF, which stands for the heating seasonal performance factor and is used to measure the efficiency of a heat pump. The U.S. government's established minimum HSPF rating for a heat pump is 6.8%. The higher the percentage is, the more efficiently the unit operates. Figure 3.1 illustrates a Lennox XP14 heat pump, which when combined with a variable speed air handler, can provide an efficiency rating of up to 16 SEER and 9.5 HSPF. The XP14 as well as the XP15 (which we examine shortly) can be combined with a gas furnace to enhance fuel efficiency by alternating between electric and gas heat, optimizing energy use and minimizing heating costs.

In Figure 3.2 the reader will find a picture of a Lennox XP15, which although considerably larger than the XP14 pictured in Figure 3.1, has slightly less efficiency. The XP15 can be obtained with an efficiency rating of up to 16.20 SEER and 9.20 HSPF in comparison to the ability to obtain a SEER of up to 16 and an HSPF of 9.5 for a smaller XP14. The reason the SEER is slightly higher for the XP15 over the XP14 is the use of additional fins in the outdoor unit. In fact, one of the "tricks" employed by heating and cooling device manufacturers to increase their SEER ratings is to increase the size

Figure 3.1 A Lennox XP14 heat pump has a SEER as high as 16 and an HSPF of 9.5.

of their products, providing additional coils that allow more efficient heat transfer to occur. It should be mentioned that the XP15 also has on-board diagnostics and a special type of compressor that according to the manufacturer provides the quietest operating heat pump on the market. However, in terms of overall heat pump efficiency the XP14 albeit smaller is more efficient. This is because its HSPF can be up to 9.5 whereas the XP15's maximum is 9.2.

Types of Heat Pumps

Similar to furnaces there are several types of heat pumps that are marketed. To add a bit of confusion, some of the terminology used to refer to different types of heat pumps can mean different things to different persons based upon how a manufacturer markets its products. Thus,

Figure 3.2 The Lennox XP15 is larger than its XP14 but slightly less efficient.

in this section we attempt to gain a basic knowledge of the different types of heat pump as well as the different terminologies used to refer to specific types of these devices.

Table 3.1 lists four common types of heat pumps. In the following sections we discuss each of the different types of heat pumps listed in the referenced table. Note that the first type of system can be a bit confusing as it refers to two distinctly different sources of use for heat pumps and a more descriptive name is probably dual fuel heat pump.

Table 3.1 Types of Heat Pumps

Hybrid heat pumps/dual fuel heat pump
Air-source heat pumps
Geothermal heat pumps
Absorption heat pumps

Hybrid Heat Pump   Although they can be very efficient, heat pumps will consume lots of energy in the form of electricity. In fact they use a considerable amount of electricity to heat and cool a home or office. A hybrid heat pump represents an attempt to reduce the cost associated with operating a heat pump by using alternate fuel. There are two basic types of hybrid heat pumps: one that uses solar energy for a portion of its electrical requirements and one that is "mated" to a high-efficiency gas- or oil-fueled furnace, more commonly referred to as a dual fuel system. The heat pump that includes a solar panel was first introduced as a product during 2009 by Lennox and is referred to as a solar-assisted heat pump and marketed under the name "SunSource."

Solar-Assisted Heat Pump   Although the first heat pump to include a solar panel reached the market in 2009, a starting point for the idea behind the use of solar panels and a heat pump was filed for a patent in 1979. That patent concerned the use of solar panels for collecting solar heat and included concentrating lenses and a heat storage chamber to store excess heat. The heat pump was actually a separate system designed to supplement solar heat when the temperature in the heat storage unit declined below a predefined value. This author does not know if the engineers at Lennox viewed this patent, however, it appears that by mating solar panels to a heat pump they developed a system that can reduce the amount of electricity needed to operate the heat pump during daylight hours when sunshine is available.

The solar panel supplied by Lennox measures 3 feet by 5 feet. This panel provides 190 watts of power, which is used to operate the system's outdoor fan. By mating a solar panel to a heat pump the SEER rating has significantly increased to 18.5.

According to Lennox the solar panel can save a customer between 8 and 12% on electric use. However, if you live in an area with a low cost of electricity your savings will be reduced. However, readers should note that the SunSource heat pump can be obtained with up to 15 solar modules. As you increase the number of solar modules you also increase the ability of the system to save electricity during daylight hours. In fact, if you go to the Lennox website at www.lennox.com and search using the term "Solar Calculator" you will find a sophisticated program you can use to determine potential savings based upon the number of solar panels and geographic region in which you're located. As you increase the number of solar panels you can vividly see your savings on energy consumption increase, however, you still need to obtain the cost of additional panels to determine if the investment provides a decent return besides making you feel good. In addition, you need to note that many so-called green energy projects need considerable government sponsorship in the form of tax credits for consumers and other economic incentives to have a chance to be economically viable. However, the mating of solar panels and heat pumps represents a start for the integration of this technology.

You can probably receive a good indication of the potential direction of solar panels combined with heat pumps by the role of the current administration. According to press reports published in October, 2010, the White House after backing the use of solar power through various tax grants said it would install solar panels on the roof during the spring of 2011 to both generate electricity and heat water. However, readers should note that solar power is a bit like the tide, rolling in and out of the White House based upon the officeholder, politics, and economics. Under President Carter solar panels were installed during 1979 to heat water, but were removed by President Reagan in 1986 as they required costly repairs. In 2003 President Bush installed solar panels to heat the White House pool and a maintenance building, which are still in use and will be expanded by the present Obama administration to generate electricity and hot water for the main building.

Dual Fuel Heat Pump A dual fuel heat pump is actually nonexistent. Instead the term is commonly used to refer to a control system that will switch between the use of a heat pump and a natural gas or oil system based upon the outdoor temperature. Thus, the control system includes wiring to an outdoor temperature sensor.

The most common device used as a control system is a thermostat. The thermostat is programmed to switch between the use of a gas- or oil-fueled furnace and a heat pump based upon a predefined outdoor temperature setting. Figure 3.3 illustrates the Lennox thermostat used to control this author's dual fuel system in his home. Note that the thermostat is shown in its default display mode, which indicates the mode of operation such as heating, emergency heat, cooling, or

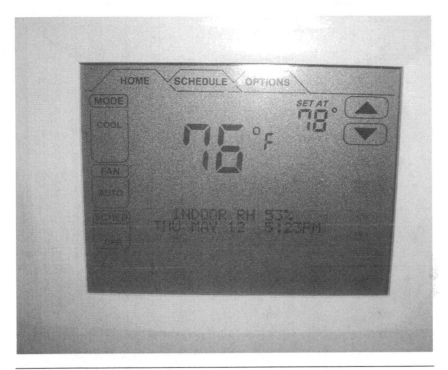

Figure 3.3   A Lennox programmable thermostat controlling a dual fuel system.

off; the fan setting; whether the schedule of operations such as cooling at certain temperatures at certain times is on or off; and the current indoor temperature; temperature setting; and a two-line display that shows either the state of the heat pump (waiting to go on) or the indoor humidity on the top line and the day and date and time on the lower line. Because the thermostat is touch sensitive you can see the author's smudges from the photograph. Because a heat pump loses efficiency as the outdoor temperature decreases, the control is commonly set to switch the heating operation to natural gas or oil when it gets really cold. Typically the switching will be predefined to occur at or below the 35 to 40°F range.

By pressing the Options tab at the top of the thermostat shown in Figure 3.3 and then performing a few additional operations you will be presented with a screen similar to the one shown in Figure 3.4. If you examine the highlighted bar you will note that it displays the message, "Dual fuel (gas/oil)," which indicates that this thermostat can be set to cut over to the use of an alternate heating by gas or oil when the temperature reaches a predefined outdoor setting.

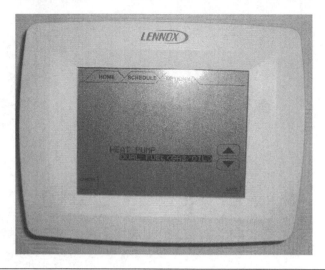

Figure 3.4   The Lennox thermostat supports dual fuel operations where a heat pump is literally mated to either a natural gas or oil-based furnace.

Cost Considerations   A key consideration concerning the use of a dual fuel system is its cost. As you might expect, it should and will cost more than a single heat pump. The additional cost includes both the control unit and the secondary heating source, such as a high-efficiency natural gas furnace.

Air-Source Heat Pump   The most common type of heat pump is referred to as the air-source device. The term "air-source" refers to the fact that the heat pump transfers heat either into or out of a home or office using the air outside. Because a heat pump transfers heat in comparison to furnaces that burn fuel, they are more efficient than furnaces. In fact, when temperatures are above 40°F a heat pump can deliver up to three times more heat energy than the electrical energy it consumes. However, when temperatures significantly drop, so does the efficiency of the heat pump, resulting in an increase in the number of dual fuel systems being installed, especially in colder climates.

Geothermal Heat Pumps   Because the temperature of the Earth is fairly constant it represents an ideal medium for exchanging heat in place of the air. In fact, geothermal heat pumps are also known as earth-coupled, GeoExchange, or ground-source heat pumps and have been in use since the late 1940s.

Geothermal heat pumps (GHPs) use the constant temperature of the earth as the exchange medium that enables the system to reach a fairly high efficiency level on cold winter nights. Because the ground temperature is warmer than the air above during the winter and cooler during the summer, the GHP takes advantage of this by exchanging heat with the earth. According to some analysts, the geothermal heat pump has the ability to transfer between three and six times more heat energy than the electricity it consumes.

Since their introduction during the late 1940s GHPs have evolved considerably, with some products including two-speed variable blowers and other models able to be configured to provide hot water in addition to heating and cooling. This type of heat pump can also be obtained as a dual fuel system. The GHP is quieter than an air-source heat pump, commonly has a longer life expectancy, requires less maintenance, and obviously is not dependent upon the temperature of the outside air. Unfortunately, the cost associated with a geothermal heat pump system can be double or more than a air-source system. Depending upon an economic analysis when you consider not only the one-time outlay for each type of heat pump but also maintenance and electricity costs, it may be beneficial to consider the installation of this type of heat pump. In fact, each year approximately 50,000 such heat pumps are installed in the United States.

Types of Geothermal Heat Pump Systems   There are four basic types of geothermal heat pump systems. Those basic types can be subdivided into two categories: closed loop and open loop. There are three types of closed-loop systems referred to as vertical, horizontal, and water based, and there is one type of open-loop system. The selection of an appropriate geothermal heat pump depends upon many factors including the cost of installation and labor rates at your facility, availability of maintenance, the climate at your location, soil conditions, and available land. In the next series of paragraphs we first quickly review the three basic closed-loop systems and then discuss the open-loop system.

Closed-Loop Systems   As previously mentioned there are three types of closed-loop geothermal systems. In the next three sections we discuss each.

Vertical   In a vertical closed-loop geothermal system holes are drilled approximately 20 feet apart and between 100 to 400 feet deep. The holes are then fitted with two pipes that are then connected with a U joint or bend at the bottom to form a loop. The resulting vertical loop is then connected with horizontal pipe lowered into a trench connected at the other end to a heat pump placed into a building. This type of heat pump is relatively expensive as holes over 4 inches in diameter must be drilled far into the ground, however, it is suitable for schools and large commercial buildings because the land area required for horizontal loops would be more extensive and possibly prohibitive to obtain in a built-up area. A geothermal heat pump system based upon the use of vertical loops is also commonly used at locations where the soil is too shallow for trenching or where a minimal disturbance to existing landscaping is desired.

Horizontal   The horizontal closed-loop geothermal system can be considerably less costly than the vertical system. This is because when land is available, the horizontal system only requires digging a trench approximately six feet below the surface to install two pipes, with the second installed two feet above the first and connected together and to an indoor heat pump. As an alternative, if sufficient land area is available it's possible to dig a wider trench and install two pipes in parallel approximately two feet apart and at least four feet from the surface. Another type of horizontal geothermal closed-loop system involves the looping of pipes. Through pipe looping it becomes possible to use a lesser area than if straight piping were installed.

Water-Based   If your location has convenient access to a sufficient amount of water, such as a lake, pond, or river you can run a pipe underground from your facility building to the water. To prevent possible freezing during winter, you could install coiled piping at a sufficient depth. Because your building can be located near the water source, it may be possible to significantly reduce the cost of trenching, resulting in a water-based geothermal heat pump offering the possibility of not costing a literal arm and a leg to install. However, as the location of the facility increases in distance from the water the cost of trenching and piping increases. Thus, this closed-loop system requires a relatively close proximity to water to be cost effective. In addition, the water must meet several criteria, such as its depth to enable coiled piping to be installed, its volume must be sufficient to enable heat transfer, and its quality should preclude industrial waste and other impurities that can play havoc with the piping.

Open-Loop Geothermal System   The open-loop geothermal system uses a well or a body of water as the heat exchange fluid that circulates directly through the system. Once the water is used it can be discharged back into its source or elsewhere. Because the water is actively used and discharged the loop is open. Obviously, this type of system requires an adequate supply of water and may also require obtaining a municipal license for the discharging of water, which in effect forces the organization to comply with local rules and regulations. In addition, there may also be state and federal regulations that can result in an additional compliance burden.

Electric Resistance Heating

Electric resistance heating converts nearly 100% of the energy in electricity to heat, however, its efficiency is actually limited when we consider the overall picture. This is because the use of coal, oil, or natural gas to generate electricity only converts about 30% of the energy of the fuel into electricity. Thus, the overall efficiency of electric resistance heating is then limited to about 30%, which usually makes the cost more expensive than heat produced using a furnace or heat pump. The exception to this general statement is twofold. First, if the cost of electricity is minimal, such as in some areas where hydro generates electricity, the use of electric resistance heating may be competitive to other types of heat generation. Second, in climates where there are a limited number of heating days the cost of heating may not be significant, making the low cost of installing electric resistance heating an affordable consideration.

Types of Electric Resistance Heaters   There are two main methods for heating via electric resistance. Those two methods are the use of a centralized forced-air electric furnace or by the use of heaters in each room. Room heaters can consist of electric baseboard heaters, electric wall heaters, electric radiant heat, or electric space heaters.

Electric Furnaces   An electric furnace is similar in concept to a natural gas furnace; however, instead of burning gas the electric furnace uses resistance coils, referred to as elements, to convert electricity to heat. A blower or large fan moves air over a group of heating coils or heating elements, with heated air delivered through supply ducts throughout a home or office. Then air is returned to the furnace through return ducts. Typically, the heating elements are activated in some sequence such that not all are turned on at the same time. This is done to avoid overloading the electrical system of the home or office and avoids a costly electrical upgrade. Thus, it's important to consider the available voltage and amperage available prior to selecting an electric furnace or you may require an expensive electrical modification.

Electric Baseboard Heaters   The second main type of electric resistance heating occurs through the use of baseboard heaters. Such heaters are zonal heaters, which means that they are controlled by thermostats located within each room unlike a furnace controlled by a common thermostat. Baseboard heaters contain electric heating elements that are placed within metal pipes. The pipes in turn are surrounded by aluminum fins similar to the coils on a heat pump or air conditioner to aid heat transfer.

There are many types of baseboard heaters, such as fixed, portable, architectural, and heavy duty. The heaters are commonly rated in BTUs as well as watts and can include 120 volts, 208 volts, and 240 volts, with different amperage, which results in its BTU and watt ratings. Inasmuch as hot air rises, it is dispensed from the top of the heater and colder air is drawn into the bottom of the heater. Some additional heat will also be radiated from the pipe, aluminum fins, and the metal housing the pipes and fins. The heater will continue producing heat until the air entering the bottom of the heater is at the same temperature as that set on the thermostat. Although radiant heaters are not a very efficient form of heating, baseboard heaters have several advantages including the use of a minimal amount of space, no requirement for ductwork, and a relatively low initial cost. In addition, as a zonal heater, the baseboard heater can be turned down or off when a person is not in his or her office. This can provide a significant reduction in the cost of heating when people are aware they should turn down or turn off the thermostat when leaving the office. In some situations this action can reduce the overall cost of heating by 20 to 25% in comparison to heating both occupied and unoccupied office areas.

Installation Although baseboard heaters can usually be installed wherever one desires, they are usually installed approximately an inch above a carpet or wood floor to allow cooler air to flow under and through the radiator fins so the air can be heated. Although usually installed under a window to counter cooling air from window glass, other considerations you need to plan for are the availability and cost of installing wiring. When installed, the heater should be placed firmly against a wall to prevent the warm air from convecting behind the heater and streaking the wall with dust particles.

If you are considering the use of electric baseboard heaters you need to know that they are like many other products in that you can expect to get what you pay for. Inexpensive models can be noisy and often give poor temperature control. Thus, you need to carefully compare and contrast the specifications of different products. In addition to comparing specifications to include warranties you need to ensure the product has labels from Underwriter's Laboratories (UL) and the National Electrical Manufacturer's Association (NEMA).

Radiators

In concluding our brief review of different types of heating we turn our attention to two of the oldest methods used to distribute heat: steam and hot water radiators.

Steam Heating Steam heating is the process of boiling, transporting the resulting steam through pipes to radiators, and then condensing the steam back into water. This process is significantly less efficient than more modern systems and is usually encountered in older homes, factories, and buildings typically constructed prior to the 1960s. In addition to being inefficient in comparison to modern heating systems, steam heating suffers from a significant delay between the boiler turning on and the heat arriving at the radiators. As a result of the delay inherent in its design, it can be difficult to implement control strategies such as a night setback system in steam systems.

Today you can still encounter steam heating in many older office buildings. Because steam moves through pipes without requiring the use of pumps it is economical to distribute over a floor or two. However, the pipes need to be insulated and if older piping is in use you may need to consider replacing it with fiberglass that is more suitable for resisting high temperatures and corrosion. In addition, periodic maintenance is required to ensure vents do not become clogged and prevent radiators from heating. Another consideration concerning steam radiators is the potential heat loss that can occur when they are placed on exterior walls. To reduce potential heat loss you can install reflectors behind such radiators.

Hot Water Radiators   A hot water radiator, as its name implies, results in the passing of hot water through a radiator to provide heat. In actuality the hot water radiator provides most of the heat by convection, with a minor portion resulting from radiant heat. This results from the radiator providing a hot surface in a room thus creating convection currents by attracting cold air at the bottom of the radiator and heating the air that rises. Although most central heating radiators are water based, you can purchase stand-alone oil-filled electric radiators.

Hot water radiators are manufactured as both vertically high devices and as lower baseboard-type devices. They can be either a one- or two-pipe system. In a single-pipe system hot water leaves the furnace where it's heated and moves in a continuous loop, returning as cooler water. That water is reheated and sent back out. In a two-pipe system one pipe moves hot water to the radiators and the second pipe provides a return path. Although a hot water system is cost effective, it does not enable humidity to be adjusted, which can represent a problem during dry winter months. Thus, the hot water system may require the use of humidifiers that increases the overall cost of providing a comfortable working environment. Another common problem in hot water systems is unwanted air in the system. This can be controlled by the use of bleed valves on radiators. However, you need to go from radiator to radiator while the system is operating and open each bleed valve slightly, then close it when water starts to escape through the valve. Thus, in an office environment this can be a time-consuming task typically given to maintenance personnel.

Similar to electric heaters, hot water heaters can be placed in zones and controlled by thermostats that work with valves on the hot water heaters. Through the use of zones it becomes possible to reduce or eliminate heating in the evening or when workers leave for the day.

Hot Water Heaters   Now that we have an appreciation of the scope of heating options we focus our attention on an area we normally forget to consider but which over the years can adversely affect our cost of energy. That area is the hot water heater. To illustrate how humans tend to forget, consider Figure 3.5, which shows a rather old and inefficient hot water heater that has been located in a UPS building for over 20 years, with its purpose in life to provide hot water to a single faucet in a building that is usually not occupied. If you closely examine the picture of the electric hot water heater shown in Figure 3.5 you can note that it has an indentation, perhaps due to being hit by the battery-operated lift being charged next to it. You can also note that it's corroding on the bottom. However, what you cannot note unless you think about it is the fact that this 40-gallon water heater is factory set to operate at 3,800 watts and uses a 30-ampere 240-volt electrical connection. The thermostat is factory set at 120°F, which is more than sufficient to warm a person's hands. Unfortunately, there are two problems with the use of this water heater in addition to it being on its literal last breath of life. First, as an electric water heater it's very easy to add an insulation jacket to reduce thermal loss. Second, although tankless electric water heaters, which we describe shortly, are debatable for use in an entire home or office, they can be effectively used for individual sinks. Thus, when this water heater heads off to the salvage yard it might be worth replacing it with a tankless model.

Types of Water Heaters

There are three basic types of water heaters: conventional tank storage water heaters, tankless water heaters, and indirect water heaters. The latter represents a water heater that is heated indirectly through the use of another device, such as a heat pump or solar panel. In the following sections we discuss each type of hot water heater.

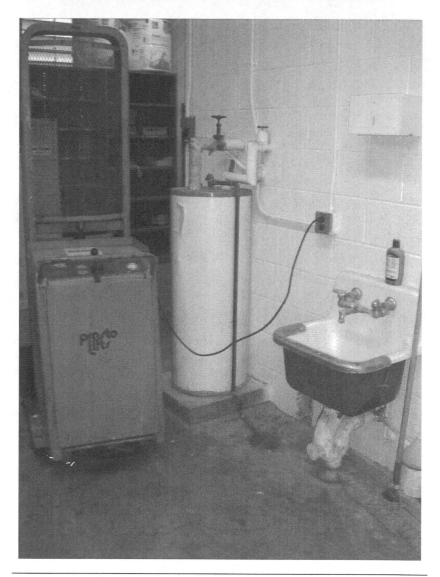

Figure 3.5   An old electric hot water heater used to provide hot water to a sink that is hardly ever used.

Conventional Tank Storage Water Heaters   Conventional tank storage water heaters remain the most popular type of water heating system for the home and office. They typically store between 20 and 80 gallons of hot water, releasing heated water from the top while cold water enters the heater at the bottom of the tank to replace the exited water. The two most common types of water heaters are operated by the use of natural gas and electricity. Other commonly used fuels include propane and fuel oil. Both natural gas and propane hot water heaters operate in a similar manner. A gas burner under the tank is used to heat cold water, with a thermostat used to open the gas valve as the water temperature falls. When the temperature rises to the thermostat's setting the valve closes. In comparison, an oil-fired water heater will mix oil and air into a mist that is ignited by an electric spark and then operates in a similar manner to gas and propane water heaters.

When an electric water heater is used it may have one or two elements, each with its own thermostat. When a water heater has two elements, on some models only one may be used and the second can be placed into use. On other models the element at the bottom of the tank is used to maintain the minimum thermostat setting and an element located in the upper part of the tank is used to facilitate hot water recovery under a demand condition.

One of the key problems associated with the use of a tank-based water heater is that it periodically heats water, even when the hot water tap or taps are not running. This is because no matter how much insulation there is in the tank it will lose heat to its surroundings. In addition, gas and oil water heaters have vents to expel combustion gases and they are also a source of heat loss. Although you need to check its thermal resistance or R value, inasmuch as a higher value is better, you can also consider the addition of an insulation blanket on certain models. Either hiring a professional or doing it yourself can reduce the effect of heat loss, which can translate into a potential savings of between 5 and 10% of its overall heating cost.

If the use of the hot water heater is periodic, such as with a restroom in a building, you may wish to consider the replacement of a conventional tank-based water heater with a different type of device. Similarly, if you have the luxury of either remodeling or building a data center from scratch you can also consider options to the use of a tank-based water heater. Two options to consider are tankless and indirect water heaters.

Tankless Water Heaters   Tankless water heaters are also referred to as demand water heaters and coiled water heaters because they do not have a tank and they provide hot water on demand instead of pre-heated water from a tank. This type of hot water heater avoids the standby heat losses associated with tank-type water heaters. When a hot water tap is turned on, cold water will travel through a pipe into the tankless water heater. Either a gas burner or an electric element (gas or electric tankless water heater) heats the water. As a result, the tankless water heaters theoretically deliver a constant supply of hot water. The reason this author uses the term "theoretically" is because the flow rate of hot water produced may not reach the level produced by a tank-type unit. Thus, although a single tankless hot water heater may not be suitable for an entire office, multiple smaller units might be suitable for installation under faucets if gas or electric is available or could become available for a nominal cost. Gas units provide a higher flow rate than electric units, but rarely will a single unit suffice for a home or office. Having experienced the use of an electric tankless unit in the United Kingdom, although sufficient for a faucet they do not produce enough hot water for other than a few seconds in a shower. However, in an office environment they can represent a good choice for providing hot water to faucets in restrooms where few people use the facilities 16 hours each day.

Indirect Water Heaters   In concluding our discussion of hot water heaters a few words are warranted concerning indirect hot water heaters. An indirect water heater uses the facility of another device, such as a furnace, heat pump, solar panel, and so on, to provide heat required for raising the temperature in a tank of water. One of the first types of indirect hot water heaters used the furnace or boiler to heat a fluid that was then circulated through a heat exchanger in the water tank. Other types of indirect hot water heaters include a heat pump hot water heater and a solar hot water heater. The heat pump hot water heater requires a sufficient amount of air space to be available around the heater whereas a solar water heater can be either one using panels for electricity to heat water in a tank or what is referred to as a solar water heating system. The latter includes a storage tank and solar collectors that use the power of the sun to heat the tank. There are two types of solar water heating systems: active, which have circulating pumps and controls, and passive, which don't. A majority of available solar water heaters require a well-insulated storage tank. Solar storage tanks have an additional outlet and inlet that are routed to and from the collector. In two-tank systems, the solar water heater preheats water before it enters the conventional water heater. In one-tank systems, the backup heater is combined with the solar storage in one tank.

Although each of these types of water heaters has certain advantages and disadvantages associated with its use, from an economic perspective, unless your data center needs to feel "green" or is located where natural gas is unavailable and the cost of electricity is high, it is usually not economical to use. However, the tax rebates offered by certain states and the federal government for certain types of energy-efficient systems can turn an uneconomic method into an economically viable project. Thus, you may wish to consider the potential tax rebates, refunds, and other enticements our elected leaders provide for literally going green.

Cooling Systems

Perhaps the major expense associated with operating a data center is cooling. We defer a detailed discussion of data center equipment heat dissipation and cooling techniques until Chapter 5, and in this section discuss several general building cooling techniques, ranging from central air conditioners and heat pumps to the use of various types of chillers.

Central Air Conditioners

Although central air conditioners are commonly used to cool homes they are also employed in many types of buildings. Sometimes they are used as a supplementary device, and other times they are used as the primary cooling device. A central air conditioner uses the ductwork within a home or building to circulate cool air. Cool air is blown through the system ducts and warmer air comes back through the return ducts. Air exits the ducts via registers that are openings in the floors, walls, or ceilings that are covered with grills that can be positioned so they funnel the air in a particular direction or can be opened fully, partially, or closed. Although it's relatively easy to ignore the grills until they become dirty or clogged with debris, sometimes the purchase of grills can alleviate the problems caused by economical grills building contractors typically install. Because building contractors seek to save money, they will typically install grills that can be either opened or closed but usually cannot be configured to deflect air to certain locations or directions. The Internet provides you with a great tool to purchase different products, but you first need to realize you need the product. This author was in the same office for 15 years and experienced the problems of a fixed grill prior to obtaining approval to install a directional one that solved a cooling problem.

Types of Central Air Conditioners   There are two basic types of central air conditioner, a split-system unit and a packaged single device or unit. In a split-system central air conditioner, an outdoor metal cabinet is used to contain the condenser and compressor as well as fins that facilitate heat transfer. An indoor cabinet will contain the evaporator coil. In many split-system air conditioners, the indoor cabinet will also contain a furnace or the indoor portion of a heat pump. If you already have a furnace but no air conditioner, a split system can be very economical to install as it will use existing ducts.

The second type of central air conditioner is referred to as a packaged central air conditioner. This type of air conditioner houses the evaporator, condenser, and compressor in one cabinet, which usually is placed on top of a roof or on a concrete slab next to the foundation of a home or office building. If you fly into the Los Angeles LAX airport you can note lots of packaged air conditioners on the roofs of one- and two-story buildings as the plane approaches the airport. Similarly, in many Western states you can view packaged central air conditioners on many roofs of homes and small commercial buildings. Many packaged air conditioners include electric heating coils or a natural gas furnace. This combination of air conditioner and central heater allows the use of a common ductwork while eliminating the requirement for a separate indoor furnace.

One of the most common functions of an air conditioner is to perform dehumidification. Although the dehumidification process results in the generation of water that requires a pan and pipe to the outside it can result in much more comfortable surroundings. Because pipes can clog, one of the things a good maintenance person or technician will do periodically is to check the drainage of the line, perhaps more frequently in hot humid areas. In addition, if installing a new system you may wish to consider having an overflow pan and water sensor switch installed. Then, if the pan fills with water the switch will cut off the air conditioner until the problem is fixed, alleviating water damage.

Sizing   The key to having a good central air-conditioning system is proper sizing. The reader is referred to a manual produced by the Air Conditioning Contractors of America (ACCA) known as *Manual J*, which is the literal bible for computing heating or cooling for residential and industrial applications. Because this manual is approximately 150 pages in length it requires a significant amount of time to become familiar with its use. In addition, because ducts will have a loss due to air filtration, humidity levels will vary by location and even by days, and heat transfer will depend upon the conductivity of materials used in a building and their locations as well as exterior temperatures. Thus, the use of the manual will require a considerable amount of time to perform the mathematics required. The result will be an estimated heat loss in BTUs, which when divided by 12,000 will provide you with the tonnage of the air conditioner required. Once properly sized a new air conditioner should reduce the amount of energy consumed by 20 to 40% or more in comparison to some models manufactured just 10 years ago. By law, new air conditioners must have a minimum SEER rating of 13.

Cost Comparison   If you are considering the installation of a new air conditioner either as a replacement for an existing device or as a totally new installation, one of the things you may wish to do is to analyze which SEER rating provides the best return on investment. A higher SEER means more efficiency, however, it also means higher cost. You can translate a SEER number directly into the energy cost because SEER 10 = 10 BTUs/watt-hour. Thus, an air conditioner that has a SEER rating of 10 will provide 10 BTUs of cooling per watt-hour (Wh) of operation, where to review, a British thermal unit represents the amount of heat energy required to raise the temperature of one pound of water by 1°F. Remember that a 1-ton air-conditioning system provides 12,000 BTUs per hour of heating, Thus, if you need a 3-ton air conditioner with a SEER of just 10 this means that the A/C unit will produce 36,000 BTUs of cooling in an hour of operation, which divided by 10 results in 3,600 watts per hour the air conditioner will use. If you assume 150 days of cooling during a year where the air runs 8 hours per day the total cooling use of electricity becomes:

$$8 \text{ hours/day} \times 150 \text{ days} \times 3,600 \text{ watts/hour}$$
$$= 4,320,000 \text{ watt hours per cooling season}$$

which when divided by 1,000 becomes 4,320 kWh. If the cost of electricity is 10 cents per kWh, then during the cooling season the use of a 10 SEER 3-ton air conditioner would cost $430. Now let's assume the SEER is 15 and the other parameters remain the same. The air conditioner would now consume 2,400 watts per hour and the total cooling use of electricity now becomes:

$$8 \text{ hours/day} \times 150 \text{ days} \times 2,400 \text{ watts/hour}$$
$$= 2,880,000 \text{ watt hours per cooling season}$$

or at 10 cents per kWh it becomes $288. Now the key question to be answered is if the difference in the cost of operating the air conditioner at $142 ($430 − $288) per season is worth the extra cost of the higher SEER device. Because you cannot legally purchase a 10 SEER air conditioner in the United States (since 2006 models must have a rating of at least a minimum of 13 SEER) the question might not be applicable, however, it illustrates the method you can use to compare the economics associated with the use of different SEER-rated devices. In addition, you will more than likely use a different cost of electricity and the number of days in the cooling system will also change, with some data centers using cooling year round. Note that you can use the previously mentioned cost methodology to compare and contrast the cost of using heat pumps and other devices.

Other Features to Consider   The air conditioner is similar to other heating and cooling products in that they have all evolved over the years to include a variety of features. From an energy savings perspective, the introduction of a variable-speed air handler has significantly reduced the cost of fan operations. Other features to consider include the quietness of the system, filter check light or display on the thermostat to remind you to check the filter, an automatic delay after running that can add life to the compressor, and a fan-only switch that enables air to circulate when you do not need cooling.

Heat Pump Cooling

Earlier in this chapter we discussed the operation and use of heat pumps to include the different types of this popular device. As a brief review we discuss its basic operation in a cooling environment in this section.

Inasmuch as we just discussed an air conditioner we should note that a heat pump and a cooling system have common mechanical components. Those common components include a compressor, evaporator coil, condensing coil, and an expansion valve. During the cooling phase, a heat pump and an air conditioner operate the same by using a refrigerant to transfer heat from inside the house or office to the outside. When operating in a cooling mode, the heat pump uses a compressor to pressurize and circulate a refrigerant that is cooled in a heat exchanger referred to as a condenser or condensing unit. The condensing unit condenses the refrigerant into a high-pressure, moderate-temperature liquid that is then passed through a pressure-lowering device and enters the evaporator, which is normally a set of coils inside the home or office. In the evaporator the refrigerant absorbs heat, is pressurized, and is returned to the outside to be dissipated into the atmosphere via a fan, assuming the heat pump is an air-source device.

Chillers

Chillers can be considered to represent a key component of air-conditioning systems for large buildings. A chiller will produce cold water to remove heat from the air in the building. They also are used in a data center to provide cooling for a file-server room or series of rooms. Similar to other types of air-conditioning systems, most chillers extract heat from water by mechanically compressing a refrigerant. Chillers can be expensive not only to purchase but also to operate as most models use an electrically driven compressor that consumes a significant amount of electricity. In addition, they are complex machines that require trained technicians to service.

A chiller will remove heat from a liquid via a vapor-compression process or through an absorption refrigeration cycle. Then the liquid is circulated through a heat exchanger to cool air or equipment as required. Chillers are used in most large buildings and typically represent 40 to 50% of the annual electricity use of many commercial and industrial facilities. Thus, their use, as a paraphrase from Willie Sutton, "is where the money is." This means that the proper operation and maintenance of building chillers should be on a list of high-priority projects to occur on a periodic basis.

Use in Air-Conditioning   In an air-conditioning environment chilled water is typically distributed to a heat exchanger. The chiller is connected to air handlers, where the air handler is commonly a large metal box containing a fan or blower, heating or cooling elements, filter racks or chambers, sound attenuators as the noise can be rather loud, and dampers, which are valves or plates that stop or regulate the flow of air inside a duct. The air handler in turn is usually connected to ductwork that is used to distribute the cooled air throughout the building, with the air returning to the air handler through the use of return ducts. The chilled water is also recirculated back to the chiller where it is again cooled. Similar to air conditioners, chillers are rated in tons, with many chillers rated between 15 and 2,000 tons, which when multiplied by 12,000 BTU/hr provides between 180,000 and 24,000,000 BTUs per hr cooling capacity. Because 1 BTU equals 0.0002928 kilowatt-hour, a 15-ton chiller is equivalent to 527 kWh whereas a 2,000-ton chiller is equivalent to 7,027 kWh. From the preceding it becomes obvious that running a chiller can consume a lot of electricity.

Types of Chillers   Similar to other heating and cooling products there is a variety of different types of chillers. Some chillers vary by the type of compression used and others vary by the type of liquid or type of compression performed. There are two basic types of chillers: those based upon mechanical compression and those based upon absorption.

Mechanical Compression Chillers   A mechanical compression chiller uses a compressor powered by electricity to compress a refrigerant. During the compression cycle the refrigerant passes through an evaporator, a condenser, and an expansion device in addition to the compressor. Let's examine the use of each of the four major components of a mechanical compression chiller as well as the cooling tower and the new controls you may be able to obtain.

Evaporator A chiller, as its name implies, generates chilled water. That chilled water is produced in the evaporator where a compressed cold refrigerant flows over the evaporator tubes. The refrigerant (which is a liquid) evaporates and changes into a gas vapor as heat is transferred from the water to the refrigerant. The resulting chilled water is pumped through the use of the chilled-water distribution system to the building's air-handling units. As the chilled water passes through coils in the air handler heat is transferred from the air to the water. The warmed water is then returned to the evaporator to be recycled and the blower in the air handler distributes the cooled air within the building.

Compressor Most of the electricity used by a chiller is due to the operation of the compressor. The function of the compressor is to take vaporized gaseous refrigerant from the evaporator and compress the gas into a high-temperature, high-pressure vapor that is transferred to the condenser.

Condenser Hot, high-pressure gas from the compressor flows into the condenser where it flows around tubes that contain condenser loop water. As the heat from the gaseous refrigerant is transferred to the water the refrigerant condenses into a liquid. The liquid then flows to an expansion valve and the condensed water is pumped from the condenser to a cooling tower where heat is transferred from the water to the atmosphere.

Expansion Valve The fourth major component of a mechanical chiller is the expansion valve. The function of this valve is to control the rate of cooling. As refrigerant flows into the evaporator through the expansion valve, the valve controls the rate at which the refrigerant expands to a lower pressure and a much lower temperature. Once the refrigerant flows around the evaporator tubes it absorbs the heat of the chilled water that's been returned from the air handlers, completing the refrigeration cycle.

Cooling Towers The fifth major component of a mechanical chiller is a cooling tower. The cooling tower is often overlooked as a component for checking inasmuch as it can reside in a place not easily accessible, such as the roof of a building. However, because it is exposed to the elements, it can gather leaves and other debris that can interfere with its operation or even clog the passage of water. Doing so can result in the compressor overheating as it attempts to work harder. In fact, according to a manufacturer of water cooling towers, for each degree Fahrenheit increase of the water coming from the cooling tower the efficiency of the chiller will decrease by an average of 2%. Thus, they should be inspected on a regular basis.

Controls   Similar to most heating and cooling products, chillers are now manufactured with sophisticated, onboard microprocessors that provide a variety of diagnostics and control functions. If the equipment should have a malfunction, depending upon its severity the microprocessor may shut it down, provide an alert, or perform both operations. In addition, depending upon the manufacturer of the chiller it may include operating controls that enable personnel to make adjustments to some chiller operating parameters. Thus, the type and scope of potential controls should be examined. For example, if the chiller is used to reduce heat in a data center you would prefer an alert to a shutdown when the problem from diagnostics is not that severe.

Classification   There are several types of fluids used for cooling. Water is commonly used and can be cooled to approximately 40°Fahrenheit. For lower temperatures the use of glycol or a brine solution is employed. Mechanical compression chillers can be further classified by compressor type. Common compression methods include reciprocating, rotary screw, centrifugal, and frictionless centrifugal.

Reciprocating   A reciprocating compression chiller has a crankshaft that is turned by an electric motor. Similar to a car engine with multiple pistons, gas is compressed by the pistons, heating it in the process. The hot gas is then discharged via the condenser instead of being exhausted out a tailpipe. In general the reciprocating compression chiller can be obtained with a capacity of up to 125 tons, making it suitable for small- to medium-size buildings.

Rotary Screw   The rotary screw compression chiller has two mating grooved rotors in a stationary housing. The rotation of the rotors is used to compress the gas. The capacity of this type of chiller can be up to approximately 450 tons, which at 12,000 BTUs per ton provides a capacity of up to 5.4 million BTUs.

Centrifugal   A third type of compression chiller is the centrifugal device. Here the centrifugal chiller operates similarly to a centrifugal water pump, with the rotating part of the compressor, referred to as an impeller, compressing the refrigerant. Centrifugal chillers provide a much higher cooling capacity than other types of chillers and also support a compact design. Typically they have a capacity beginning at 150 tons or 1.8 million BTUs of cooling capacity.

Frictionless Centrifugal   The fourth type of compression chiller can be considered to be similar to some lubrication-less fans commonly installed in heating and air-conditioning systems over the past decade although they employ a different technology. Referred to as frictionless centrifugal chillers, they use magnetic bearing technology so that the compressor docs not require lubrication. Typically the frictionless centrifugal compressor includes a variable-speed DC motor with direct-drive for the centrifugal compressor. Capacities range from 60 to 300 tons. This is equivalent to between .72 million BTUs and 3.6 million BTUs of cooling capacity.

Absorption Chiller   Absorption chillers use a heat source, such as natural gas or steam to create a refrigeration cycle that does not use mechanical compression. Thus, this type of chiller has no moving parts.

Absorption chillers are driven by hot water, which in turn can be generated from natural gas or even an oil-based boiler or furnace as well as from a number of industrial sources to include waste heat from industrial processes, or even heat from solar thermal installations. Because they use heat generated from natural gas, oil, or another nonelectric source to produce chilled water, they consume a relatively small amount of electricity to operate pumps in comparison to the electricity used by mechanical compression chillers.

The principle behind the operation of an absorption chiller is based on the interaction of gases and solids. With absorption chilling, the interaction between the solid and the gas allows gas to be absorbed into a solid. This results in the adsorption chamber of an absorption chiller being filled with silica gel or another type of solid material, eliminating both the need for moving parts and the noise associated with those moving parts. That noise can be considerable. In fact, in many buildings you will encounter a sign stating you need to wear earplugs when going into a mechanical equipment room that contains a chiller and associated air handlers due to the noise level in the room. When an absorption chiller uses silica gel, its use creates an extremely low humidity condition that causes the water refrigerant to evaporate at a low temperature. As the water evaporates in the evaporator, it cools the chilled water.

Factors to Consider

The selection of a new or replacement chiller can be a lengthy process that requires considering numerous factors beyond the scope of this book, however, we now turn our attention to factors of importance to the data center. In doing so we examine several factors that you need to consider not only to economize on the cost associated with the operation of a chiller but factors that can facilitate the operation of the data center.

Rapid Restart Capability   One of the key items you need to consider is what happens when your data center loses power. Assuming you have a UPS capability that can alleviate many problems, what happens if you cannot afford to power everything and the UPS is used to provide power for an orderly shutdown? Then when power returns you need to consider how long it takes for the chiller to provide an appropriate level of cooling prior to heat buildup causing equipment problems. Thus, both the time to restart a chiller and its ability to cool the data center within a predefined period of time are important considerations.

Operating Multiple Chillers   Depending upon the size of a data center and the building it's housed in you may have more than one chiller in use. When you have two or more chillers used for the building and a separate one for the data center it becomes possible to match the building loads to the chillers. By reviewing the use of chillers it might be possible to match the loads more efficiently, which in effect reduces electrical consumption.

Checking the Refrigerant Line   Similar to automobile brakes, you do not want air in your refrigerant lines. Although modern chillers include air purgers, not all do so. Thus, air in a line will cause the compressor to work harder, expending additional energy. Having maintenance check the refrigerant line on a periodic basis may allow you to uncover a small problem prior to its becoming a major one. In addition to looking for air you need to maintain the refrigerant level based upon the manufacturer's specifications. In addition to having maintenance personnel perform a periodic pressure test, you can set a regular schedule to take temperature readings and compare those readings to the manufacturer specifications, providing a method to determine if the system is within specification or if a potential problem has arisen that requires investigation.

Optimize Cooling during Cold Weather   Some chillers include a bypass and heat exchanger referred to as a water-side economizer. In effect, the water-side economizer eliminates the need for cooling via compressors when the outdoor temperature is sufficient to provide cooling. In a chiller environment the water-side economizer produces chilled water without requiring the chiller to run. In a data center environment cold water is supplied to air handlers that cool at the floor level. To provide sufficiently cold water from outside air in some locations might be limited to evenings and a part of the day, thus it may be hard to justify the cost of an economizer. Instead, if the data center uses containment by having cold or hot aisles they may be able to raise their chilled water set point, which can extend the use of an economizer.

To illustrate the potential effect of economizing upon the use of energy you can refer to a short "bits" published in the September 23, 2010 issue of *Network World* magazine titled "Yahoo! opens 'chicken coop' data center." In that "bit" it was mentioned that Yahoo! was opening at that time the most eco-friendly data center, using a radical new design to reduce the use of energy by 40%. Apparently Yahoo! designed their data center in some ways similar to a chicken coop, hence its name. Using long halls and located near the Niagara Falls area in upstate New York, the data center uses the air to cool servers, avoiding the use of a chiller. Although you may have an existing data center that does not have the luxury of relocation, the note indicates that you can significantly reduce your electric bill by using cooler air when it's available. Even if your data center is located in a hot humid climate, there will be evenings when the cooler outside air could be used.

Examine Ductworks   Although the examination of ductworks is presented under our examination of chiller considerations, this topic is applicable for any ductwork where heated or cooled air flows.

Ductwork leaks present a problem whenever air escapes to the outside. Ducts running through an office ceiling as well as through unconditioned spaces are common sources of such leaks. In addition, some buildings use cavities created during construction as ducts, allowing air to easily escape as it flows around a joist or wall plate. It's important to seal heating and cooling ducts but at the same time you need to consider the level of insulation or its absence from ductwork. In fact, this author remembers a two-story data center where the ceiling tiles when lifted revealed sheet metal ducts, which during the summer would periodically drip condensation. Once the ducts were insulated the condensation problem was alleviated and the use of electricity substantially decreased.

One of the easiest methods used to determine ductwork leakage is to purchase a laser temperature sensor. By targeting the ductwork with the laser the outside temperature of the sheet metal will be recorded. That temperature should be fairly uniform until a leak is uncovered, where the sensor will then record an abnormality, represented by a significant increase or decrease in the temperature depending upon whether cooling or heating is being used. Often this $30 tool can save its weight in gold by pointing out a leak in ductwork that might not otherwise be noticed.

Examining Air Filters   Although maintenance requirements will vary based upon the type of equipment, one thing they have in common that you need to consider is the air filter or filters being used. Dirty filters will hamper the operation of the air handler, slowing down the flow of air and making the system waste energy as it operates to perform heating or cooling. Thus, you should at a minimum follow the manufacturer's guidelines concerning the replacement of air filters. In addition to facilitating the flow of air, a clean filter will remove most dust and dirt particles from circulating, making for a better working environment.

Heating and Cooling Items to Consider   At the beginning of this chapter we mentioned that a checklist of items to consider would be included at the end of the chapter. This checklist, which is presented in Table 3.2, should be used as a guide for both acquiring and maintaining general heating and cooling devices. Because data centers can range in scope from a small office with a single server in a small building to racks upon racks of servers and mainframes located in a very large building there is no "one size fits all" methodology concerning items to consider. Thus, although some items listed in the referenced table will be applicable for some readers, other items may not.

Considering the Long Term

In concluding this chapter a few words about the long-term effect of a decision on heating or cooling equipment is warranted. When considering a new building or the potential replacement of an existing building's heating you need to consider carefully the type of fuel to use. This is because over a period of time the cost of fuel consumed can easily exceed the cost of equipment used to burn the fuel. For example, in certain locations a significant amount of natural gas has been found based upon a horizontal drilling technique that enabled the recovery of deep shale gas. This has resulted in the cost of gas declining over the past few years while reserves have significantly increased. Thus, if your organization is located in an area served by natural gas it might be practical to consider the replacement of an existing furnace that uses a different and more expensive type of fuel.

Table 3.2 Guide for Acquiring and Maintaining Heating and Cooling

Boilers
    Capacity in horsepower, R pounds of steam per hour or BTUs
Radiant heating systems
Type
        Panel in wall, floor, or ceiling
        Radiator
            Pumps, blower, and piping considerations
Heat pump
    Capacity in tons
    Type
    Hybrid heat pumps/dual fuel heat pump
    Air-source heat pumps
    Geothermal heat pumps
    Absorption heat pumps
SEER and HSPF ratings
    Dual fuel support
Features—variable-speed fan, filter check display, compressor turn-on delay
Electric resistance heating
    Type
        Centralized furnace
            Voltage and current requirements
        Room heaters: baseboard or electric radiant heater
        Baseboard heater types: fixed, portable, heavy-duty, architectural
            Voltage, current, BTU, and watt rating
            Zones and thermostats
    Cost of electricity
    Number of heating days per year
Radiators
    Steam heating
        Delay
        Pipe insulation
        Reflectors behind radiators
Hot water radiators
        Fluid: water or oil
        Size
        Zone control
Hot water heater
    Type
        Tank-based
        Tankless
        Indirect
    Heat source

Table 3.2 (*Continued*)   Guide for Acquiring and Maintaining Heating and Cooling

Gas
Electric
    Number of heating elements
    Number of thermostats
Propane
Oil
Solar
    Active or passive
    Tax rebates
Insulation—R value
Hot water flow gal/minute
Air conditioner
Type—split system or packaged
Size/capacity in BTUs or tons
Vents and grills adjustability
Features—variable-speed fan, filter check display, compressor turn-on delay
Chiller
Rating in tons or BTUs
Type
    Mechanical compression chillers
        Evaporator
        Compressor
        Condenser
        Expansion valve
        Cooling tower
        Controls
    Classification
        Reciprocating
        Rotary screw
        Centrifugal
        Frictionless centrifugal
    Absorption chiller
Controls
Cooling tower capacity and location
Type of fluid
Selection factors to consider
    Rapid restart capability
    Operating multiple chillers
Checking the refrigerant line
Optimize cooling during cold weather
Examine ductworks
Examine air filters

4

READING AND UNDERSTANDING YOUR ELECTRIC, GAS, AND WATER METERS

In this chapter we concentrate on something that we often take for granted, the ability to understand and read different types of meters. In doing so we describe and discuss various types of meters, such as the standard analog type dialed electric meter as well as the more recently developed "smart meter" that provides utilities with the ability to make the most use of time-of-day pricing for electricity. In addition to discussing electric meters, we also focus our attention upon natural gas and water meters. Although for many data centers the vast majority of their monthly bills may be for electrical service, the use of natural gas and water can result in significant cumulative expenditures that may be possible to reduce. In both this chapter and in later chapters in this book we describe and discuss several actions that we can consider to reduce the cost of electric, natural gas, and water service.

The Electric Meter

In this section we focus our attention upon the electric meter. As we do so, we first discuss the various types of meters prior to going into specifics regarding how to read different categories of meters.

Electric Meter Categories

There are two general categories of electric meters we can define: dumb and smart. The so-called dumb meter is an electromechanical device that currently represents the vast majority of meters installed and their basic design dates back to the late 1800s. The second category of meters, referred to as smart meters, represents electronic meters that have a microprocessor or controller and logic built into the device. This type of meter is rapidly being installed at many locations and probably represents the literal wave of the future as it will enable utilities to bill customers based upon time-of-day consumption and be capable of being integrated into the so-called smart grid, as well as provide customers with the ability to integrate personal computers with smart meter software to obtain usage statistics that they may be able to use to reduce or postpone certain types of electrical consumption.

Unfortunately, although many millions of smart meters are being installed they represent only a small fraction of the population of electric meters. In the United States there are two states out of 50 where the installation of smart electric meters now represents over 10% of the electric meter population: California and Texas. Electric utility companies in other states are either considering installing smart meters or have field trials, however, with the exception of the two previously named states their usage represents a tiny fraction of the installed base of electric meters.

Electric meters can also be categorized as to their support of single-phase or three-phase alternating current (AC), by their type of display, such as a dial or numeric display, whether they support variable rates, and if they support prepayment. The variable-rate electric meters are used by organizations that commonly operate multiple shifts. This type of meter supports two or more readings, enabling energy consumption to be computed for different shifts such that the off-peak consumption usually is less expensive than peak consumption. The prepayment meter is found in the United Kingdom and other countries and is typically installed at rental-type properties. This type of meter can use tokens or prepaid cards to provide electricity and contains a relay that will trip to cut off the supply when the balance is used up.

Examining the Electric Meter

One of the more obvious things in this book is that to learn how to read a meter requires us to have access to one for illustrative purposes. Fortunately, this author was able to take pictures of his electric, gas, and water meters, which should be sufficient for illustrative purposes. Figure 4.1 illustrates the electric meter installed by Georgia Power

Figure 4.1   The electric meter used at this author's home.

approximately 34 years ago and, which although not a smart meter by any standard, like a Timex watch, it keeps on ticking, counting off the energy consumption in this author's home. The utility company, which in this service area is Georgia Power, a subsidiary of The Southern Company, brings either overhead or underground electrical service via the use of feeder wires from a transformer located within close proximity to the home or office. The feeder wires will be connected to the top inside of the meter, which is referred to as the line side.

If you remove the face of the meter, which should only be done by an appropriate utility person, you would note that there are two hot wires that are usually left black in color. The third wire is the neutral wire that is generally marked with white tape. The two hot wires are connected to terminals at the top of the meter and a third connection terminal in the middle is where the neutral wire will be connected. The two hot wire connection points used for the outgoing connection represent the load connection points. This is the portion of the inside of the meter that also feeds the service panel in your home or office. Similar to the line connection, the load connection has two hot feeds with the center being the neutral connection. In addition to the two hot wires, there will also be a ground wire that will be connected to the neutral connection on the meter and to the ground rod. In Figure 4.1 the electric meter shown is for single-phase, 120-VAC operations, however, it should be noted that for large industrial operations and many data centers the meter will be for three-phase AC.

If you turn your attention to the meter shown in Figure 4.1 you will note that it is primarily focused upon the glass enclosure, which to a degree resembles an oversized Mason jar. Because the glass enclosure is clear, it allows you as well as the meter reader who probably visits your home on a monthly basis to observe the positions of the pointers on the five dials you can see inside the glass. One of the problems associated with reading an electric meter is that over the years a home or building may be repainted or it could be re-stuccoed. Depending upon the neatness of the person or persons doing the work the ability to observe the meter dials may be hampered by paint or stucco dripped onto the glass, which is why the glass should be protected when work on the home or office is performed.

Figure 4.1 shows the meter display very well, but it does not show the metal box that makes the connections weatherproof as well as the tamper-resistant tag. That tag is used to lock the box so that if an unauthorized person attempts to modify the meter the attempt will be noted. Although the utility is responsible for the meter and its connection to the electrical service, the locking tag is both employed to keep the general public out of harm's way as well as to indicate if any tampering occurred. If the latter has occurred, the wrongdoer may be fined or even have the utility disconnect the premises from electrical service.

The meter shown in Figure 4.1 is technically referred to as an electromechanical meter which, as briefly mentioned earlier, dates to the 1880s. This type of meter operates by counting the number of revolutions of the aluminum disk that is shown located under the label, which in turn is located under the dials in the referenced figure. This meter measures electricity in kilowatt hours, however, there are meters that measure electricity in terms of megajoules. As a refresher, a kilowatt hour (kWh) represents 1,000 watts expended during an hour, or the electricity consumed by a 100-watt bulb turned on for 10 hours. In comparison, the joule is named after James Prescott Joule and technically represents the energy expended in applying a force of one newton for a distance of one meter; it is better known by the relationship where the joule represents the work required to produce

one watt of power continuously for a duration of one second, the latter being called a watt second (Ws). Thus, 3,600 joules is equal to one
watt hour inasmuch as there are 3,600 seconds in an hour.

Returning our attention to Figure 4.1 and the aluminum disk,
because the disk rotates at a speed proportional to the power, the
number of revolutions is proportional to the energy used including a
tiny amount of approximately two watts used by the meter. Thus, the
vast majority of power that the electric meter records represents power
used by the consumer.

The amount of energy represented by one revolution of the aluminum disk is denoted by the symbol Kh, which represents the number of
watt-hours per revolution. Many electric meters use a value of 7.2 Kh.
Knowing the value of Kh it becomes possible to compute the power
consumption at a moment in time by using a chronometer or stopwatch.
For example, if the time in seconds required for the aluminum disk to
complete one full revolution is t, then the power in watts becomes:

$$P = \frac{3,600 \times Kh}{t}$$

If we assume Kh has a value of 7.2 watt-hours per revolution and
that the aluminum disk completes a revolution in 10.8 seconds, then
the power in watts becomes:

$$P = 3,600 \times 7.2/10.8 = 2,400 \text{ watts}$$

Although you can time the number of seconds per rotation and
switch devices on and off to compute their power consumption you
have to ask yourself if you really want to do this and how accurate
your results will be. The answer to the first question is more than
likely a resounding NO, and the answer to the second question is
probably not too accurate. The reason for the latter response is that
many devices that you might consider OFF actually consume some
power, such as all the devices with clocks, certain power strips that
have an illuminated LED, refrigerators, personal computers in a sleep
mode of operation, and perhaps not so obvious are thermostats and
hardwired controls that measure certain parameters.

Currently a vast majority of electric meters including the one
illustrated in Figure 4.1 must be read manually. With the gradual

introduction of newer meters it becomes possible for meter readings either to be transmitted via wireless technology or via the power line to the utility, saving a considerable amount of money by not having to employ as many meter readers going to customer locations on a monthly basis. Thus, one of the more immediate benefits from the installation of so-called smart meters is a reduction in the cost of meter reading. Whether this will lower the ultimate cost of electricity to the consumer remains to be seen.

If you stand directly in front of the electric meter you will observe a series of five round dials near the top of the face of the meter. If you carefully examine each dial you will note that each has 10 digits (0–9) and a black pointer that resembles many clock dials. You will also note that from the right-most dial, the first, third, and fifth dials are numbered 0 through 9 clockwise, whereas the second and fourth dials are numbered essentially backwards from 9 through 0 counterclockwise. As electricity flows through the meter the pointers will advance and so will your monthly cost for the use of electricity. Each dial from right to left indicates the unit: tens, hundreds, thousands, and ten thousands of kWh of energy consumed. However, the first, third, and fifth dials rotate in the clockwise direction whereas the second and fourth dials rotate in the counterclockwise direction. Figure 4.2 illustrates an example of the five dials and a setting taken at random that we use to illustrate how to read an electric meter.

One additional piece of information concerning the dial electric meter that uses a rotating aluminum disk that you might want to consider is lubrication or the lack of it. As the meter ages it's obvious that some friction occurs, which may very slightly decrease the rotation speed of the disk. The effect of this decrease in rotation speed is to make the meter indicate a drop less of power consumption than actually occurs. Perhaps this might explain why some homeowners and businesses that were upgraded to smart meters received a shock from their bill due to the accuracy of the new meter.

Figure 4.2   Electric meter dial rotation.

Reading an Electric Meter

When you read the settings of the pointers on each dial you should select the lower number when the pointer is between numbers. For example, if the pointer is between 3 and 4 you would select 3 as the number. Reading from right to left on the set of dials in Figure 4.2, we note that the right-most dial is between 1 and 2, therefore we select one (1). This position represents digits, so the last number in our sequence will be 1. Next, continuing to the left, the second pointer on the second dial is between 4 and 5, therefore its value will be 4. Because it represents tens, we now have a cumulative reading of 41. As you examine the dials in Figure 4.2, note that from the right the second and fourth dials are numbered counterclockwise.

The third dial in Figure 4.2 is exactly at 9 and represents the hundreds position, so we now have the value of 941 on the meter. Continuing to the fourth dial, its pointer is between 8 and 9 and it represents thousands, so we select 8 and our reading is now 8,941. Finally, the fifth and last dial has the pointer between 7 and 8 and represents the ten thousand position. Thus, the value of the electric meter shown in Figure 4.2 becomes 78,941 or seventy-eight thousand, nine hundred forty-one kilowatts of power. By the way, if you read the electric meter at the same time tomorrow you can then determine the number of kilowatt-hours used in one day. Whether this is meaningful to a great extent depends on the weather. For example, a nice Spring day with a temperature of 72 degrees would minimize cooling costs and provide a good indication of the baseline power used by a data center. Then, measuring the consumption that occurs in August might provide you with the ability to determine the added cost above the baseline associated with cooling and removal of humidity from the data center.

If you want to get an estimate of your potential electric bill, the meter provides you with some general consumption information that can be helpful. For example, assume that the reading you take at the same time tomorrow is 79,997. Then, subtracting 78,441 from 79,997 you obtain 1,556 kWh of power consumed during a 24-hour period. Assuming the cost of electricity is 10 cents per kilowatt hour, this means that your business or an extremely large home consumed $156.60 worth of electricity for that 24-hour period. We could return to the dumb meter day after day to take additional readings to compute the cost of electricity consumed each day, but chances are high we would more than likely forget to do so. Thus, we could assume that during the month unless the weather changed drastically we would consume $156.60 per day. Then, if we multiply by 30 days, we would obtain an estimate of monthly consumption of $4,668. Note that this estimate reflects only the cost of energy consumed and does not include such easy-to-forget (until you get the utility bill) billing additions as municipal and state taxes, minimum connection fees, and other fees that can easily drive up the cost of electrical service. To be fair, this author should also mention that depending upon the contract your organization has with the utility, you may be eligible for a variety of discounts, such as allowing power to be reduced during peak periods of electrical usage by utility customers. Whether a data center should accept what is essentially a "brownout" provision depends upon whether your organization has a standby generator and the cost associated with operating that generator.

Load Meters

Prior to moving on to discuss a relatively new type of electric meter referred to as "digital" or "smart," a few words about load meters are in order. A load meter as its name implies is designed to measure the highest peak demand for electricity flowing through the meter. Most load meters are used by organizations that consume in excess of 1,000 kilowatt-hours of electricity per month. If your serving utility has a peak load clause in your electric agreement your organization will have a peak load meter. The load meter can be either analog with dials similar to those shown in Figure 4.1 but with an additional meter that indicates the peak demand normally measured in 30-minute time periods or digital, which we discuss shortly. If your organization has an analog load meter it will resemble the meter shown in Figure 4.1 and you would read power consumption the same as before. However, the load meter will usually have a large needle that moves along a calibrated scale around the meter face, with this scale measuring the load in kilowatts. Here the position of the needle will indicate the highest peak load since the last time the meter was read. Similar to automobiles, there is a range of different types of load meters, with some having a single large needle to indicate the maximum load whereas other load meters might have multiple dials, with some meters capable of being programmed for time-of-day operations and even having a telephone connection to contact the utility.

Recording Data

Prior to discussing smart meters in detail a few words about data recording are in order. Some electric meters, such as certain models manufactured by Landis & Gyr, a company based in Zug, Switzerland but with offices worldwide, developed electric meters that can be used to record information. In Figure 4.3 the reader will view a Landis & Gyr AXRS4 meter used by the Georgia Power Company and installed at one of its nonresidential sites. This digital meter is a combination of active energy, demand, and time-of-use and includes a load profile recorder.

The AXR device is approved for metering kWh and kilovolt-ampere (kVA) both as energy quantities and as demand quantities for

Figure 4.3   The Landis & Gyr meter has a data recording capability. Modem box is circled.

block intervals, sliding window, and even thermal demand. The meter includes a 15-channel solid-state programmable pulse recorder that can be used for recording energy pulses. The meter has an optical port and a demand reset switch located on the front of the cover and as shown, includes an alphanumeric liquid crystal display (LCD).

Operation   The AXRS4 samples voltage and current pairs at a rate of 3.33 MHz, automatically detecting the service type and voltage. The values are filtered digitally, providing a single 20-bit analog-to-digital converter (ADC) and the meter will then transmit the signal to a digital signal processor. Data are calculated by the DSP with the exception of VA, which is calculated by a microcontroller. If you carefully examine Figure 4.3 you will note that there is a box next to the word "Modem," (circled) which is not checked. This meter can be equipped with an internal modem board to enable data to be accessed and read via a telephone line and is even capable of having an optional meter transmitter unit module (STAR MTU) added that can link individual meters to a fixed network, allowing two-way communication that enables any of the meter fields to be read and managed remotely.

Digital "Smart" Meters

Newer electric meters are digital and contain an LCD display that records usage in a manner similar to a vehicle's odometer. Such meters have an added feature as they are actually read from the utility company's office. Because they include a microprocessor that is programmable and adds intelligence to the meter it is commonly referred to as a smart meter.

There are several types of smart meters. Although they are based upon the use of a microprocessor their method of communication can differ considerably among devices. Some smart meters are essentially one-way transmission devices, designed to receive a utility company query and then transmit its readings, eliminating the need for a meter reader to visit the home or office. Other smart meters are truly two-way transmission devices, designed to receive and transmit a variety of information. Regardless of the type of meter there are several methods being used to enable communications.

In Europe, where there are a large number of homes and offices connected to each transformer broadband over power lines (BPL), a method where communication occurs at a frequency different from the 50-cycle AC used in European countries is popularly used. BPL commonly employs frequency shift keying (FSK) where marks or binary ones and spaces or binary zeros are transmitted using two different frequencies, hence the name of the technique. Under FSK the carrier is below 500 kHz and widely spaced mark and space frequencies are used to minimize errors, however, the data rate is relatively low, at approximately 100 kbps. In the United States, Canada, and other countries that have a power distribution system with a lesser number of consumers per transformer the preferred mode of communication is 900 MHz wireless, which is usually implemented as a mesh network instead of using a star network topology.

Smart Meters and the Smart Grid

Unless we have been in hibernation for the past few years we have probably encountered the term "smart grid" numerous times, used both by itself and with the term, "smart meter." Some authors were correct in the manner in which they used the terms; other articles were a bit off the mark. Thus, this author takes this opportunity to clarify the terms and how they relate to one another.

The "smart grid" represents the integration of intelligent two-way communication and control in a secure manner to the electrical grid infrastructure. The goal of the smart grid is to provide utilities with detailed information that will allow the utility to enhance its operations. That enhancement can include improving its reliability by monitoring load and fault conditions that could result in brownouts or even blackouts as well as managing the delivery and consumption of electricity that can reduce energy costs by optimizing consumption and allowing customers to manage their demand. Concerning the latter, the smart meter is a key part of the evolving smart grid. At the home or office the smart meter is designed to connect via one of several types of networks to different equipment. Those types of networks can include the well-known IEEE 802.11 WiFi standard, ZigBee, another wireless standard that uses the 2.4 GHz band to obtain a data rate of approximately 250 kbps, the HomePlug transmission method, which turns wall outlets into transmitter/receivers at data rates up to 200 Mbps, home telephone wire, and even coaxial cable. By allowing communication to occur from the smart meter to devices within the home or office it becomes possible to install one or more LCD panels inside the home or office that can instantly inform you of the cost associated with running various types of electrical devices as well as commence some action, such as raising or lowering the temperature on a thermostat, deferring running a dishwasher until the evening when rates are lower, and performing other energy-associated actions.

Reading the Smart Meter Display

Although it has many functions, a digital smart meter measures the amount of electricity you used and displays this usage on a liquid crystal display. You read the numbers from left to right, such that the fifth number represents the ten thousands position, the fourth number represents the thousands position, and so on. Thus, if the meter shows the following number:

52345

This would indicate that the reading was 52,345 (fifty-two thousand, three hundred and forty-five) kilowatt-hours.

Suppose the next month your digital meter showed the following number:

63486

Then, in one month your energy consumption would be 63,486–52,345 or 11,141 kilowatt-hours. Once again you can compute a reasonable estimate of your electric bill by multiplying the kWhs used by the rate per kWh to obtain an estimate of the energy charge. This author uses the term "reasonable estimate" because there are a number of different billing categories used by electric utilities, with most utilities having a base rate you must pay regardless of whether you consume any power. For example, consider Figure 4.4 that is an extract from a Georgia Power Electric Service Tariff Power and Large Light Schedule, which is applicable for customers that use 500 or more kWh per month and have one service delivery point. If you examine the excerpt illustrated

MONTHLY RATE:

Energy Charge Including Demand Charge:

Base Charge $16.75

All consumption (kWh) not greater than 200 hours times the billing demand:

    First 3,000 kWh   @   10.8471¢ per kWh

    Next 7,000 kWh   @   9.8355¢ per kWh

    Next 190,000 kWh   @   8.3880¢ per kWh

    Over 200,000 kWh   @   6.4648¢ per kWh

All consumption (kWh) in excess of 200 hours and not greater than 400 hours times the billing demand   @   1.1062¢ per kWh

All consumption (kWh) in excess of 400 hours and not greater than 600 hours times the billing demand   @   0.8730¢ per kWh

All consumption (kWh) in excess of 600 hours times the billing demand   @   0.6292¢ per kWh

Minimum Monthly Bill:

A. $16.75 Base Charge plus $7.80 per kW of billing demand plus excess kVAR charges plus Environmental Compliance Cost Recovery plus Fuel Cost Recovery, as applied to the current month kWh, plus Franchise Fee.

Figure 4.4   Excerpt from Georgia Power Company Power and Large Light Schedule PLL-5 Electric Service Tariff.

in Figure 4.4 you will note that the monthly base charge is $16.75 and that consumption is on a sliding scale, with the first 3,000 kWh billed at 10.8471 cents per kWh, decreasing to a bit over 6 cents per kWh when consumption tops 200,000 kWh in a month. In addition, if you read note A concerning the minimum monthly bill you will note it includes the cost of several additional fees, such as an excess kVA charge, an Environmental Compliance Cost Recovery fee, a Fuel Cost Recovery fee, and a Franchise fee.

Smart Meter Problems

If you watch the evening news on television or have read one of several articles published in both local newspapers and nationwide publications you might have noted how some persons complained that their electric bill literally skyrocketed after a smart meter was installed. This is especially true for customers of two utilities that have rolled out millions of smart meters: Pacific Gas & Electric of California and CenterPoint Energy located in Texas. According to some reports in 2008, customers complained that in the prior year a $140 electric bill was now $350 with little change in temperature. Other customers complained that they were being billed $600 for electricity on a 1,300-square-foot trailer when a new smart meter was installed, whereas in prior months the cost of electricity using the older electro-mechanical meter was slightly over $100 for the month.

The number of complaints from electric utility customers has well exceeded 10,000, so a logical question is how accurate are the new meters and why do some customers receive what appear to be outrageous electric bills? The next few paragraphs explain what is probably happening and although a few customer complaints continue, it is hoped we will shed some light on a few of the possible culprits. In addition, the results of a report that examined the new smart meters is mentioned that was published in the later part of 2010.

Beginning in 2008 several million smart meters were installed by electric utility companies, most notably Pacific Gas & Electric and CenterPoint Energy. These advanced meters produce readings that are sent to the electric utility, usually at 15-minute intervals and are used to generate a bill without requiring a meter reader to visit the premises. Because the number of smart meters being installed exceeded 10,000 per day during portions of 2009 and 2010, just a slight percentage of defective meters could be a cause for alarm. For example, consider a defective rate of one per thousand meters or .001%. This would result in one meter being installed each day that would literally not be kosher. Although this defect rate is low, you would not want to be the consumer who had a defective meter installed. By the way, a defect rate of .001 is actually not unreasonable. When you consider the error-free installation of heat pumps, refrigerators, servers, and other electronic devices, a failure rate of 1 in a thousand would actually be very good. Considering that in the 1970s this author worked for a minicomputer manufacturer where products rolling off the assembly line only underwent a "smoke test," where the computer was powered on and employees looked for smoke, we have come a long way in terms of quality assurance, however, you can still expect defects to occur. One example to consider is the well-known Six Sigma business strategy pioneered by Motorola, in which 99.99966% of the products manufactured are statistically expected to be free of defects. This equates to 3.4 defects per million, which seems quite reasonable. However, if two component manufacturers meet the Six Sigma standard but their components are used by a third manufacturer in a series environment then the availability of the two components will be less than each individual component. Because it's easier to be Six Sigma compliant on a component level than a system level this means that you need to check the reliability and availability data of systems you are considering.

Standards

Currently there are a number of standards governing the electrical requirements of smart meters. The International Electrotechnical Commission (IEC) is the international standards and conformity assessment body for all fields of electronic technology. Its 61036 standard defines the power dissipation, voltage, and performance guidelines to include a meter's absolute voltage and overcurrent maximums. In addition to the IEC, the American National Standards Institute (ANSI) developed its C12.20 standards for solid-state electric meters, which when followed make electric meters twice as accurate as older electromechanical meters, such as the one shown in Figure 4.1. With this in mind and the fact that the millions of meters recently installed complied with these standards, why do some persons have significant billing problems? Literally the jury is still out on this issue according to some irate consumers, however, the following are several possibilities.

Possible Causes of Billing Inaccuracies

In this section we examine several potential causes of billing problems when utility customers are migrated to a smart meter environment. First, it's possible that the older electromechanical meter, which in some situations could be 30 or more years old, has became inaccurate due to the rotating disk becoming worn or failing to spin properly, and its lack of self-lubrication. Thus, the smart meter installed to replace the electromechanical meter might not be inaccurate. Second, the goal of the smart meter from the viewpoint of the utility is to provide a time-of-day rate capability and tariffs by some utilities reflect the fact that electricity will cost more during the day than at night. For example, consider the Pacific Gas & Electric Time of Use tariff that can be found at the following website: http://www.pge.com/tariffs/tm2/pdf/ELEC_SCHEDS_A-6.pdf.

In examining an extract of that tariff note Figures 4.5 and 4.6. In Figure 4.5 an extract from sheet 3 of the PG&E tariff is shown. Note that under the "Small General Time-of-Use Service" the energy rates during the summer can vary from 11.691 cents per kWh during the off-peak time period to 45.331 cents per kWh during the peak summer period. This represents an increase of approximately a factor of four between peak and off-peak periods. Now what we need to determine is the schedule of times for peak and off-peak periods.

If we turn our attention to Figure 4.6 we can note that PG&E has three defined periods of time, referred to as Peak, Partial-peak, and Off-peak. During the summer the peak period of time where the rates are rather high is defined from 12:00 noon to 6:00 p.m. Monday through Friday with the exception of holidays. The partial-peak period of time ranges from 8:30 a.m. to 12:00 noon and from 6:00 p.m. to 9:30 p.m., again Monday through Friday except for holidays. Finally, the off-peak period is defined ranging from 9:30 p.m. to 8:30 a.m. Monday through Friday and all day on Saturday, Sunday, and holidays. With this rate schedule if an organization continued what it was doing without consuming additional electricity during many days

Sheet 3
ELECTRIC SCHEDULE A-6
SMALL GENERAL TIME-OF-USE SERVICE

TERRITORY:	This rate schedule applies everywhere PG&E provides electric service.
RATES:	Total bundled service charges are calculated using the total rates shown below. Direct Access (DA) and Community Choice Aggregation (CCA) charges shall be calculated in accordance with the paragraph in this rate schedule titled Billing.

TOTAL RATES

Total Customer/Meter Charge Rates

Customer Charge Single-phase ($ per meter per day)	$0.29569
Customer Charge Poly-phase ($ per meter per day)	$0.44353
Meter Charge (A-6) ($ per meter per day)	$0.20107
Meter Charge (W) ($ per meter per day)	$0.05914
Meter Charge (X) ($ per meter per day)	$0.20107

Total Energy Rates ($ per kWh)

Peak Summer	$0.45331	(R)
Part-Peak Summer	$0.20061	(R)
Off-Peak Summer	$0.11691	(R)
Part-Peak Winter	$0.16567	(R)
Off-Peak Winter	$0.12084	(R)

Figure 4.5 PG&E small general time-of-use service rate schedule.

and liked a cool environment they could easily see their electric bill literally skyrocket by a factor of approximately four once a smart meter was installed. Thus, it's quite possible that the smart meter is operating just fine but they are getting shocked by the time-of-use tariff.

As a matter of interest, due to the number of consumers being shocked by their electric bill when a smart meter was installed, both the California Public Utilities Commission and the consulting firm Navigant Consulting hired by Texas regulators investigated the accuracy of those meters. Both investigations reported by early September 2010 that the meters were accurate with respect to industry standards, recording electrical consumption within a band between 98% and 102% of the amount of actual energy consumed. In fact, in an article appearing in the *Wall Street Journal*'s Thursday, September 7, 2010 edition titled, "Probe Finds Energy Meters Accurate, Service Lacking," it was pointed out that in testing the older electromechanical meters they were found to have an accuracy of 96%. In the referenced article the California and Texas utility companies were faulted for not educating customers about the meter switch and that some

Sheet 5

ELECTRIC SCHEDULE A-6

SMALL GENERAL TIME-OF-USE SERVICE

TIME PERIODS: Times of the year and times of the day are defined as follows:

SUMMER (Service from May 1 through October 31):

Peak:	12:00 noon to 6:00 p.m.	Monday through Friday (except holidays)
Partial-peak:	8:30 a.m. to 12:00 noon AND 6:00 p.m. to 9:30 p.m.	Monday through Friday (except holidays)
Off-peak:	9:30 p.m. to 8:30 a.m. All day	Monday through Friday Saturday, Sunday, and holidays

WINTER (Service from November 1 through April 30):

Partial-Peak:	8:30 a.m. to 9:30 p.m.	Monday through Friday (except holidays)
Off-Peak:	9:30 p.m. to 8:30 a.m. All day	Monday through Friday (except holidays) Saturday, Sunday, and holidays
Holidays:	"Holidays" for the purposes of this rate schedule are New Year's Day, President's Day, Memorial Day, Independence Day, Labor Day, Veterans Day, Thanksgiving Day, and Christmas Day. The dates will be those on which the holidays are legally observed.	

Figure 4.6   PG&E time periods for small general time-of-use service.

trouble reports transmitted wirelessly from the meters were ignored, resulting in the possibility that a meter could malfunction and corrective action would not occur in a timely manner.

Why Rates Matter

To illustrate the considerable effect of the cost of electricity upon a data center let's examine the billing that occurred over an 11-month period to which this author had access. Table 4.1 lists the kWh consumed and the costs associated with that consumption for an 11-month period. The data center that consumed the electricity indicated in Table 4.1 operates approximately 50 servers and has approximately 100 employees, each with his or her own computer. Located in the southeastern portion of the United States, this data center is located in a two-story building with the top floor holding mostly offices and conference rooms, and the lower floor holding two data centers and a data communications center. The facility contains 70,000 square feet so we can compute energy consumption in several different ways. Those methods include consumption per square foot, which may not be meaningful as it doesn't consider the use of equipment such as servers, personal computers, and copiers; on a server basis that excludes employees and other equipment; or on an employee basis, which although excluding equipment, is perhaps the most meaningful as you always need

Table 4.1   The Cost of Electricity for a Data Center

MONTH	TOTAL $	KWH	FROM:	TO:
Oct-09	22,722.02	314000	09/10/09	10/10/09
Nov-09	22,835.12	223000	10/09/09	11/09/09
Dec-09	31,426.52	402000	11/09/09	12/09/09
Jan-10	28,922.11	402000	12/09/09	01/09/10
Feb-10	29,003.35	415000	01/09/10	02/10/10
Mar-10	27,725.97	384000	02/10/10	03/11/10
Apr-10	27,266.58	347000	03/11/10	04/09/10
May-10	26,758.81	344000	04/09/10	05/10/10
Jun-10	28,710.29	343000	05/10/10	06/10/10
Jul-10	30,764.25	366000	06/10/10	07/12/10
Aug-10	28,471.70	341000	07/12/10	08/11/10
Sep-10	39,506.68	360000	08/11/10	09/13/10
TOTAL	344,113.40	4241000		
AVERAGE	28,676.12	353416.67		

a certain level of operators and other employees to run a data center. Based upon the population of employees being approximately 100 we can compute the average cost of electricity per employee as being $28,676/100 or $2,867 per month. The average kWh consumed per employee becomes 353,416/100 or 3,535 kWh per month. These figures can be used as a reasonable guide for other data centers, although the billing structure, cost of electricity, and the method or methods used by a utility to provide power generation all play an important role in the cost of electrical service.

Now that we have a basic understanding of the electric meter and the potential problems associated with the use of smart meters by some consumers let's turn our attention to the natural gas meter.

The Natural Gas Meter

Once we become familiar with the electric meter the natural gas meter should be relatively easy to read. In Figure 4.7 a relatively new natural gas meter is shown. This meter was provided by the Atlanta Gas Light Company during 2009 due to the presumed inability of the previously installed 34-year-old meter to pass a sufficient quantity of gas at a given pressure when new high-efficient heating units were installed at the author's residence. If you carefully examine Figure 4.7 you will note that although a natural gas meter does not look exactly like an electric meter the basic steps associated with reading each type of meter is the same. Natural gas meters are designed to measure the flow of gas in cubic feet (ccf) instead of the kWh that an electric meter measures. They typically have four or five main dials that can be considered large and labeled with such metrics as 100,000, 10,000, and so on that represent the amount of ccfs that flow through the meter. They also have one or two smaller dials under the larger dials. Usually, the lower and smaller dials are used by gas company personnel for testing and calibration purposes.

Types of Gas Meters

Similar to electric meters there are a number of different types of gas meters. Most residential meters have chambers with movable diaphragms that fill and expel gas. As the diaphragms fill and expel

Figure 4.7   A typical natural gas meter based upon flow measuring diaphragm.

gas the linear motion of the diaphragms is converted into the rotary motion of a crankshaft that produces a mechanism to operate counters, resulting in the dials on the meter being turned. Other types of gas meters include orifice meters that consist of a length of pipe that is commonly used in industrial locations; ultrasonic flow meters that measure the flow of gas via its speed and are used in large gas-consuming facilities or in pipelines to measure gas flow; turbine gas meters that measure the flow of gas to determine volume and are commonly used in tank farms, pipelines, and terminals; and rotary meters, which are precise volume-measuring instruments that operate according to the displacement principle and are commonly used for measuring higher volumes of gas at higher pressures than are capable of being handled by diaphragm-based gas meters.

Meter Reading

Similar to reading an analog electric meter you read a gas meter by selecting the lower value of each of the pointers when it is between two numbers. For the example shown in Figure 4.7 (which is the "new" gas meter installed at this author's home) reading from right to left, the 1,000 position pointer is a bit over 9 but less than 0, hence it represents 9,000 ccf. Moving to the second pointer or dial from the right, it is more than 6 but slightly less than 7, so we select 6. Thus, this pointer is in the 10,000 position and represents 60,000 ccf of natural gas. Note that this dial as well as the fourth dial from the right is a counterclockwise dial, similar to the dials on an electric meter. Thus, you have to look at the dials carefully and cannot assume that from afar the pointer is between 3 and 4 as it would be if the dial were numbered clockwise, which it isn't. Next, the third dial or pointer from the right is exactly on the number 3, representing 300,000 ccf. Finally, the fourth and last dial from the right is between 4 and 5, thus we select 4, which represents 4,000,000 ccf. Thus, our meter reading becomes 4,369 that represents four million, three hundred sixty-nine thousand ccf of natural gas.

To reduce the cost of labor associated with meter reading, many natural gas utilities read your meter every other month. When the meter is located in an inaccessible place, such as a basement or carport turned into a garage, the utility may use a formula to estimate your gas consumption. That estimate, although fairly accurate, may continue for several months until the utility can arrange to read your meter.

It should be noted that many gas meters now include an automated meter reading (AMR) capability. The AMR capability can vary by utility as well as within a utility's service area. Some AMR gas meters use IEEE 802.11 wireless technology commonly referred to as WiFi, whereas other meters use a different wireless technology or even telephone lines to report the meter reading. Some wireless technologies are one-way, with the reading of the meter and its identifier transmitted every few seconds. In comparison, other wireless technologies are two-way, with the reader transmitting a message to the meter which, when recognized, results in the meter reading being transmitted. Both licensed and unlicensed frequency bands are used by different wireless technologies. Through the use of AMR technology the gas utility no longer has to send a meter reader to each location. Instead, depending upon the technology used, the utility may be able to send a truck down the road recording wireless meter readings or simply process received data at a central location as it polls each meter remotely.

Estimating the Monthly Gas Bill

Similar to the electric bill, there is a wide variance between gas utility companies that can make the estimation process associated with attempting to determine your natural gas bill most interesting. For example, under deregulation you may have to pay a basic fee for the gas line routed to your home or office by one company as well as another fee to a different company for the gas provider you selected. Fortunately, the bill you receive is usually a consolidated one, making it easier to make one electronic payment or use one check and stamp, however, this may not always be the case.

To illustrate some of the potential rates and charges you can face on your natural gas bill this author went to the Gas-South web page located at www.gas-south.com. Figure 4.8 illustrates the business rate plans available for customers in the service area of the company. Note that organizations willing to sign a 6- or 12-month contract can receive a better rate than organizations that are not willing to make such a commitment. Also note that there is a customer service fee that is added to each rate plan. This decreasing cost for a long-term commitment is a common practice of most natural gas companies in that a customer agreeing to purchase a commodity over a longer period of

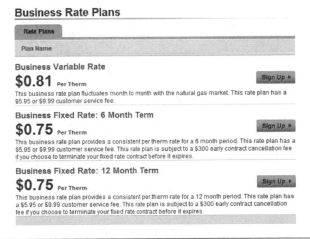

Figure 4.8   Gas-South business rate plans in September 2010.

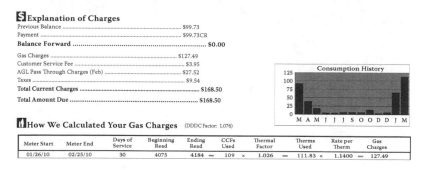

Explanation of Charges

Previous Balance	$99.73
Payment	$99.73CR
Balance Forward	**$0.00**
Gas Charges	$127.49
Customer Service Fee	$3.95
AGL Pass Through Charges (Feb)	$27.52
Taxes	$9.54
Total Current Charges	**$168.50**
Total Amount Due	**$168.50**

How We Calculated Your Gas Charges   (DDDC Factor: 1.076)

Meter Start	Meter End	Days of Service	Beginning Read	Ending Read	CCFs Used	Thermal Factor	Therms Used	Rate per Therm	Gas Charges
01/26/10	02/25/10	30	4075	4184 =	109 ×	1.026 =	111.83 ×	1.1400 =	127.49

Figure 4.9   Extract from a monthly natural gas bill.

time receives a more favorable rate than a customer who desires the flexibility to hook up with a different company whenever they want or who for company policy reasons cannot sign a long-term contract. Although a few years ago the cost of natural gas appeared to rise near daily during the winter, today the use of horizontal drilling has resulted in a significant increase in gas reserves and a lower price for customers without a contract. Thus, you need to consider the evolution of technology as it alters the supply and demand curve as well as weather, the ability to engage in long-term contracts, and other criteria prior to deciding whether to initiate a long-term contract.

To illustrate why simply multiplying the ccf used or consumed by the therm factor to obtain the number of therms used and multiplying that amount by the rate or cost per therm may not provide an accurate picture of your monthly natural gas bill, consider Figure 4.9. In this illustration of an actual gas bill note that the number of therms consumed was 111.83 and the cost per therm was $1.14. This resulted in an estimated fee of $127.49, however, the actual bill was for $168.50 or approximately 32% higher. If you focus your attention to the upper left portion of Figure 4.9 under the "Explanation of Charges" you will note that although the gas charges were indeed $127.49, to that amount the utility added a customer service fee of $3.95, an Atlanta Gas Light (AGL) pass-through fee of $27.52, and taxes in the amount of $9.54, resulting in a $127.49 gas consumption bill becoming a bill for $168.50. Thus, for budgeting purposes you need to consider carefully how your natural gas utility bills you to include taxes and pass-through fees as well as any customer service fee. Now that we have an appreciation for the operation, reading, and billing associated with a natural gas meter let's turn our attention to the water meter.

The Water Meter

As its name implies, a water meter is a device used to measure the volume of water usage. Similar to electric and gas meters there are many types of water meters. In this section we discuss the reading of water meters as the different types can be summarized by their dials: analog and digital. However, prior to discussing the types of meters we need to say a few words about where the meter may be located.

Locate Your Meter

Although it might be obvious where your meters are located, especially if you have occupied a building or home for a long time, this author learned never to take anything for granted. The water meter is usually located near the curb in front of your home or place of business in a direct line with the main outside underground pipe, however, sometimes it may reside at the side or rear of your home or building. The water meter could also be housed in a concrete box usually marked "water" or can be located in a rectangular hole in the ground that has a heavy steel covering lid. Other water utilities may even place the water meter next to your home or building, so the first thing you typically want to do is to determine where the meter is located. A second thing you may want to do is determine where the main shutoff valve is located in the event you need to turn off water to your home or building. The shutoff is usually located near or next to your water meter but that may not always be the case. In addition, some shutoff valves require the use of a special tool to operate the valve correctly. Thus, you should consider how to turn off the water supply in the event of an emergency until a licensed plumber reaches your facility.

Most water meters this author has seen have a large analog dial as well as an odometer style digital dial. Figure 4.10 illustrates the water meter installed at this author's home. At the time this picture was taken the reading under the words, "CUBIC FEET," shows the total amount of water the meter has read. The meter in Figure 4.10 shows a reading of 135685, which is the total number of cubic feet of water recorded since the meter was installed or after it cycled through its maximum reading. Because our charge is based on units of 100 cubic feet, the meter reader discards the last two numbers (the ones with the

Figure 4.10 Viewing the author's Neptune water meter.

black background). Thus, this reading would actually be 1,356 or one thousand three hundred and fifty-six ccf.

If you turn your attention to the Neptune water meter shown in Figure 4.10 you will see a dark (in the figure but red in actual color) triangle pointing upward and a red colored pointer that it is shown as slightly above .1. The red triangle is a flow indicator and rotates whenever water flows through the meter. If you turn off all water to your home or business and the red triangle continues to rotate this can be used to indicate that you may have a leak and require some investigation. The large dark (red) colored pointer is known as the sweep arm. Each full revolution of the sweep arm indicates that one full gallon of water or approximately 7.48 gallons have passed through the meter. The odometer style register is referred to as a register and provides a running total of all the water that has passed through the meter.

Suppose that 30 days later your water meter read 1782, indicating that in the 30-day period you had used 42,600 (1,782 − 1,356 = 426 × 100) cubic feet of water. What is your water bill? The answer to this question depends upon the type of service plan you are under and the method by which the water utility or authority bills customers. Thus, let's discuss some of the variances that can occur in your monthly water bill.

Water Bills

Most organizations and homeowners receive a monthly bill from a local water and sewerage authority. That bill can literally have a variety of components inasmuch as there are thousands of water authorities around the world. What we discuss here are some of the more prominent factors that can affect your monthly water bill.

One of the key factors that affect your monthly bill is the size of your water connection. The typical single-family domestic customer has a 3/4-inch meter whereas some larger homes may have a 1-inch meter. The total monthly bill you can expect to receive represents a combination of the monthly meter base fee, which is based on the size of the meter, and the amount of water used in hundreds of cubic feet (hcf or many times expressed as ccf) where each hcf or ccf is equal to 748.05 gallons of water. The monthly meter base fee can vary from a few dollars per month in some locations to $30 or more dollars per month in other locations. In addition, to discourage the use of water, many water authorities employ a tiered cost structure where the cost per hcf or ccf increases as usage increases. In addition to charging for water consumption the water utility or authority will normally have a sewerage fee component. Adding the two together will normally result in a monthly water and sewerage bill.

To illustrate the potential pricing complexity associated with the monthly water and sewerage bill you receive let's return to this author's hometown of Macon, Georgia to examine the rates charged during 2010 to Macon and Bibb County customers. For residential customers the base fee shown at the top of Table 4.2 (which increases as the size of the connection to the water authority increases) is added to the water consumption rate of $1.52 per every 100 cubic feet of water consumed up to 300 cubic feet, at which point the rate increases to $1.62 per 100 cubic feet of consumption. For example, if we return to our example in which we used 426 ccf of water during the month and

Table 4.2 Macon Water Authority Residential and Nonresidential Water and Sewerage Base Rates

Residential Rates
Water Rate: $1.52/CCF for up to 3 per month, thereafter $1.62/CCF
Sewerage Rate: $1.61/ CCF for up to 3 per month, thereafter $1.71/CCF

METER SIZE (IN.)	WATER BASE FEE ($)	SEWERAGE BASE FEE ($)
5/8	7.50	5.00
1	10.00	6.67
1.5	22.50	15.00
2	45.00	30.00

Nonresidential Rates
Water Rate: $1.62 per CCF
Sewerage Rate: $1.71 per CCF

METER SIZE (IN.)	WATER BASE FEE ($)	SEWERAGE BASE FEE ($)
5/8	7.50	5.00
1	10.00	6.67
1.5	22.50	15.00
2	45.00	30.00
3	67.50	45.00
4	112.50	75.00
6	187.50	125.00
8	300.00	200.00
10	375.00	250.00

assume our meter was a 1-inch connection, our monthly bill would be the sum of $10 for the base rate plus $1.52 multiplied by 3 for the first 300 ccf of water plus $1.62 multiplied by 1.26 for the remaining 126 ccf of water consumed, or a total of $16.60. This seems reasonable, but we have yet to consider the sewerage component of the monthly bill.

Similar to the manner by which base fees are determined according to the size of the meter, the Macon Water Authority also charges a base fee for sewer services based upon the size of the water meter. The base fee for 5/8-inch residential meters is $5 per month, and larger meter sizes have increased monthly fees. Those fees are also listed in Table 4.2. For all rate classes, the consumption charges are currently $1.61 per ccf for sewerage for the first 3 ccf, and $1.71 per ccf for consumption above 3 ccf. Thus, the sewerage portion of the bill, again assuming a 1-inch meter connection is $6.67 plus $1.61 per ccf × 3 plus $1.71 × 1.26 for a total of $13.65, resulting in a total monthly bill of $30.25 when the water component of $16.60 is added to the sewerage component of $13.65. This example was for residential service, however, nonresidential computations occur in a similar manner, with the main difference being the base fees charged for varying meter-size connections with nonresidential rates slightly higher than residential rates.

Abnormalities in the Water Bill

One of the abnormalities of the rate structure occurs during the summer when both residential and nonresidential customers may be tempted to water their lawns and shrubbery. Although the water is not recycled and has nothing to do with sewerage the customer winds up paying what can be a hefty fee during those hot Georgia summers or elects to plant cactus or not to water. Actually, as a side note, this pricing appears to favor restaurants where customers get sick from the food and need to immediately use the facilities, while penalizing landscaping firms, but because this book is concerned with the efficiency of data centers we do not probe deeper into the pricing schedule just mentioned.

To illustrate why the water bill must be considered in budgeting, consider Table 4.3 that contains an extract of the monthly cost of

Table 4.3 Extract of Water Bill for a 100-Employee Data Center

MONTH	METER READING	GAL USED	USAGE/100 CU FT	FROM:	TO:	COST
Oct-09	9287	42,750	57	10/08/09	10/29/09	$281.01
Nov-09	9330	32,250	43	10/29/09	11/30/09	$235.79
Dec-09	9381	38,250	51	11/30/09	12/23/09	$307.33
Jan-10	42*	31,500	42	12/23/09	01/27/10	$277.36
Feb-10	106	79,500	106	01/27/10	02/26/10	$490.48
Mar-10	280	130,500	174	02/26/10	03/29/10	$716.92
Apr-10	460	135,000	180	03/29/10	04/23/10	$736.90
May-10	613	114,750	153	04/23/10	05/26/10	$646.99
Jun-09	882	201,750	269	05/26/10	07/02/10	$1,033.27
Jul-09	1135	189,750	253	07/02/10	08/02/10	$979.99
Aug-09	1419	213,000	284	08/02/10	09/01/10	$1,083.22
Sep-09	—	—	—	—	—	—
—	—	—	—	—	—	—
—	—	—	—	—	—	$6,789.26

* Meter reached its maximum and started anew.

water and sewerage service for a data center with approximately 100 employees. This bill indicates that for an 11-month period the total water and sewerage bill was $6,789.26, or approximately $67 per employee. Your data center may be more or less efficient with respect to its water usage, however, a good place to start for budgeting purposes is to allocate approximately $100 per employee on an annual basis. Then, you may wish to consider such factors as to whether your organization operates an underground or aboveground sprinkler system during the summer, if your data center uses a water chiller, and the rate structure of the water authority or municipality to fine-tune your water budget.

In concluding our brief examination of pricing, we mention that many water authorities have a number of billing fee variances, with some billing based upon the number of gallons of water consumed whereas other water authorities may incorporate a multitiered fee schedule that either raises or lowers the cost of water consumption based upon usage during the month. Because the water bill is similar to death and taxes in that it will eventually appear, although most likely monthly, you need to examine the bill and also to understand for what your organization is paying. In certain situations, such as a building with over 20-year-old water closets (WCs), simply placing

Table 4.4 Rationale for the Use of Smart Water Meters

Curb water demand
Enable water leak detection when it occurs
Provide software-based tools for consumers to monitor water usage
Enhance the ability of the utility to perform preventive maintenance
Obtain meter readings at a lower cost

a brick in each toilet tank may reduce the water usage by .5 gallons without causing any problems to occur. If you assume each employee visits the WC 20 days per month, a 200-employee building might reduce its water consumption by 100 gallons per day or 2,000 per month for the cost of a few bricks. Similarly, on a weekend it might be appropriate to watch the water meter to determine if there are one or more leaks adversely increasing your organization's monthly water bill.

Smart Water Meters

According to various articles recently published in several trade publications approximately a third of all water authorities are considering acquiring smart water meters. Although the reason given is to promote conservation, another key reason is the fact that the smart water meter allows utilities simply to drive through a neighborhood to obtain meter readings instead of having to go to each meter to read its setting. The smart water meter is based upon the use of a long-life battery and wireless transmission. Depending upon the type of meter, it may be polled and respond to a poll by broadcasting its setting or periodically transmit an identifier and value. Some smart water meters include an Internet protocol (IP) address and allow consumers to view their consumption via an Internet connection. Table 4.4 lists five key reasons often cited for the deployment of smart water meters by a water authority.

5

Data Center Equipment Energy Consumption

The goal of this chapter is twofold. First, as the title of this chapter implies, we obtain an appreciation for the energy consumption of equipment typically found in a data center. Such equipment can include personal computers and tablets, a variety of servers, and even mainframes. In addition, we also examine the energy consumption of monitors, printers, and most important, communications equipment. Concerning the latter, unlike personal computers and tablets that are usually powered off 16 hours per day, communications equipment is typically powered on 24/7, which means that they can be considered similar to the Energizer Bunny in that they keep on consuming electricity. Second, as we examine equipment we discuss tools and techniques we can use to reduce the cost of operating equipment. As we investigate the consumption of energy by different devices we note how we can use two tables contained in this chapter to facilitate the computation of the monthly operating cost of a device. Although the tables assume an energy operating cost of 10 cents per kWh, we note later in this chapter that we can easily adjust the cost to other kWh costs based upon the utility that provides service to our data center and the type of contract negotiated.

Because employees bring to work a variety of devices that obtain power from a battery charger this author would be negligent if he did not mention what is referred to as phantom power. To do so, we examine the battery charger and why the charging of cell phones, laptops, notebooks, tablets, and other devices can result in the cost of electricity increasing while the device is fully charged, a situation that may make the electric utility happy but provides our organization with a bill that with a little effort could be smaller each month. Similarly, we also discuss the electrical consumption of other devices and methods that can be used to reduce the cost of electricity. If your data center is located in an area where cooling occurs most of the year due to hot humid weather, your savings can actually be significantly more than what we compute. This is because devices that consume electricity generate heat, which then requires the expenditure of additional electricity to remove.

Operational Modes to Consider

When considering the use of chargers there are two modes of operation you need to consider that this author refers to as always-on versus partially-on. An always-on charger, as its name implies, both charges a device and consumes power when the plugged-in device is fully charged. In comparison, a partially-on device charger will charge a plugged-in device, but when charging is complete or the plugged-in device is removed only a trickle of energy is then consumed. You can actually feel the difference between devices by holding your hand on top of each type of charger inserted into a wall outlet but without a device plugged in. The always-on charger will be a lot warmer than the partially-on charger, because the former turns more wasted energy into heat.

Power Loads

The waste of charger energy is referred to as vampire and phantom energy and can even include electrical cords, power strips with LEDs and other devices, such as televisions, DVD players, and even printers and scanners. Although there are no precise measurements of the waste of electricity in offices, according to some projections the phantom load accounts for between 5 and 10% of all electrical consumption. Based upon information from the Arizona Department of Energy Office, a few examples of the loads consumed by different devices in watts are listed in Table 5.1.

In examining the entries in Table 5.1 this author selected some typical devices found in the office. Note that a computer in sleep mode consumes approximately 1.7 watts per hour. Although this may appear insignificant, let's perform a small calculation to determine the cost for a 500-employee organization that allows employees to place their computer into a sleep mode when they go home.

Table 5.1   Power Loads of Various Equipment

Cell phone charger	varies, 3 watts
Computer, in sleep mode	1.7 watts
Computer printer, turned off	5 watts
DVD player	4.2 watts
Microwave	2.9 watts
Television w/remote	5–20 watts

Assuming the employee works 8 hours per day or 40 hours per week, this means their computer is in sleep mode of operation 168 – 40 or 128 hours per week inasmuch as there are 168 hours in a 7-day week and the typical work week has an employee at his or her desk for 40 hours. With 52 weeks per year, this means the computer is in sleep mode 128 hours/week × 52 weeks/year or 6,656 hours/year. At 1.7 watts/hour consumed in sleep mode this means the computer consumes 11,315 watts/year or approximately 11.3 kWh as we divide by 1,000 to obtain kWh. At 10 cents per kWh, this works out to $1.13 per computer or for 500 employees $565. This doesn't appear to be an exorbitant cost, however, you need to consider the fact that this is more than likely a minimum cost. This is because some computers may not be configured to go into sleep mode after no activity occurs for a predefined period of time and some employees may have configured their computers to wait for a long period of time prior to going into sleep mode of operation. Because a computer may consume 100 watts when active, if employees configured their computers to wait 30 minutes prior to going into sleep mode and touched their keyboard prior to leaving the office each day, this would result in 2.5 hours per week of each computer consuming 100 watts, or for a 500-employee office 50,000/1,000 or an additional 50 kWh of energy consumption per week. Thus, for a 52-week year this could result in the additional consumption of 50 kWh/week × 52 weeks or 2,600 kWh per year. In addition many employees leave their cell phone charger plugged in all day and there are numerous printers around the office that probably consume a lot more than 5 watts when in sleep mode. When you start adding each of these actions together and in addition consider the variety of power strips that exist in most offices and all of a sudden you might be capable of saving $5,000 to $10,000 you begin to note how they can add up to a considerable amount of energy consumption.

Commonsense Items to Consider

By making employees follow some commonsense rules it becomes possible to considerably reduce the amount of energy consumed in a data center. Because each kWh of energy not consumed results in a lesser amount of heat buildup, your cooling costs will be lower. Thus, your organization will actually realize more than a kWh of savings for each kWh not used. Some of the commonsense items to consider are indicated in the following paragraphs.

Obtain Smart Power Strips

Obtain smart power strips for employees. By plugging computers, printers, cell phone chargers, and other devices into smart power strips your employees can easily make sure power is off to all devices when they leave the office. In addition, the smart power strip knows when power is not needed and will turn itself off. The smart power strip has three types of outlets typically labeled Control, Hot, and Switched. The Control outlet is for use by a computer or in the home it is used by a television. The Hot outlet is always on whereas the Switched outlets are tied to the Control outlet. Thus, if the device plugged into the Control outlet is off then the switch automatically turns off the switched outlets. This means that if a computer printer and monitor are plugged into two switched outlets, when the computer is turned off the printer and monitor will not draw power. This can result in a significant reduction in kWh consumed, as both devices draw power even when they are rated as Energy Star devices, a topic we discuss later in this chapter.

Check Cell Phone Charger Ratings

If your organization purchases cell phones for employees consider phones with a five-star charger rating. Because two-thirds of the energy used by chargers is wasted, a group of vendors including Apple, LG, Motorola, Nokia, Samsung Electronics, and Sony Ericsson agreed to a rating system that indicates how much energy a cell phone charger uses in a standby mode of operation. Five stars designate the most efficient chargers that use 0.03 watts or less energy, and chargers that consume more than 0.5 watts receive no stars. In January, 2009 the European Union (EU) announced that 10 cell phone manufacturers signed a memorandum of understanding that will result in cell phones being charged via USB computer ports, limiting the need for every cell phone to be sold with a charger. Not to be outdone, in October 2009 the International Telecommunications Union announced a universal charger solution that enables chargers to be interoperable across manufacturers. Now an ITU recommendation, once adopted by industry it will result in the use of USB charging that will provide an energy efficiency of at least four stars or approximately three times more energy efficient than an unrated charger.

However, from a practical standpoint a word about USB cables is in order. Having used several cell phones over the years that were USB compatible, a key problem noted by this author is the lack of a standard cable. The USB connector is standardized, however, the other end of the cable appears anything but standardized. I have used three cell phones in the past year, each unfortunately requiring a different cable to connect the phone for hot syncing via a USB port. Thus, although the elimination of charges might be desirable, you need to check the type of cable connection required for USB charging. Obviously, if your organization decides to unify behind one type of cell phone this should not be a problem, however, if your organization allows employees to have a mixture of devices it could represent a potential problem.

Unplug Rarely Used Devices

Unplug devices that are rarely used. One device that comes to mind is a network plotter that was added over eight years ago for the use of a manager who left the company many years ago. The plotter resides in a corner closet and from observing its paper tray that stays full, is more than likely never used today. In addition to unplugging such devices, it might be a good time to question the wisdom of having such devices in the first place. Thus, this might be an opportunity to rid the organization of hardware of dubious necessity.

Ensure Monitors Are Turned Off When Not Used

An old-fashioned cathode-ray tube (CRT) monitor that draws approximately .8 watts when turned off can consume 65 watts when powered on and about 12 watts when in a sleep mode. If we fast forward through technology progress, an LCD display on average consumes about 1.1 watts when turned off and it uses 28 when turned on and about 1.3 when in sleep mode. Thus, there are significant differences in energy consumption between operating modes, especially between the on and sleep modes. For the modern LCD display the ratio of power consumption between on and sleep modes is 28:1.3, or approximately a factor of 21.5 higher when on than when in sleep mode. Thus, if you have employees who turn on a screen saver and leave work they are actually wasting a lot of energy. This is because the screen saver requires the computer and attached monitor to operate at full power. When screen savers were first introduced they were designed to prevent screen burn occurring on CRT monitors. Unless your organization is using an old CRT monitor or plasma display, there is no reason to use screen savers today. In fact, they will cause the monitor to use approximately 21.5 times the power it needs, because it could be placed in sleep mode of operation.

Although we have heard the expression "bigger is better," in the wonderful world of monitors another term to use is, "bigger means more energy consumption." Those attractive 32- to 42-inch monitors that can display two pages of text are certainly attractive, but they consume a significant additional amount of energy in comparison to smaller monitors. Thus, the need for a larger monitor should be based upon necessity.

Turn Off or Place Computers in a Standby Mode

A typical desktop computer consumes approximately 75 watts of energy when powered on. In comparison, when in a sleep mode the computer consumes about 20 watts, whereas when off it will consume approximately 3 watts of energy. Thus, the ratio of powered on to sleep mode is 75:20 or 3.5 for the typical desktop computer. This means that simply instructing employees to place their computers into a sleep mode of operation when they go to lunch, leave the office, or are not using the computer can reduce energy consumption by a factor of 3.5. In addition to a letter or memorandum to employees, a walk-through by management to note the use of any screen savers can be helpful as some employees either do not read memos or decide that they would prefer to use old technology because the cost of its use is usually hidden from direct view.

Favor Energy Star Equipment

Although Energy Star is considered by many people to represent an energy-efficiency rating system for consumer products in the United States, in actuality it has an international presence. First created in the United States during the early 1990s, its use has spread to the European Union as well as Canada, Australia, New Zealand, Taiwan, and Japan. Devices that carry the Energy Star logo represent products that are commonly 20 to 30% more energy efficient than other products. If you recently went into an appliance store to look for a new washer, refrigerator, or other consumer product you would have seen the Energy Star logo on most products as well as a tag showing the estimated annual operating cost in comparison to a range of similar products. Today, it is difficult in some areas to find a non-Energy Star computer or monitor, however, in certain locations as well as via the Internet it is still possible to purchase energy hogs. Thus, by focusing your attention upon acquiring Energy Star compliant products you will also be focusing your attention upon energy-efficient products.

It should be noted that the U.S. government provides a wealth of information concerning the energy consumption of different types of computers in addition to appliances and other devices. In fact, the U.S. Environmental Protection Agency and the U.S. Department of Energy sponsor an Energy Star website that has a variety of Excel spreadsheet and PDF files that list Energy Star qualified desktop computers, workstations, thin clients, notebook products, and small scale servers. The main URL for accessing this information is: http://www.energystar.gov/index.cfm?fuseaction=find_a_product. showProductGroup&pgw_code=CO.

Although tablet computers were not listed at the time this book was prepared, due to several vendors introducing new products during 2011 it is expected that this new category of computers will be added in the near future. By using the data on the Energy Star website you can not only determine if the computer you have or are considering is qualified, but, in addition, obtain a wealth of information concerning the manner by which a computer uses energy. For example, you can obtain the amount of power consumed when a computer server is powered off, in the idle mode, the default sleep mode time, operating system, and major markets where the computer is sold. For other types of computers you may be able to obtain additional information that can assist you in making an educated procurement decision.

General Cost Computations

One of the metrics in this book that is worth repeating due to its importance concerns computing the cost of electricity that a device consumes. Although the metrics are the same for computers as for such appliances as dishwashers, refrigerators, and other devices, their hours of operating use can vary considerably. Whereas a dishwasher might be used several times a week, its operating cycle is typically 30 to 60 minutes. In comparison, a computer will operate at least 8 hours per day if it's a workstation, and servers and communications equipment are usually considered to represent 24/7 devices; that is, always on.

Many devices found in a data center include a label that provides information about its electrical rating. Unfortunately, that label is typically located near the bottom or side of the device, which periodically represents a challenge to locate unless you do so when the device is installed. If the label notes the number of amps and not the power consumption in watts, you need to multiply the amps by 120 if your device operates on 120 VAC. If your office or data center is located in a country that uses 240 volts instead of 120 you would then multiply the amps by 240 to obtain the energy consumption in watts. Note that if the device for which you are computing energy consumption has a stand-alone transformer that converts AC to DC you need to multiply the amps by the DC voltage on the label of the transformer. For example, if the transformer label says "input 24 V, 1.5A," then the power consumption would become 24 volts $\times$ 1.5 amps or 36 watts. Because the cost of electricity is measured based upon the consumption of thousands of watts over time, we need to determine the consumption in kWh or kilowatt-hours. Then, we can use the cost per kWh our organization pays to determine the operating cost of the device.

Let's continue our assumption concerning a device that uses a transformer and consumes 36 watts. Thus, over an hour it consumes

36 watts of electricity. Assuming the device operates 24/7, then in a 30-day month it consumes 30 days/month × 24 hours/day × 36 watts/hour or 25,920 watts, which when divided by 1,000 is 25.92 kWh. At a dime per kWh, the operating cost of these devices is $2.59 per month. If the transformer is connected to a printer and only operates 8 hours per day, let's compute its energy consumption. Instead of a 30-day month, the printer is (one hopes) turned off when employees leave for the day and the month now has an average of 22 working days. Then, the energy consumption becomes: 22 days/month × 8 hours/day × 36 watts/hour or 6,336 watt hours, which when divided by 1,000 is 6.336 kWh. If your organization has 300 employees, each having her own printing device, then your monthly bill for the energy used just by the printers becomes 6.332 kWh × 300 × .10 cents/kWh or $189.96. On a yearly basis, multiplying by 12 we obtain a cost for operating the printers of $2,279.52, assuming our organization pays 10 cents per kWh. Later in this chapter we become acquainted with Tables 5.2 and 5.3 that facilitate the computation of costs associated with the operation of different devices as well as how to compute the energy consumption cost when the price per kWh varies from a dime to a different amount.

Device Consumption

Originally the intention of this author was to provide readers with a list of devices, such as blade servers, mainframes, monitors, and other equipment found in a data center that could be used to measure energy consumption among different devices. Although this was proposed with good intentions, as the material for this book was developed, technological progress interfered with his good intentions. That is, the introduction of different multicore processors, energy-efficient printers, and other products would make any listing obsolete by the publication date. Thus, instead of listing individual devices by manufacturer and model number this author decided that readers could request such information when they ask for a bid quotation or use the resources on the Internet to determine the energy consumption of a specific product or products. In addition, previously in this chapter this author gave the URL of the Energy Star website where readers can obtain energy consumption data for a range of devices commonly found in a data center, ranging from different types of personal computers to servers.

To assist readers in computing the cost of equipment, two tables are included in this chapter. The first table, Table 5.2, is from an Excel spreadsheet created by this author that provides the cost associated with power consumption at 10 cents per kWh where the device consumes 1, 10, 20, 50, 100, or 1,000 watts and operates between 1 and 24 hours per day. Through the use of this table you can easily compute the operating cost of devices that consume amounts of power other than the amounts listed horizontally across the top of the table. For example, let's assume you want to compute the cost of a device that operates 24/7 and consumes 1,500 watts of energy. To do so you

Table 5.2   Power Consumption Costs per 30-Day Month[a]

OPERATION HOURS/DAY	WATTS = AMPS × VOLTS						
	1	10	20	30	50	100	1,000
1	0.00	0.03	0.06	0.09	0.15	0.30	3.00
2	0.01	0.06	0.12	0.18	0.30	0.60	6.00
3	0.01	0.09	0.18	0.27	0.45	0.90	9.00
4	0.01	0.12	0.24	0.36	0.60	1.20	12.00
5	0.02	0.15	0.30	0.45	0.75	1.50	15.00
6	0.02	0.18	0.36	0.54	0.90	1.80	18.00
7	0.02	0.21	0.42	0.63	1.05	2.10	21.00
8	0.02	0.24	0.48	0.72	1.20	2.40	24.00
9	0.03	0.27	0.54	0.81	1.35	2.70	27.00
10	0.03	0.30	0.60	0.90	1.50	3.00	30.00
11	0.03	0.33	0.66	0.99	1.65	3.30	33.00
12	0.04	0.36	0.72	1.08	1.80	3.60	36.00
13	0.04	0.39	0.78	1.17	1.95	3.90	39.00
14	0.04	0.42	0.84	1.26	2.10	4.20	42.00
15	0.05	0.45	0.90	1.35	2.25	4.50	45.00
16	0.05	0.48	0.96	1.44	2.40	4.80	48.00
17	0.05	0.51	1.02	1.53	2.55	5.10	51.00
18	0.05	0.54	1.08	1.62	2.70	5.40	54.00
19	0.06	0.57	1.14	1.71	2.85	5.70	57.00
20	0.06	0.60	1.20	1.80	3.00	6.00	60.00
21	0.06	0.63	1.26	1.89	3.15	6.30	63.00
22	0.07	0.66	1.32	1.98	3.30	6.60	66.00
23	0.07	0.69	1.38	2.07	3.45	6.90	69.00
24	0.07	0.72	1.44	2.16	3.60	7.20	72.00

[a] Cost per kWh 10 cents.

Table 5.3   Power Consumption Costs per 22-Day Month[a]

OPERATION HOURS/DAY	WATTS = AMPS × VOLTS						
	1	10	20	30	50	100	1,000
1	0.00	0.02	0.04	0.07	0.11	0.22	2.20
2	0.00	0.04	0.09	0.13	0.22	0.44	4.40
3	0.01	0.07	0.13	0.20	0.33	0.66	6.60
4	0.01	0.09	0.18	0.26	0.44	0.88	8.80
5	0.01	0.11	0.22	0.33	0.55	1.10	11.00
6	0.01	0.13	0.26	0.40	0.66	1.32	13.20
7	0.02	0.15	0.31	0.46	0.77	1.54	15.40
8	0.02	0.18	0.35	0.53	0.88	1.76	17.60
9	0.02	0.20	0.40	0.59	0.99	1.98	19.80
10	0.02	0.22	0.44	0.66	1.10	2.20	22.00
11	0.02	0.24	0.48	0.73	1.21	2.42	24.20
12	0.03	0.26	0.53	0.79	1.32	2.64	26.40
13	0.03	0.29	0.57	0.86	1.43	2.86	28.60
14	0.03	0.31	0.62	0.92	1.54	3.08	30.80
15	0.03	0.33	0.66	0.99	1.65	3.30	33.00
16	0.04	0.35	0.70	1.06	1.76	3.52	35.20
17	0.04	0.37	0.75	1.12	1.87	3.74	37.40
18	0.04	0.40	0.79	1.19	1.98	3.96	39.60
19	0.04	0.42	0.84	1.25	2.09	4.18	41.80
20	0.04	0.44	0.88	1.32	2.20	4.40	44.00
21	0.05	0.46	0.92	1.39	2.31	4.62	46.20
22	0.05	0.48	0.97	1.45	2.42	4.84	48.40
23	0.05	0.51	1.01	1.52	2.53	5.06	50.60
24	0.05	0.53	1.06	1.58	2.64	5.28	52.80

[a] Cost per kWh 10 cents.

would go to the 24 hours/day row at the bottom of the table. Then you would move across the table to the 1,000 watts column, where the cost entry is $72. Because an additional 500 watts would be half the cost of 1,000, you can add $36 to $72, obtaining a monthly cost of $108. You could also take the entry in the 100-watt column for 24 hours/day of operation which is $7.20 and multiply that amount by 5 and add it to the $72, which also results in a cost of $108, so the table provides you with a sufficient amount of flexibility.

Varying the Cost per kWh

Because Tables 5.2 and 5.3 were computed using a cost per kWh of 10 cents, a logical question readers might have is how to use the table if your organization pays a different amount per kWh. The answer to this question is to multiply the result obtained by the use of the table by the percentage difference between your organization's cost and the assumed 10 cent per kWh cost used in the table. For example, if your organization pays 12 cents per kWh, you would multiply the result obtained from the use of the table by 1 + .2 or 120%. For our prior example where we computed the cost of operating a device to be $108 at 10 cents per kWh, if our actual cost was 12 cents per kWh we would multiply $108 by 120%, obtaining $126. Now suppose your organization pays 8 cents per kWh instead of the 10 cents used in the referenced table. You would then multiply $108 by 80%, obtaining $86.40.

Now that we have a good understanding of the use of the two tables presented in this chapter to facilitate the computation of energy consumption costs, let's turn our attention to one of the most intensive users of energy in a data center, the server. In doing so we discuss computer memory including understanding why modern double data rate (DDR)3 memory significantly reduces the amount of power required by a server.

Servers

Over the past few years several vendors including Dell, HP, and IBM among others have concentrated their server offerings by incorporating Opteron and Xeon multicore products into their servers. As a refresher for some readers and new information for others, we briefly discuss each product. Opteron represents AMD's x86 server and workstation series of processors. Opteron was the first AMD processor to implement its 64-bit instruction set architecture and it competes with Intel's Xeon processor. A recently released version of the Opteron supports 8 and 12 cores, resulting in a very powerful microprocessor. Concerning the Intel microprocessor, there are literally hundreds of models of Xeon processors, ranging in scope from uniprocessors through the so-called Beckton processor announced in March 2010, which is a processor with up to eight cores and which uses buffering inside the chipset to support up to 16 standard DDR3 dual in-line memory modules (DIMMs) per CPU socket. Both the latest versions of the Opteron and Xeon processors enable the use of low-voltage DDR3 memory. To understand why this represents a significant potential for reducing the amount of power consumed by a server, we briefly digress and discuss memory.

Computer Memory   Similar to personal computers, servers require random access memory (RAM). However, most servers are configured with more memory than personal computers, so the voltage used by memory and the resultant use of energy by the server can be more of an issue. Although this book is not concerned with the various types of computer memory from a processing standpoint, it should be noted that the greater the clock speed of memory the faster a computer can normally process data. In the evolution of computer memory DDR was commercialized in 1996 and generally available through 2000. This type of memory supported high data transfer rates by controlling the timing of the electrical data and clock signals. In doing so a double pumping technique was used, where the transfer of data occurred on both the rising and falling edges of the clock signal, resulting in the ability to lower the clock frequency. The name of this type of memory "double data rate" refers to the fact that a DDR synchronous dynamic random access memory (SDRAM) with a defined clock frequency achieves nearly twice the bandwidth of a single data rate (SDR) running at the same clock frequency. DDR memory requires 2.5 volts, which was lower than other memory then available, resulting in a lower energy consumption and the ability to operate cooler.

As memory evolved, DDR was supplanted by DDR2. DDR2 SDRAM superseded the original DDR SDRAM specification and the two are not compatible. In addition to a double data transfer capability, DDR2 allows a higher bus speed and requires lower power (1.8 volts) by running the internal clock at one quarter the speed of the data bus. The two factors enable a total of 4 data transfers per internal clock cycle. With data being transferred in 64-bit chunks, DDR2 SDRAM results in a transfer rate in bytes per second computed as follows:

$$(\text{memory clock rate}) \times 2 \ (\text{bus clock multiplier}) \times 2 \ (\text{dual rate})$$
$$\times \ 64 \ (\text{number of bits transferred})/8 \ (\text{number of bits/byte})$$

Thus, with a memory clock frequency of 100 MHz, DDR2 SDRAM gives a maximum transfer rate of 3,200 megabytes per second (MB/s).

Similar to DDR, DDR2 has a low voltage requirement of 1.8 volts, which is even lower than DDR's 2.5 volts. Thus, DDR2 memory conserves additional energy and enables cooler operations. According to specifications reviewed by this author, DDR2 memory can operate at up to 3.2 gigabytes per second (GB/s).

In the evolution of memory, DDR3 represents the latest type of available memory, whereas DDR4 may appear in 2012. DDR3 or double data rate three SDRAM represents an evolution of improvement over DDR2 and similar to DDR2 versus DDR, DDR3 is not compatible with DDR2. A key benefit of DDR3 is its ability to transfer data at a rate twice that of DDR2 memory, enabling higher bus rates. DDR3 memory provides a 30% reduction in power consumption in comparison to DDR2 memory, operating at 1.5 volts in comparison to the 1.8 volts used by DDR2. Thus, computers using DDR3 memory will generally operate at a lower cost than those using DDR2 memory.

With data being transferred in 64-bit chunks, DDR3 SDRAM provides a transfer rate capability of:

$$(\text{memory clock rate}) \times 4 \text{ (bus clock multiplier)} \times 2 \text{ (data rate)}$$
$$\times 64 \text{ (number of bits transferred)}/8 \text{ (number of bits/byte)}$$

Thus, with a memory clock frequency of 100 MHz, DDR3 SDRAM gives a maximum transfer rate of 6400 MB/s. Although this may appear high, in actuality some types of DDR3 memory support peak transfer rates of 17 GB/s.

In general, DDR3 memory provides greater speeds than DDR2 memory. This should enable a server to support multiple programs or processor-intensive demanding programs better than a computer using slower memory. In fact, according to advertisements from Samsung in *Bloomberg Businessweek* during 2010, their 30-nano 4-G bit DDR3 server memory chip saves 86% more energy than its DDR2 predecessor. Thus, using DDR3 memory in servers in a server farm could result in a significant lowering of the monthly electric bill. In addition, as each new version of DDR memory requires less power than the previous version, this results in a lower amount of energy consumption and less cooling requirement.

Rack Pack Considerations   Until recently most computer manufacturers incorporated multiple core processors as a platform for building
a server. This architecture was challenged in 2010 by the introduction of the SeaMicro 10U system. The 10U rack consists of 512 1.6
GHz Z530 Intel Atom processors and 1 Tbyte of dynamic random
access memory (DRAM). The use of single core processors instead
of multicore processors resulted from a computation of the system
performance per watt, which at full CPU utilization was anticipated
to be more than three times better than multicore solutions such as
the use of Xeon or Opteron multicore processors. Another SeaMicro
system referred to as the SM10000 supports up to 2,048 Intel Atom
processors in a single rack. With a suggested price near $140,000 and
a system bandwidth of 1.28 Tbits/s, the SeaMicro SM10000 system is targeted for large organizations running web services. Because
on average it uses 1 kW of power and a maximum of 2 kW, the
SM10000 can significantly reduce the cost of server power for systems that operate 24/7.

Communications Equipment

Communications equipment can be similar to servers and mainframes due to the fact that they are operational 24/7, perhaps taken
down to replace a failing power supply or to resolve another problem.
Because most modern routers, firewalls, and LAN switches can be
obtained with dual power supplies, even the failure of one may allow
the device to remain operational while being repaired. According
to an article in the January 11, 2010 edition of *Scientific American*
titled, "Can the World's Telecoms Slash Their Energy Consumption
1,000-Fold?" the global network to include equipment required for
its operation produces 250 million tons of carbon dioxide emissions
annually, which is roughly the equivalent of the emissions produced
by 50 million automobiles each year. To put the amount of CO_2 generated by communications in perspective, it would take a forest the
size of the United Kingdom to absorb 250 million tons of CO_2. The
referenced article mentioned how the world's telecoms were attempting to reduce their use of energy inasmuch as it is both costly and
harmful to the environment. A similar rationale can be made for

reducing the consumption of energy by data communications equipment within a data center. However, in addition to savings upon the cost of energy and reducing emissions it's a topic that is often overlooked by the data center manager.

In the past there were probably a few good reasons to ignore the energy consumption of communications devices, however, this is now no longer the case. Today, many manufacturers of data communications equipment have redesigned their products both from a performance and an energy consumption level. Through the addition of the double data rate and advances to include DDR2 and DDR3 memory modules that operate at higher clock rates than older memory but use a lower voltage (1.35 V for DDR3 versus 1.8 V for DDR2 versus 2.5 V for DDR), resulting in lower energy consumption and in effect less heat dissipation. This allows fans to consume less energy in dissipating heat and reduces the overall energy footprint of communications equipment. Thus, a LAN switch purchased just a few years ago that might have had a power consumption of 370 to 400 watts can be obtained with a power consumption of approximately 150 watts and more functionality. The difference may appear trivial, after all it's only a minimum of 220 watts (370 less 150), but over a year this equates to:

$$220 \text{ watts} \times 24 \text{ hours/day} \times 365 \text{ days/year}/1{,}000 \text{ watts/kWh}$$
$$= 1927 \text{ kWh}$$

If your organization is only paying 10 cents per kWh, then a small LAN switch is costing you $192 per year in additional electricity cost. If you have a fairly large data center you easily have at least 10 to 20 LAN switches, however, instead of being small units they are probably 48- or 64-port devices. In such cases the savings per device in energy consumption can easily amount to over $300 per year per device, or approximately $6,000 per year for a data center with 20 switches, which migrates to more efficient energy consumption products. Should you change your LAN switches based just upon energy efficiency? Here to be truthful the answer is probably not. However, at the very least energy efficiency should be a key criterion in determining the operational cost of different equipment over its useful life. Thus, if your acquisition process includes performing a detailed analysis of the lifetime cost of owning equipment then you need to consider the cost of electricity consumed by different products that meet or exceed your technical requirements in addition to maintenance, reliability, and how service is performed, with the latter including such possibilities as having an additional device to facilitate swapping equipment or the number of hours it takes for a technician to reach your data center location.

Due to the inclusion of many types of data communications devices with a data center it would be impossible to cover all of the possible options managers should consider. Instead, we focus our attention upon one common device included in just about every data center to illustrate how it is possible to both improve performance and reduce the consumption of energy when doing so by turning our attention to the Cisco 3750 series of stackable LAN switches.

Cisco 3750 Series At the time this book was written the Cisco Catalyst 3750 represented a series of stackable switches ranging from the Model 3750FS-24 with 24 Ethernet 10/100 megabits per second (mbps) ports to the model 3750G-12S-SD with 12 Ethernet 1-Gigabit ports. Some of the models include a power over Ethernet (PoE) capability, which enables the switch to provide power for digital telephones, webcams, IEEE 802.11 Wireless LAN access points, and other devices. Table 5.4 provides a summary of the different stackable 3750 switches that can be updated by searching the Cisco website as the vendor periodically introduces new products to the marketplace. A key feature of the Cisco 3750 series is its ability to pool power among switches in a

Table 5.4 Cisco Catalyst 3750 Series Switch Models

MODEL	TOTAL ETHERNET PORTS	UPLINKS DEFAULT	AC POWER SUPPLY RATING (W)	DEFAULT PoE POWER (W)
C3750-24FS-S	24	2×1G	125	—
C3750V2-24T-S	24	2×1G	60	—
C3750V2-48TS-S	48	4×1G	130	—
C3750-24TS-E	24	2×1G	60	—
C3750V2-24P-S	24 PoE	2×1G	525	370
C3750V2-48P-S	48 PoE	4×1G	525	370
C3750V2-24PS-E	24 PoE	2×1G	525	370
C3750V2-48PS-E	48 PoE	4×1G	525	370
C3750G-128-S	12×1G	—	100	—
C3750-12S-E	12×1G	—	100	—
C3750G-12S-SD	12×1G	—	72	—

stack that enables both capital and operational costs, with the latter including energy consumption to be reduced.

Although the 3750 switches offer a variety of features including switching at layer 2 and layer 3 of the International Standards Organization (ISO) Open System Interconnection (OSI) model, an integrated wireless LAN controller in certain models and other features, we do not focus on those features inasmuch as we are concerned with energy efficiency in this book. Thus, our discussion of the 3750 series concentrates on the Cisco "EnergyWise" technology included in the 3750s.

Cisco StackPower and EnergyWise Technology   Cisco's EnergyWise technology can be considered to represent an architecture added to its 3750 series of switches, which has the effect of reducing energy consumption as well as enabling an organization to measure the power consumption of its network infrastructure. Being able to stack switches via the use of pooled power supplies resulted in the term StackPower used by Cisco to identify the technology that enables power to be made available to any switch within a stack or on an as-needed basis. This enables the savings of both power and power supplies. In addition, by stacking switches you can obtain a smaller footprint that can be important in a crowded communications closet or data center.

StackPower   Under StackPower a single 1,100-watt power supply can provide power to four switches, with up to nine switches being able to share power in a star topology by using an expandable power system. Through the use of 3750 switches that are interconnected to form a power stack, unused power from switches that have lower power requirements can be allocated from a literal power pool to switches that require additional power. The power pool can be considered to represent a dynamic reserve of power allocated to switches as their power requirements change. For example, consider a ring formed by the interconnection of four switches, each having an input power of 1,100 watts and 500 watts of actual consumption. Under StackPower the available power pool is 4,400 watts or 4 switches × 1,100 watts per switch. Then, inasmuch as 2,000 watts is in use (500 × 4 switches), the difference or 1,100 watts (4 switches × (1,100 watts – 500 watts)) of power would be considered to represent reserved power that could be allocated to different switches as their loads increase, whereas the amount of reserved power would grow when switches consumed less power.

Because LAN switches are key devices whose failure can result in the inability of networked users to perform effectively, many organizations obtain dual power supplies to ensure high availability through critical component redundancy. Through the use of StackPower it becomes possible to purchase a lesser number of power supplies while obtaining an $N + 1$ redundancy for power supplies configured in a ring. For example, assume each of four switches in a stack consumed 130 watts, resulting in a total power draw of 520 watts. With 130-watt power supplies, full $N + 1$ redundancy would require eight 130-watt power supplies for conventional switches, however, under StackPower as few as two 525-watt power supplies could be used, resulting in a savings of six power supplies. Although the cost of power supplies varies based upon wattage as well as efficiency, size, and other factors, you can be sure that the cost of two 525-watt power supplies will be significantly less than the cost of eight 130-watt power supplies, resulting in an economic savings added to a power reduction capability. In actuality, there are four power supply options available for use in Cisco 3750-X series switches: 350 watt, 440 watt, 715 watt, and 1,100 watt. Thus, instead of our earlier example where switches used 130-watt power supplies the minimum wattage for load sharing would require two 715-watt power supplies for redundancy as the use of 440-watt power supplies would not be sufficient.

EnergyWise Technology   It's important to note that there are many types of communications equipment located within a data center, such as firewalls, routers, communications servers, print servers, and other devices that are in effect powered on and operational 24/7. At a Cisco Networkers conference in 2009 in Barcelona, Spain, Cisco Systems introduced its EnergyWise technology for certain Cisco switches that will measure, report, and provide the ability to reduce the energy consumption of such Internet protocol (IP) devices as digital phones, computers, and even network access points. Included in the Cisco announcement was the fact that a number of industry partners would work with the vendor that would ultimately allow the management of power consumption throughout a building by enabling elevators, lighting, air conditioning, and heating to be managed through the use of EnergyWise technology.

Operation   EnergyWise represents a system that initially polls the enterprise to discover manageable devices. By examining IP traffic it switches off devices that do not need to be on, or resets them to use less power. By automatically switching devices with no activity into a low power mode it becomes possible to remove human forgetfulness to turn off devices as they leave the office, either for the day or for a break or long lunch. According to one article this author read, simply turning off the digital telephones within a 1,000-employee organization during evening hours could save between 30 and 40 tons of greenhouse gases a year. In addition, EnergyWise includes a toolkit that enables the integration of third-party management systems, such as IBM's Tivoli and VMware's Orchestrator as well as such legacy building devices as access control systems, climate control, and lighting. Through the use of EnergyWise it becomes possible to measure how much power is being consumed by each device on the network. This in turn enables one to decide upon potential actions to reduce energy cost with facts and not simply estimations. In addition, because the system provides factual data in real-time you can use this information to enact policies and procedures that will affect the overall power consumption within a building. For example, if a building has multiple elevators you may obtain information that enables you to consider turning off one or more elevators between certain hours of the day.

The first version of EnergyWise, announced in 2009, operated on Cisco Catalyst 2xxx and 3xxx Series switches and was limited to monitoring and controlling IP phones, access points, and network-attached devices running off power over the Ethernet provided by those switches. A second release that extended support to Catalyst 4500 Series switches added the control of other network-attached devices, such as PCs and servers. In 2010 Cisco added supports for its Catalyst 6500 series switches and via a toolkit support for a wide range of lighting, heating, air conditioning, and even other vendor management systems. Readers should consider the use of a search tool using "energy-efficient LAN switches," "energy-efficient network devices," "energy-efficient network attached devices," or similar terms

to determine if a new product that provides energy-efficient operations needs to be considered during the procurement process.

Other Techniques to Reduce Energy Consumption

Now that we have an appreciation for some potential methods to
reduce the energy consumption of communications devices let's turn
our focus to a handful of general techniques we can use to reduce
energy consumption within a data center. In doing so we examine a
variety of techniques, from understanding why we should keep the
temperature within a data center at or below 77°Fahrenheit to the use
of diffusers.

Fan Speed Considerations Most modern communications devices,
including routers, firewalls, and switches as well as computers, including all types of server platforms include one or more variable-speed
fans. As the temperature increases above approximately 77°F the fan
will significantly increase its rotational speed, consuming additional
power. In fact, power consumption increases near exponential as the
fan speed increases, resulting in a fan speed increase of 10% resulting
in a 33% increase in power consumption. This means that it is critical
to keep the temperature within equipment located in the data center at
or below 77°F if you are attempting to minimize the consumption of
electricity. One of the more prominent sets of methods that can be uti-
lized to do this can be referred to as the placement of equipment racks
and their cooling considerations upon which we now turn our focus.

Rack Placement and Cooling Considerations There are several methods you can consider to minimize electoral consumption within a
data center. One is to optimize airflow, enabling equipment racks to
increase their density from approximately 5 kW to 25 kW or more
if the data center design permits. Another possibility is to arrange
racks of equipment such that you have an arrangement of hot aisle
and cold aisle equipment racks. A third method is to consider supplemental cooling for areas where the heat dissipated by equipment
could represent a problem and a fourth method involves considering
a change in the cooling method used. Let's briefly look at each of
these methods.

Optimize Airflow   There are several techniques you can consider to optimize the flow of air within a data center. One key technique is to maximize the return air temperature by supplying air directly to the equipment loads, especially when equipment racks would otherwise generate the temperature beyond 77°F that causes fans to run faster, consuming additional energy. In doing so, cooling air should be supplied directly to the equipment air intake locations. To accomplish this you can consider using applicable diffusers or positioning supply and return ducts to minimize the mixing of airflow.

Use Appropriate Diffusers   As a refresher, a diffuser represents a flow passage. There are several types of diffusers you can consider using. If you can obtain a data center diffuser you should pass on the availability to use standard office-style diffusers. This results from the fact that a standard office diffuser is designed to create a fully mixed environment. Thus, this type of diffuser is not appropriate for data centers. Diffusers should be selected that deliver air directly to the IT equipment; those without regard for drafts dominate the design of most office-based diffusers.

Position Supply and Returns to Minimize Airflow Mixing   When considering the placement of diffusers in a data center they should be located to deliver air directly to heat generation equipment and racks. Diffusers should be placed so they direct cool air to the areas where equipment draws in such air. Thus, you should not place diffusers so that cool air is directed to the hot air exhaust of equipment. If you watch the weather channel or the weather report on your news channel you probably have viewed the effect of a hot air front mixing with a cold air front, generating a near perfect storm. Although you probably will not generate a storm in your data center, you do not want to have cold air directly mixing with hot air.

Minimize Air Leaks in Raised Floor Systems.   The raised floor found in most data centers represents an often-overlooked area that wastes energy. If your data center uses a raised floor as a supply plenum you need to check the plenum for air leaks as often it is installed one year and used over and over again as new systems replace older computers. As air flows through the plenum the sheet metal may pop at improperly sealed joints and the flow of cables through the plenum can result in air leaks at their entry and exit points. In addition, you should verify that floor tiles are located where there are equipment loads, which will prevent the short circuiting of cooling air directly to the returns. Another area of concern you need to verify is the use and placement of perforated tiles. Such tiles should not be placed near computer room air-conditioning return ducts as they will interfere with the ducts used as a return air path.

Optimize Location of Computer Room Air Conditioners   As most people know, as the distance between the devices to be cooled and air conditioners increases, more power is required to blow cool air. Thus, any method you can perform to minimize the distance between air conditioners and equipment will reduce the cost of electricity required to flow cool air to its intended locations.

Use Insulation   One of the great mysteries of life is how many data center managers do almost everything right but neglect to consider the obvious. That obvious item is the ceiling. In one building this author is familiar with, if you took a ruler and pushed up the ceiling tile you would see the uninsulated concrete ceiling. Simply insulating the ceiling resulted in a reduction of electrical consumption by over 30% as most of the cool air from air handlers was literally going up the roof!

Provide Adequately Sized Return Plenum   When planning or reviewing the use of return plenum you need to ensure that they are correctly sized. Obstructions such as cabling trays, piping, electrical conduits, or other types of wiring run through plenums should be accounted for when calculating the amount of plenum space required for your data center. It's important to note that any blockage within the plenum can result in significant pressure drops and uneven airflow.

Consider Ceiling Height   When an organization gets an attractive deal on real estate, many times the result is a data center operating in a former bank that has 12-foot-high ceilings. Although nice to view for customers of the bank, high ceilings are a significant expense to heat and cool. Thus, the data center manager needs to consider carefully the height of ceilings in the data center to determine if they need to be lowered.

Hot Aisle/Cold Aisle Zone Arrangement   By carefully segregating equipment into "hot" and "cold" aisles that are installed in zones you can develop a hot and cold aisle data center that may optimize airflow. Under the hot aisle/cold aisle scheme cabinets or racks of equipment are placed into a series of rows, with each cabinet or rack on a raised floor. The fronts of the cabinets or racks in an aisle all face the same way, resulting in a second aisle having racks or cabinets that face in the opposite direction. Because the fronts of equipment in two aisles face each other and fans move heat upward and to the rear, the aisles with equipment facing each other are referred to as cold aisles. The racks or cabinets in two aisles that have the rear facing each other are referred to as hot aisles. The hot aisle in between racks can be covered at the top of the racks or cabinets and at the end of the rows and ducted back to the computer room air-conditioning unit. The result is a full separation between supply and return air, allowing normal air to cool the cold racks.

Note that for a hot aisle/cold aisle configuration to be effective you cannot use glass-enclosed cabinets. Early versions of server enclosures and communications equipment were often manufactured with "smoked" or glass-front doors. Although you can still obtain glass doors for different equipment cabinets, if you want to use a hot aisle/cold aisle configuration you need to change your doors to the perforated type for this method to work. Perforated doors are a necessity for server enclosures, however, the amount of perforated area needed for effective cooling depends upon the manufacturer. Some server doors utilize 65% perforation, whereas other doors are manufactured with 80% or more perforation. Cabinet doors and their amount of perforations are important, but the remainder of the enclosure can have an important effect in maintaining airflow as well. Thus, any cabinet or rack accessories should not impede airflow and other accessories, such as blanking panels, can actually facilitate the cooling of equipment as they prevent exhaust air from returning to the equipment intake. In addition, heat removal will be influenced by raised floor height, tile placement, the level of cabinet door perforation, air handler locations, and even the architecture of the room.

Although the hot aisle/cold aisle configuration is commonly used in data centers around the world, the design is not standardized, nor is there uniformity concerning whether hot aisle or cold aisle containment should be used. In a paper from Emerson Network Power that looked at both hot and cold aisle containment, it came to the conclusion that cold aisle containment is a better solution. The paper made this case because cold aisle containment is a more focused cooling approach when using central air-conditioning, inasmuch as it enables you to focus where you want to direct cold air. An opposite recommendation is from American Power Conversion (APC) which supports hot aisle containment. The rationale for their recommendation is based on the fact that hot aisle containment will enable the capture of heated equipment exhaust air very close to its point of origin, cooling it immediately. In effect this method reduces the risk of hot air flowing into locations within the data center that could be adversely affected. According to a project manager in the Energy Technologies Division at the United States Lawrence Berkeley National Laboratories who studied the effectiveness of both hot aisle and cold aisle containment, both approaches offer significant improvements in the efficiency and effectiveness of data center cooling. Although the experts may disagree on which approach offers a better potential, either method will reduce your organization's use of electricity.

Use Supplemental Cooling In most data centers you will encounter what is referred to as a "hot spot." Most often, you can actually feel the presence of the hot spot as you walk by an aisle with rack after rack of equipment and suddenly the temperature feels a lot warmer until you pass the area and the temperature returns to the cooling temperature you are attempting to maintain in the data center. To counteract the hot spot you can first examine where cooling vents are located to determine if it might be possible to direct the flow of cool air toward the hot spot. However, to do so you should actually direct cool air toward the inflow areas of equipment generating the hot spot and the location where the hot spot occurs. Although this represents a minimum cost cooling effort, it could save your organization a considerable amount of energy if the hot spot results in fans within equipment running at a higher than normal speed to expel warm air.

Assuming the obvious low-cost method cannot be performed, another potential solution to the problem of hot spots within the data center is to consider the use of supplemental cooling, referred to as closely coupled cooling where a chilled liquid, such as water or glycol is piped into the middle of the raised floor space resulting in an air-to-liquid heat exchange within a row of racks or even within a rack. There are different types of closely coupled cooling with corresponding different costs associated with installing the plumbing as well as the cost of the system in terms of BTUs removed per unit of time. For some organizations with one or more hot spots, the cost of a supplementary cooling method may be a viable solution. However, similar to other methods of reducing hot spots, you need to consider the cost of installation, operation, and maintenance to determine if it represents an economically viable method to removing data center hot spots while permitting rack densities to increase.

Available Calculators

The Internet can be a valuable tool. However, it can also provide information that does not quite tell the full story. Thus, in concluding this chapter a few words about the use of so-called "ROI" (return on investment) and other types of calculators focused upon selling servers are warranted.

In developing material for inclusion in this book this author examined several ROI type calculators on web pages operated by IBM, HP, and other server manufacturers. Some of the calculators appeared to be very comprehensive, making the user consider the type of enterprise software packages to be used, current workload, hardware, and server costs and many additional metrics, however, several calculators were deficient in omitting the cost of energy, which over the life of the equipment could easily exceed its cost. Thus, when using a calculator you need to consider how comprehensive it is. If it omits energy costs, this does not mean that the calculator should not be used, but that you might consider modifying the results to better reflect your operational conditions.

Prior to using any calculator you should develop a spreadsheet that lists projected hardware and software costs, operating costs, and even strategic costs that can be used to form a baseline for cost comparisons.

When listing hardware and software costs you can consider listing such costs under the term "Equipment Costs," which will allow separate entries for hardware, software, and even energy use. In fact, you should also list any communications equipment there as such devices typically operate 24/7 and their energy consumption can easily add up. Table 5.5 illustrates an example of a potential cost table you can construct that will facilitate the use of web-based ROI calculators.

Although completing the information asked for in Table 5.5 may appear to represent a time-consuming task, not all information may be necessary. For example, if you are only considering the replacement of one type of server you can skip over other entries and focus your attention upon obtaining the required metric that is commensurate with the action you are planning. However, if the replacement of one or more devices will require additional cooling you then need to consider both the cost of electricity and water, if the cooling will be based upon the use of a chiller.

According to some ROI calculators, it's possible to obtain a return on your investment in as little as two months. To obtain this near-financial miracle one vendor includes the consolidation of approximately 30 servers onto one, which reduces licensing fees from over $27,000 to under $1,000 per year. Although it's possible your organization may be able to consolidate servers due to new technology such as virtualization, it is highly doubtful if most organizations can obtain anywhere near a 30:1 consolidation ratio. As my financial advisor likes to point out, when a return significantly exceeds that commonly available, be suspicious. Similarly, when you review the use of different ROI calculators carefully examine the potential entries as you may have to make some adjustments, especially if the calculator has predefined entries that require modification to reflect your organization's location, such as a higher electric or water rate.

Table 5.5 Equipment Cost Sheet

SERVER HARDWARE COST
Database servers _____
Application servers _____
Web servers _____
Other servers _____

SERVER SOFTWARE COST
Monthly/yearly cost _____

PC/TABLET HARDWARE COSTS
PC/tablet hardware _____

PC/TABLET SOFTWARE COST
Programs _____

CELL PHONE/SMART PHONE
Type and cost _____

COMMUNICATIONS EQUIPMENT
Routers _____
Firewalls _____
LAN switches _____
Print servers _____
Other devices _____

MAINTENANCE COST
Servers _____
PC/tablets _____
Communications equipment _____

ENERGY COST
Cost per kWh _____
Consumption _____
Servers _____
PCs/ tablets _____
Communications equipment _____

OTHER COSTS TO CONSIDER
Additional cooling _____
Electricity _____
Water _____

6

MINIMIZING COMPUTER
ENERGY CONSUMPTION

In every data center a majority of electrical consumption results from the use of computers and the networking devices used within the data center. Thus, the focus of this chapter is upon obtaining a firm understanding of several methods we can consider for reducing the energy consumption of different types of computers, ranging from personal computers to servers as well as networking devices. To do so we review the characteristics of sleep mode under the Windows operating system as well as discuss several standards associated with saving energy by providing different mechanisms to control the consumption of energy. Because it would be difficult to impossible to cover every operating system that exists, this author focuses his attention on the Windows series of operating systems from Microsoft as they represent the vast majority of operating systems used by personal computers and servers.

Sleep Mode Considerations

When we discuss energy consumption, one of the parameters many people do not understand is that in a data center the monitors attached to most computers actually consume more electricity than the computer. Perhaps the key exception to the preceding are the large servers typically located in a data center. However, when you consider the fact that there are typically hundreds of employees within a data center, each with his own personal computer and monitor, on a cumulative basis it is possible that the consumption of electricity by monitors contributes to a large portion of an organization's monthly electric bill. Thus, any method that we can use to reduce that bill warrants discussion.

Power Options

Beginning with late versions of Microsoft's Windows NT operating system, most modern operating systems support Energy Star sleep mode settings. Even if you are operating an older version of an operating system it is still possible to conserve power by employing smart power strips that can sense when a computer is idle and temporarily shut down the monitor. In Chapter 5 of this book we discussed the use of smart power strips and readers may consider rereading the relevant section in that chapter for additional information concerning these power strips. Sleep mode is now one of several power options you can configure from the control panel under Windows 7. Because its access can at times be a bit confusing, let's examine how we can access the power options when using Windows 7 and the options available for selection.

Accessing Power Options   For those of us who are literally old-timers, in earlier versions of Windows the collection of hardware and system settings that managed how your computers use power was known as a power scheme. Under more modern versions of Windows including Vista and Windows 7, the name has been changed to power plans. Thus, other than the name used there is no difference between a power scheme and a power plan.

One method you can use to access a power plan is to click on the Start button, click on the Control Panel, select Systems and Security, and then click on Power Options. In actuality, there are several methods that can be used to access the power plan built into Windows, ranging from the use of a command prompt window for those of us who never gave up on the Disk Operating System (DOS) to the use of the Registry Editor, and even a local group policy editor. You can even use the Start Search box and type Power Options to go directly to a dialog box that will list the plans available and the one currently set as the default plan. For the purposes of this book we concentrate our efforts on the use of point and click technology, which for the majority of readers will be easy to follow. Thus, from the Start menu you would select the Control Panel option, which allows you to customize the appearance and functionality of the computer. Under Windows 7 the Control Panel would initially appear similar to the screen illustrated in Figure 6.1.

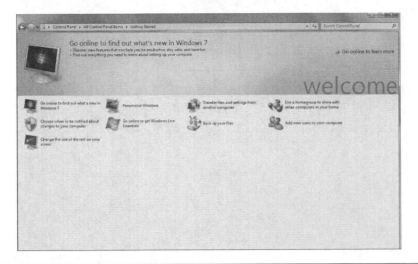

Figure 6.1   The Windows 7 control panel.

In examining Figure 6.1 you might initially be at a loss in attempting to determine which entry you should click upon to be able to access power options available under this operating system. Fortunately, there are only nine icons to select from, so any trial-and-error method will eventually allow you to select the applicable icon. However, it should be noted that by clicking on View by the use of a drop-down menu and selecting "Large Items" or "Small Items" this action would result in a list of items being displayed to include "Power Plans" that, when clicked upon, would result in the display of the Power options window similar to the one illustrated in Figure 6.2. Although any shortcut method that produces the same result should be considered by readers, because this author is explaining power plans to readers with different backgrounds he takes a longer route to arrive at the same point. Thus, we take the long way to arrive at the same destination.

If you select the Presentations icon your screen display will be similar to the one illustrated in Figure 6.3. Note that by clicking on the screen saver icon a dialog box labeled "Screen Saver Settings" is automatically displayed, however, for clarity this dialog box was dragged to the right of the screen by this author. In examining this dialog box note that by default the Screen Saver is set to none and a good technique is to ensure that no employee uses any screen saver in a modern work environment. This is because a screen saver ensures that the monitor is fully active and precludes any savings occurring from

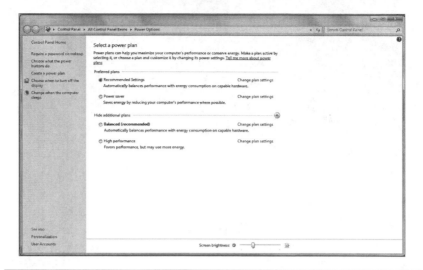

Figure 6.2   Selecting a power plan.

one of the biggest energy hogs in a data center, the monitor found on every employee's desk.

If you turn your attention to the lower left portion of the Screen Saver Settings dialog box illustrated in Figure 6.3 you will note a Power management section, where Power management is first described and under the description is a link you can select to both view and change settings, so let's select that link and investigate the options available under Windows 7.

Figure 6.2 illustrates the power plans available under Windows 7. Basically, as previously stated, a power plan represents a collection of hardware and software settings that enable a computer user to manage the manner by which the computer uses energy. Under Windows 7 users can utilize power plans to reduce energy consumption, maximize computer performance, or strike a balance between the two. By default, the power plan used by Windows 7 is set to "balanced." This option provides full performance when required; however, it saves power during periods of inactivity. As the default setting, this option is considered by Microsoft to represent the best power plan for a majority of users. However, you need to understand that "balanced" represents settings for the typical or average computer user and your employees may not be represented by this average.

If you carefully examine Figure 6.2 you will note that you can select a different power plan or you can consider changing either an existing

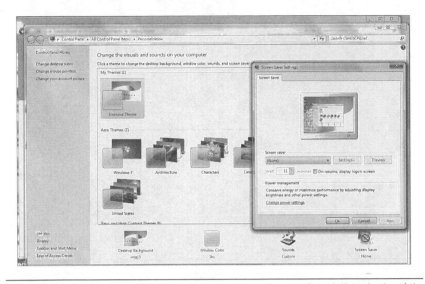

Figure 6.3   Under Windows 7 access to power management occurs through the selection of the screen saver settings dialog box.

or changed power plan setting. Concerning the additional power plans, the power saver plan reduces energy consumption by reducing system performance and screen brightness. This power plan is probably more suitable for laptop or notebook users attempting to conserve battery power on a long flight rather than a desktop computer user. The third power plan, high performance, maximizes screen brightness and under certain conditions can increase a computer's performance. Although the high performance option is applicable for many desktop users, a word of caution is warranted if you use this setting on a laptop or notebook computer. Because the use of this setting results in a maximum level of screen brightness it will result in a significant use of battery power, which in turn will reduce the amount of time you can use the computer prior to its automatically shutting down.

Editing a Power Plan   By clicking on the "change plan settings" associated with a power plan you obtain the ability to view, change, or accept a variety of options associated with the plan. To illustrate this, click on the Change plan settings associated with the recommended settings entry at the top right area of Figure 6.2. As a result of the selection just made you will be able to directly control four aspects of the selected power plan. This is illustrated in Figure 6.4, which shows the defaults setting for the "Recommended Settings" power

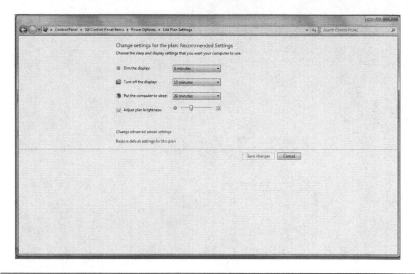

Figure 6.4   Default settings for the selected power plan.

plan. Note that you can change the time associated with dimming the display from a default value of 5 minutes, turn off the display that has a default value of 15 minutes, put the computer into a sleep mode of operation whose default setting is 20 minutes, and adjust the brightness of the monitor, whose default value is a bit under the halfway mark. In addition, you can also restore the default settings associated with the power plan selected or select the advanced power settings option.

Although this author recognizes that each person will use a computer in a different manner, he has difficulty with two default settings. If the monitor is turned off after 15 minutes, it doesn't make much sense to allow the computer an extra five minutes prior to putting it into a sleep mode of operation. If you consider the fact that employees typically take two 20- to 30-minute breaks and at least a 30-minute lunch, then there are at least three periods per day where the employee leaves the computer and the computer consumes an extra amount of energy for 5 minutes while the monitor is turned off. If you multiply 15 minutes per day by 22 working days per month and then multiply the result by 12 months per year you obtain an extra period of over 66 hours per year where the monitor is turned off but the computer is not in a sleep mode of operation. If the computer consumes 100 watts, this equates to 6.6 kWh of energy use per computer, or for an organization with 500 employees over 3,300 additional kWh of energy consumption that could be reduced by simply changing one entry in the power plan so that the monitor is turned off and the computer goes into a sleep mode of operation at the same time. As a friend of mine once said, save a few bucks here and a few there and soon you have some significant savings.

CPU States   Concerning the sleep mode, in actuality there are four sleep states within one of a series of four general CPU states that are defined under an open standard referred to as the Advanced Configuration and Power Interface (ACPI) specification. Originally developed by Intel, Microsoft, and Toshiba, other computer manufacturers are now behind this specification that defines a platform-independent series of interfaces that enables the discovery of hardware, configuration management, power management, and monitoring. Beginning with state S0 to indicate the CPU is working, under the sleeping state it is subdivided into four states referred to as S1 through S4. Table 6.1 indicates the four CPU sleep states defined by the ACPI specification.

In addition to the four sleep states and the working state, the ACPI specification defines two additional states referred to as S5, known as soft off and what this author refers to as state S6, which is called mechanical off. S5 is similar to S6, however, activity on the keyboard, mouse, or another device can wake the computer when it is in an S5 state. Under the mechanical off state the computer's power consumption is reduced to near zero as only the real-time clock operates and it obtains power from its own battery, which is usually installed

Table 6.1   CPU Sleep States Defined by the ACPI Specification

STATE	DESCRIPTION
S1	Power to CPU and RAM maintained but processor caches are flushed and CPU stops executing any instructions and devices that do not indicate they need to be powered on can be powered off. S1 is not normally used.
S2	The CPU is placed in a power off state while RAM is refreshed. S2 actually is a lower power mode than S1 but, like S1, is not normally used.
S3	This is the true standby mode where RAM remains powered on and refreshed but the CPU only draws a few watts of power so it can wake up. This state is normally used.
S4	Known as suspend to disk or the hibernation mode, all contents of main memory are saved to disk so power can be removed from RAM. When placed in the hibernate mode the computer takes longer to activate than when in the standby S3 mode.

as a rechargeable circular battery on the motherboard. When in the mechanical off state the computer can be safely moved as it is not in effect consuming AC power.

When selecting a sleep state you need to consider the activity of personnel versus the likelihood of a power loss to determine an applicable sleep state. Although you would most likely select S3, under certain conditions you might prefer to select S4, which can be considered as a hybrid sleep option. This results from the fact that in a hybrid sleep mode your computer system saves any open documents and programs to your hard disk, and then places your computer into a low-power state, similar to an S3 state. A key advantage of hybrid sleep is that if a power failure occurs, Windows can restore your work from your hard disk. Thus, if your data center has an uninterruptible power supply (UPS) that backs up your servers but does not provide a backup for employee computers and you frequently lose power, you might consider the S4 mode. Then, if a power failure occurs, users can still recover their last working state because all data in memory are saved to disk. However, a disadvantage of the S4 state results from the time this mode takes to save memory to a hibernation file as well as additional time to return to a working state than if the computer were placed into an S3 state.

Returning to Figure 6.4, which illustrates the default settings for the recommended power plan, note that you can control the time to dim your display, turn off the display, place the computer into a sleep mode of operation, and select the brightness level of the display. In addition to directly setting three values and screen brightness you can restore default settings for the power plan and select some advanced settings. Concerning the latter, assuming you select the advanced settings option, your resulting display would be similar to that shown in Figure 6.5, with the dialog box labeled Power Options moved to the right of the screen by this author for clarity of illustration.

Advanced Settings   If you turn your attention to the dialog box labeled Advanced Settings, as shown in Figure 6.5, perhaps the first thing you will note is that by default no password is required. If you select Yes, thereafter a password will be required whenever the computer is in a standby, sleep, or hibernate mode and wakes up. Because employees take breaks and go to lunch and unless constantly reminded are

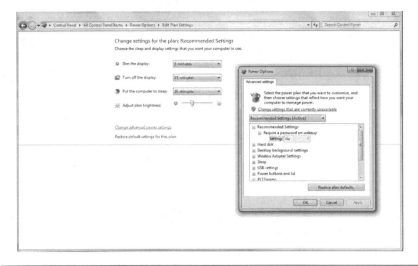

Figure 6.5   Viewing the advanced options dialog box.

prone to let their computer remain powered on and unlocked, sometimes forcing the issue by requiring a password when a computer goes
into a sleep mode is a good idea. However, if your employees are in a
secure building, are trustworthy, and you receive no visitors, then you
can consider not requiring employees literally to go the extra mile by
requiring the extra step associated with having to log on each time the
computer resumes operation and you can leave the option set to "NO."
However, if you get confused about what you have done by not keeping a record of changes you can consider starting anew by clicking on
the "Restore plan defaults" option.

In addition to assigning or removing a wake-up password, you
can customize a variety of options that affect different hardware that
makes up the computer platform. There are 10 options you can consider, ranging from controlling the hard drive to multimedia settings
described in the following paragraphs.

Hard Drive   Selecting the hard drive option enables you to control
when the hard drive is turned off after no activity. A default value of
20 minutes is used, which this author finds a bit excessive for normal
office environments and would probably be more comfortable with a
value of 15 minutes. You can adjust the hard disk settings by simply
clicking on the default value, which displays a counter that can be

incremented or decremented by one per click on an upper or lower pointing arrow or you can enter a value directly.

Wireless Adapter   There are four settings available for selection under the wireless adapter power plan option. The default setting is "maximize performance," and the options available for selection include low, medium, and maximum power savings. Because wireless LAN adapters do not consume much power and their performance is critical, you should probably leave the setting on maximum performance for laptops and notebooks. However, if your computer is a desktop that uses a wired Ethernet connection to the corporate network, then setting this option to maximum power savings should be considered.

Sleep   The sleep option defines the period of inactivity, which when reached places the computer into a sleep mode. By default the value is set at 20 minutes, which again is considered to be too high by this author inasmuch as he feels 15 minutes is a more reasonable period of time. You can change the setting in a manner similar to how you change the hard drive setting, by clicking on the value that results in a "Sleep after" display that allows you to either click on an upward or downward facing arrow or directly enter a value.

USB Setting   By default the USB (universal serial bus) selective suspend setting is disabled. This option can be either enabled or disabled. For organizations that for security reasons do not allow employees to use USB ports you should more than likely consider enabling this option.

Power Buttons and Lid   There are three options under the power buttons and lid entry. Those options include power button action, sleep button action, and start menu power button. The power button action is used to specify the action that occurs when you press the power button. There are three potential settings: do nothing, sleep, and shut down with the defaults set to sleep. The sleep button option specifies the action that occurs when the computer user selects the sleep option. The available options are do nothing and sleep, with sleep being the default option. The last entry is the start menu power button, with sleep and do nothing as the available options, with sleep selected as the default option. Although these options appear reasonable, there are certain operating environments where you might consider selecting an option other than the default option. Thus, you need to consider your operating environment prior to selecting an option.

PCI Express The PCI express option (PCIe) is used to specify the active state power management (ASPM) policy to use for compliant capable links when the link is idle. ASPM allows power to be incrementally reduced to individual serial links in a PCI express bus-based computer as a link becomes less active. As a refresher for some readers, prior PCI and PCI-X buses consumed no power when no data were transmitted. However, in evolving into the high-speed PCI express bus, even when no data are transmitted the serial links continuously exchange data to provide synchronization. This additional activity consumes more power than the earlier PCI and PCI-X buses. Because a serial-based PCIe bus device, such as the common IEEE 1394 (FireWire) becomes less active it becomes possible to reduce power consumption by placing the link into a low-power mode of operation. Unfortunately, invoking a low-power mode of operation for the PCIe bus results in an increase in latency because the serial bus will have to wake from its low-power mode and may even require the host-to-device link to be re-established, further increasing the delay time.

Under Windows 7 there are three settings you can select. The default setting is Maximum Power Savings; however, you can also select Moderate Power Savings or turn power savings off. The Maximum and Moderate settings correspond to the two low-power modes specified under the PCI 2.0 specification referred to as L0 and L1. The first setting is for one direction of the serial link, and the second mode is bidirectional and results in additional power savings.

Processor Power Management

Under the processor power management option you can view and change the minimum and maximum processor states. A third option that is not presently shown, System cooling policy, can be viewed and changed if you first click on the link "Change settings that are currently unavailable," which is above the Recommended Settings bar

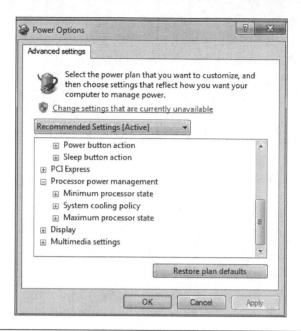

Figure 6.6   Viewing a portion of settings that were not previously displayed.

in Figure 6.5. Once you click on that link and scroll slightly down the resulting dialog box, the Power Options dialog box will appear similar to the box illustrated in Figure 6.6, showing a System cooling policy between the Minimum processor state and Maximum processor state entries. By default the Minimum processor state is set at 5%, whereas the Maximum processor state is set to 100%. The Minimum processor state is used to set the minimum performance state of the processor in percent and when selected you can either use the upper or lower arrows or directly enter a percentage in the resulting box. Similarly, the Maximum performance state is used to define the maximum performance state of the processor in percent and is changed in the same manner as the Minimum processor state.

Between the minimum and maximum processor states is the System cooling policy. This option lets you change the cooling mode of your system. There are two options available: Active, which increases the fan speed before slowing the processor to maintain cooling, and Passive, which slows down the processor before speeding up the fan. Passive saves a lot more power as it reduces the clock on your processor. Although the System cooling policy is usually implemented on laptops and notebooks to enhance battery time, you can consider its use for desktops where employees primarily use a computer for word processing and do not need the full capability of a modern processor.

Display

Through the use of the display entry you can define the time in minutes after a period of inactivity that will cause the display to turn off. You can also use this entry to extend the time that the operating system waits to turn off the display, which is referred to as the Active display. In addition, you can control the brightness of the display. By default the display is set to turn off after 15 minutes of inactivity and you can change this entry by either entering another period in minutes or clicking on an upper or lower facing arrow to adjust the time. The Active display entry by default is set to on, which means that by simply clicking a mouse or keyboard entry the display period for inactivity begins anew. You can consider setting this entry to off if you observe that your user community is abusing the default setting. The third setting, Display brightness, by default is set to 100% and when clicked upon can be adjusted by either clicking on an arrow or directly entering a percentage.

Multimedia Settings

The last entry in the Power Options dialog box is the multimedia settings entry. This entry is used to configure power settings when a device is playing media from the computer. Currently, when sharing media there are three options from which a selection can be made. The default option is to prevent idling to sleep, whereas other options include allowing the computer to sleep and allowing the computer to enter Away Mode. Concerning the latter, this is a feature that enables the computer to appear off to the user when it is actually operational and processing one or more background media tasks, such as recording a television program or streaming media to another device. In an office environment you probably do not want computers to enter the Away mode of operation. In addition to many office environments not having a reason to use this setting, when employees have the ability to use it, it will result in an inability to allow the computer to go into a full sleep mode of operation.

Computer Power Efficiency

When you have used Windows 7 for a while you probably discovered that it contains a wealth of features that are not well publicized. One of those features is the ability to generate an energy-efficiency report. That report will analyze the energy efficiency of the computer as well as indicate any problems and if the machine is a laptop or notebook, can be used to determine if one or more settings are consuming a significant amount of battery power.

The literal key to the use of the energy report occurs through the command line interface, which for old DOS users is easy to recognize; however, for other readers it may not be so obvious and warrants a degree of explanation concerning its use. In addition, you need to run the command prompt as an administrator even if you are logged onto Windows with administrator settings.

Accessing the Command Prompt

You can access the command prompt by clicking on Start and then typing "command prompt" into the search box, right-clicking on Command Prompt, and then selecting "Run as Administrator" option from the resulting menu list. Figure 6.7 illustrates the selection of the Run as Administrator option from the drop-down menu. The reason this is important is that it changes the directory from where you were previously to the C:\windows\windows32 directory where the file you are invoking resides.

To obtain an appreciation for the power of the program this author used his knowledge of DOS to display the options associated with the program. Using the "/?" after the command results in a listing of the program options, however, because they are considerable they will rapidly scroll off the screen, although you can use the scroll bar to view the listing. As an alternative, you can pipe the listing to a file through the use of the greater than sign (>) and then read the file into Word, which this author did by the following command:

```
powercfg /? >myfile.01
```

As a result of the use of the above DOS command the options associated with the use of the powercfg command are placed onto the file

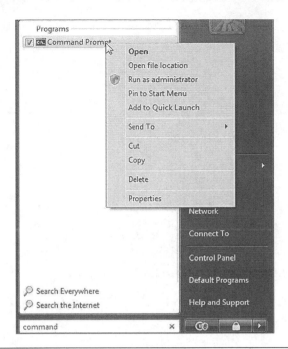

Figure 6.7   Running the command prompt as administrator.

named myfile.01, which is then imported into Word and duplicated as Figure 6.8 so we can review some of the many options associated with this program.

As indicated in Figure 6.8, the powercfg command line provides you with another tool to control the power settings on a computer. By entering the command followed by either the dash (–) List or –L you can list the power schemes applicable to the computer's environment. Through the –Query or simply the –Q command, you can display the contents of a specified power scheme. Note that the –Change or simply the –C option allows you to change a value in the current power scheme. Although some people may prefer to work with DOS, for the majority of commands you will more than likely prefer to use the graphic user interface previously covered in our discussion of power options. However, there are many options, such as devicequery and energy that are restricted to use via the command line in the present version of Windows. For example, –devicequery can be used to return a list of devices that meet a specified criterion, such as devices that support hibernation. Another key example is the use of the –energy option, so let's turn our attention to its use.

```
POWERCFG <command line options>
Description:
  This command line tool enables users to control the power settings on
  a system.

Parameter List:
-LIST, -L    Lists all power schemes in the current user's environment.

             Usage: POWERCFG -LIST

-QUERY, -Q   Displays the contents of the specified power scheme.

             Usage: POWERCFG -QUERY <SCHEME_GUID> <SUB_GUID>

             <SCHEME_GUID>(optional) Specifies the GUID of the power
                          scheme to display, can be obtained by using
                          powercfg -l.
             <SUB_GUID>   (optional) Specifies the GUID of the subgroup
                          to display.     Requires a SCHEME_GUID to
                          be provided.

             If neither SCHEME_GUID or SUB_GUID are provided, the set-
             tings of the current user's active power scheme are dis-
             played. If SUB_GUID is not specified, all settings in the
             specified power scheme are displayed.

-CHANGE, -X Modifies a setting value in the current power scheme.

             Usage: POWERCFG -X <SETTING> <VALUE>

             <SETTING>        Specifies one of the following options:
                              -monitor-timeout-ac <minutes>
                              -monitor-timeout-dc <minutes>
                              -disk-timeout-ac <minutes>
                              -disk-timeout-dc <minutes>
                              -standby-timeout-ac <minutes>
                              -standby-timeout-dc <minutes>
                              -hibernate-timeout-ac <minutes>
                              -hibernate-timeout-dc <minutes>

             Example:
               POWERCFG -Change -monitor-timeout-ac 5

             This would set the monitor idle timeout value to 5 minutes
             when on AC power.

  -CHANGENAME        Modifies the name of a power scheme and optionally
                     its description.
             Usage: POWERCFG -CHANGENAME <GUID> <name> <scheme
             description>
```

Figure 6.8   Powercfg command line options.

```
                    If the description is omitted only the name will be
                    changed.

-DUPLICATESCHEME
                    Duplicates the specified power scheme. The resulting GUID
                    which represents the new scheme will be displayed.

                    Usage: POWERCFG -DUPLICATESCHEME <GUID> <destination GUID>

                    <GUID>  Specifies a scheme GUID obtained by using the pow-
                            ercfg -l.

                    If <destination GUID> is omitted, a new GUID will be cre-
                    ated for the duplicated scheme.

-DELETE, -D Deletes the power scheme with the specified GUID.

                    Usage: POWERCFG -DELETE <GUID>

                    <GUID>   obtained by using the LIST parameter.

-DELETESETTING
                    Deletes a power setting.

                    Usage: POWERCFG -DELETESETTING <SUB_GUID> <SETTING_GUID>

                    <SUB_GUID>      Specifies the subgroup GUID.
                    <SETTING_GUID>  Specifies the power setting guid.

-SETACTIVE, -S
                    Makes the specified power scheme active on the system.

                    Usage: POWERCFG -SETACTIVE <SCHEME_GUID>

                    <SCHEME_GUID>   Specifies the scheme guid.

-GETACTIVESCHEME
                    Retrieve the currently active power scheme.

                    Usage: POWERCFG -GETACTIVESCHEME

-SETACVALUEINDEX
                    Sets a value associated with a specified power setting
                    while the system is powered by AC power.

                    Usage: POWERCFG -SETACVALUEINDEX <SCHEME_GUID> <SUB_GUID>
                    <SETTING_GUID> <SettingIndex>

                    <SCHEME_GUID>   Specifies a power scheme GUID and may be
                                    obtained by using PowerCfg /L.
```

Figure 6.8 (*Continued*)   Powercfg command line options.

                           `<SUB_GUID>`   Specifies a subgroup of power setting GUID and may be obtained by using "PowerCfg /Q."

          `<SETTING_GUID>` Specifies an individual power setting GUID and may be obtained by using "PowerCfg /Q".

          `<SettingIndex>` Specifies which of the list of of possible values this power setting will be set to.

Example:

   POWERCFG -SetAcValueIndex `<GUID>` `<GUID>` `<GUID>` 5

This would set the power setting's AC value to the 5th entry in the list of possible values for this power setting.

-SETDCVALUEINDEX

Sets a value associated with a specified power setting while the system is powered by DC power.

Usage: POWERCFG -SETDCVALUEINDEX `<SCHEME_GUID>` `<SUB_GUID>` `<SETTING_GUID>` `<SettingIndex>`

`<SCHEME_GUID>` Specifies a power scheme GUID and may be obtained by using PowerCfg /L.

`<SUB_GUID>`   Specifies a subgroup of power setting GUID and may be obtained by using "PowerCfg /Q."

`<SETTING_GUID>` Specifies an individual power setting GUID and may be obtained by using "PowerCfg /Q".

`<SettingIndex>` Specifies which of the list of possible values this setting will be set to.

Example:

   POWERCFG -SetDcValueIndex `<GUID>` `<GUID>` `<GUID>` 5

This would set the power setting's DC value to the 5th entry in the list of possible values for this power setting.

-HIBERNATE, -H

Enables-Disables the hibernate feature. Hibernate timeout is not supported on all systems.

Usage: POWERCFG -H `<ON|OFF>`

          POWERCFG -H -Size `<PercentSize>`

-Size   Specifies the desired hiberfile size in percentage of the total memory. The default size cannot be smaller than 50.

       This switch will also enable the hiberfile automatically.

-AVAILABLESLEEPSTATES, -A

Reports the sleep states available on the system Attempts to report reasons why sleep states are unavailable.

Figure 6.8 (*Continued*)   Powercfg command line options.

```
-DEVICEQUERY
          Return a list wof devices that meet the specified criteria.

          Usage: POWERCFG -DEVICEQUERY <queryflags>

          <queryflags>    Secifies one of the following criteria:

          wake_from_S1_supported   Return all devices that support
                                   waking the system from a light
                                   sleep state.
          wake_from_S2_supported   Return all devices that support
                                   waking the system from a deeper
                                   sleep state.
          wake_from_S3_supported   Return all devices that sup-
                                   port waking the system from the
                                   deepest sleep state.
          wake_from_any            Return all devices that support
                                   waking the system from any sleep
                                   state.
          S1_supported             List devices supporting light
                                   sleep.
          S2_supported             List devices supporting deeper
                                   sleep.
          S3_supported             List devices supporting deepest
                                   sleep.
          S4_supported             List devices supporting
                                   hibernation.
          wake_programmable        List devices that are user-
                                   configurable to wake the system
                                   from a sleep state.
          wake_armed               List devices that are currently
                                   configured to wake the system
                                   from any sleep state.
          all_devices              Return all devices present in
                                   the system.
          all_devices_verbose      Return verbose list of devices.
          Example:
            POWERCFG -DEVICEQUERY wake_armed

-DEVICEENABLEWAKE
          Enable the device to wake the system from a sleep state.

          Usage: POWERCFG -DEVICEENABLEWAKE <devicename>

          <devicename>    Specifies a device retrieved using
                          "PowerCfg -DEVICEQUERY wake_programmable".

          Example:
            POWERCFG -DEVICEENABLEWAKE

                                   "Microsoft USB IntelliMouse
                                   Explorer"
```

Figure 6.8 (*Continued*) Powercfg command line options.

```
-DEVICEDISABLEWAKE <devicename> disable the device from waking the
system
                Disable the device from waking the system from a sleep
                state

                Usage: POWERCFG -DEVICEDISABLEWAKE

                <devicename>     Specifies a device retrieved using
                                 "PowerCfg -DEVICEQUERY wake_armed".

-IMPORT         Imports all power settings from the specified file.

                Usage: POWERCFG -IMPORT <filename> <GUID>

                <filename>       Specify a fully-qualified path to a file
                                 generated by using "PowerCfg -EXPORT
                                 parameter".
                <GUID>           (optional) The settings are loaded into a
                                 power scheme represented by this GUID. If
                                 not supplied, powercfg will generate and
                                 use a new GUID

                Example:
                  POWERCFG -IMPORT c:\scheme.pow

-EXPORT         Exports power scheme, represented by the specified GUID, to
                the specified file.

                Usage: POWERCFG -EXPORT <filename> <GUID>

                <filename>       Specify a fully-qualified path to a desti-
                                 nation file.
                <GUID>           specifies a power scheme GUID and may be
                                 obtained by using "PowerCfg /L"

                Example:
                  POWERCFG -EXPORT c:\scheme.pow
                                        381b4222-f694-41f0-9685-
                                        ff5bb260df2e

-LASTWAKE       Reports information about what woke the system from the
                last sleep transition

-HELP, -?       Displays information on command-line parameters.

-ALIASES        Displays all aliases and their corresponding GUIDs. The
                user may use these aliases in place of any GUID on the
                commandline.
```

Figure 6.8 (*Continued*)   Powercfg command line options.

```
-SETSECURITYDESCRIPTOR
            Sets a security descriptor associated with a specified
            power setting, power scheme, or action.

            Usage: POWERCFG -SETSECURITYDESCRIPTOR <GUID|ACTION> <SDDL>

            <GUID>          Specifies a power scheme or a power set-
                            ting GUID.
            <ACTION>        Can be one of the following strings:
                            ActionSetActive, ActionCreate,
                            ActionDefault
            <SDDL>          Specifies a valid security descrip-
                            tor string in SDDL format. Call POWERCFG
                            -GETSECURITYDESCRIPTOR to see an example
                            SDDL STRING.

-GETSECURITYDESCRIPTOR
            Gets a security descriptor associated with a specified
            power setting, power scheme, or action.

            Usage: POWERCFG -GETSECURITYDESCRIPTOR <GUID|ACTION>
            <GUID>          Specifies a power scheme or a power set-
                            ting GUID.
            <ACTION>        Can be one of the following strings:
                            ActionSetActive, ActionCreate,
                            ActionDefault

-REQUESTS
            Enumerate application and driver Power Requests. Power
            Requests prevent the computer from automatically powering
            off the display or entering a low-power sleep mode.

-REQUESTSOVERRIDE
            Sets a Power Request override for a particular Process,
            Service, or Driver. If no parameters are specified,
            this command displays the current list of Power Request
            Overrides.

            Usage: POWERCFG -REQUESTSOVERRIDE <CALLER_TYPE> <NAME>
            <REQUEST>
            <CALLER_TYPE>   Specifies one of the following caller type:
                            PROCESS, SERVICE, DRIVER. This is obtained
                            by calling the POWERCFG -REQUESTS command.
            <NAME>          Specifies the caller name. This is the name
                            returned from calling POWERCFG -REQUESTS
                            command.
            <REQUEST>       Specifies one or more of the following
                            Power
                            Request Types: Display, System, Awaymode.
            Example:
              POWERCFG -REQUESTSOVERRIDE PROCESS wmplayer.exe Display
              System
```

Figure 6.8 (*Continued*)   Powercfg command line options.

```
-ENERGY
                Analyze the system for common energy-efficiency and battery
                life problems. The ENERGY command should be used when the
                computer is idle and with no open programs or documents.
                The ENERGY command will generate an HTML report file in
                the current path. The ENERGY command supports the follow-
                ing optional parameters:

                Usage:   POWERCFG -ENERGY [-OUTPUT <FILENAME>] [-XML]
                                          [-DURATION <SECONDS>]
                         POWERCFG -ENERGY -TRACE [-D <FILEPATH>]
                                                  [-DURATION <SECONDS>]
                -OUTPUT <FILENAME>        - Specify the path and filename to
                                            store the energy report HTML file.
                -XML                      - Format the report file as XML.
                -TRACE                    - Record system behavior and do
                                            not perform analysis. Trace files
                                            will be generated in the current
                                            path unless the -D parameter is
                                            specified.
                -D <FILEPATH>             - Specify the directory to store
                                            trace data. May only be used with
                                            the -TRACE parameter.
                -DURATION <SECONDS> - Specify the number of seconds
                                            to observe system behavior.
                                            Default is 60 seconds.
-WAKETIMERS
                Enumerate the active wake timers. If enabled, the
                expiration of a wake timer wakes the system from
                sleep and hibernate states.
```

Figure 6.8 (*Continued*)   Powercfg command line options.

Examining an Energy Report

The best method to illustrate a point is by performing an operation, therefore this author used his mini-notebook as a platform to run an energy report. To do so he entered the administrative mode at the command prompt and then typed the following command:

```
powercfg -energy
```

As a result of the previously described action the computer will display several lines of information, with the first line informing you that tracing is enabled for 60 seconds, followed by a line informing you that system behavior is being observed and another line stating that the trace data are being analyzed. After what may appear to be a long time but in actuality is about two minutes or less you will receive an "analysis complete" message followed by a list of any energy efficiency problems categorized as errors, warnings, and informational.

To view the report that was generated as an HTML report you would enter the following command:

```
energy-report.html
```

Depending upon the browsers installed and which is set as the default browser, the reports first page in Internet Explorer would appear as shown in Figure 6.9. In Figure 6.10 you will find a copy of the complete report that examined the power efficiency of this author's HP small notebook computer that was purposely configured so it would generate a variety of errors and warnings. Note that instead of illustrating the report as a series of web pages this author piped the output of the report to a file that was then imported into Microsoft Word and pasted as in Figure 6.10.

In examining the first page of the power efficiency diagnostic report shown in an Internet Explorer window in Figure 6.9 note that you can view the first six errors. Remember that in this example the computer upon which the report was run was a notebook, which means that certain errors that occurred may not be applicable for a desktop where your concern for battery life does not normally come into play.

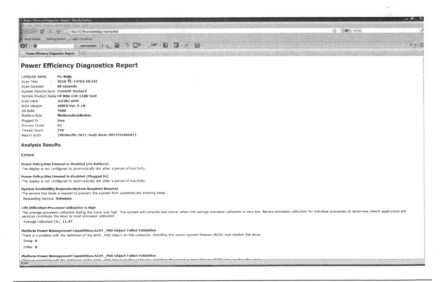

Figure 6.9 A portion of a power efficiency diagnostic report.

Power Efficiency Diagnostics Report

Computer Name	PC-MINI
Scan Time	2010-11-14T02:49:33Z
Scan Duration	60 seconds
System Manufacturer	Hewlett-Packard
System Product Name	HP Mini 110-1100 Tord
BIOS Date	10/06/2009
BIOS Version	308F0 Ver. F.18
OS Build	7600
Platform Role	PlatformRoleMobile
Plugged In	true
Process Count	62
Thread Count	776
Report GUID	{9b48e7fb-7073-4ed9-8a4e-8071f5abb681}

Analysis Results

Errors

Power Policy: Dim timeout is disabled (On Battery)

The display is not configured to automatically dim after a period of inactivity.

Power Policy: Dim timeout is disabled (Plugged In)

The display is not configured to automatically dim after a period of inactivity.

System Availability Requests: System Required Request

The service has made a request to prevent the system from automatically entering sleep.

Requesting Service   **Schedule**

CPU Utilization: Processor utilization is high

The average processor utilization during the trace was high. The system will consume less power when the average processor utilization is very low. Review processor utilization for individual processes to determine which applications and services contribute the most to total processor utilization.

Average Utilization (%)   **11.37**

Platform Power Management Capabilities: ACPI _PSD Object Failed Validation

There is a problem with the definition of the ACPI _PSD object on this computer. Installing the latest system firmware (BIOS) may resolve this issue.

Group   **0**
Index   **0**

Platform Power Management Capabilities: ACPI _PSD Object Failed Validation

There is a problem with the definition of the ACPI _PSD object on this computer. Installing the latest system firmware (BIOS) may resolve this issue.

Group   **0**
Index   **1**

Warnings

Power Policy: Display timeout is long (Plugged In)

The display is configured to turn off after longer than 10 minutes.

Timeout (seconds)   **900**

Figure 6.10   The complete power efficiency diagnostic report.

Power Policy: 802.11 Radio Power Policy is Maximum Performance (Plugged In)

The current power policy for 802.11-compatible wireless network adapters is not configured to use low-power modes.

CPU Utilization: Individual process with significant processor utilization.

This process is responsible for a significant portion of the total processor utilization recorded during the trace.

Process Name	**svchost.exe**
PID	**932**
Average Utilization (%)	**4.72**
Module	Average Module Utilization (%)
\SystemRoot\system32\ntkrnlpa.exe	1.84
\Device\HarddiskVolume2\Windows\System32\ntdll.dll	0.72
\Device\HarddiskVolume2\Windows\System32\msxml3.dll	0.42

CPU Utilization: Individual process with significant processor utilization.

This process is responsible for a significant portion of the total processor utilization recorded during the trace.

Process Name	**System**
PID	**4**
Average Utilization (%)	**3.40**
Module	Average Module Utilization (%)
\SystemRoot\system32\ntkrnlpa.exe	0.90
\SystemRoot\system32\DRIVERS\bcmwl6.sys	0.76
\SystemRoot\System32\drivers\tcpip.sys	0.45

CPU Utilization: Individual process with significant processor utilization.

This process is responsible for a significant portion of the total processor utilization recorded during the trace.

Process Name	**svchost.exe**
PID	**892**
Average Utilization (%)	**0.33**
Module	Average Module Utilization (%)
\Device\HarddiskVolume2\Windows\System32\sysmain.dll	0.24
\Device\HarddiskVolume2\Windows\System32\msvcrt.dll	0.06
\SystemRoot\system32\ntkrnlpa.exe	0.00

CPU Utilization: Individual process with significant processor utilization.

This process is responsible for a significant portion of the total processor utilization recorded during the trace.

Process Name	**javaw.exe**
PID	**3476**
Average Utilization (%)	**0.28**
Module	Average Module Utilization (%)

Figure 6.10 (*Continued*)   The complete power efficiency diagnostic report.

\Device\HarddiskVolume2\Program Files\Hewlett-Packard\	
HP QuickSync\jre\bin\client\jvm.dll	0.07
	0.06
\SystemRoot\system32\ntkrnlpa.exe	0.06

CPU Utilization: Individual process with significant processor utilization.

This process is responsible for a significant portion of the total processor utilization recorded during the trace.

Process Name	**explorer.exe**
PID	**3056**
Average Utilization (%)	**0.21**
Module	**Average Module Utilization (%)**
\SystemRoot\System32\win32k.sys	**0.08**
\SystemRoot\system32\ntkrnlpa.exe	**0.04**
\Device\HarddiskVolume2\Windows\System32\ntdll.dll	**0.01**

Information

Platform Timer Resolution: Platform Timer Resolution

The default platform timer resolution is 15.6ms (15625000ns) and should be used whenever the system is idle. If the timer resolution is increased, processor power management technologies may not be effective. The timer resolution may be increased due to multimedia playback or graphical animations.

Current Timer Resolution (100 ns units)   **156000**

Power Policy: Active Power Plan

The current power plan in use

Plan Name	**OEM Balanced**
Plan GUID	**{381b4222-f694-41f0-9685-ff5bb260df2e}**

Power Policy: Power Plan Personality (On Battery)

The personality of the current power plan when the system is on battery power.

Personality   **Balanced**

Power Policy: Video Quality (On Battery)

Enables Windows Media Player to optimize for quality or power savings when playing video.

Quality Mode   **Balance Video Quality and Power Savings**

Power Policy: Power Plan Personality (Plugged In)

The personality of the current power plan when the system is plugged in.

Personality   **Balanced**

Power Policy: Video quality (Plugged In)

Enables Windows Media Player to optimize for quality or power savings when playing video.

Quality Mode   **Optimize for Video Quality**

Figure 6.10 (*Continued*)   The complete power efficiency diagnostic report.

USB Suspend: Analysis Success

Analysis was successful. No energy efficiency problems were found. No information was returned.

Battery: Battery Information

Battery ID	**Hewlett-PackardPrimary**
Manufacturer	**Hewlett-Packard**
Serial Number	
Chemistry	**LION**
Long Term	1
Design Capacity	**27540**
Last Full Charge	**26428**

Platform Power Management Capabilities: Supported Sleep States

Sleep states allow the computer to enter low-power modes after a period of inactivity. The S3 sleep state is the default sleep state for Windows platforms. The S3 sleep state consumes only enough power to preserve memory contents and allow the computer to resume working quickly. Very few platforms support the S1 or S2 Sleep states.

S1 Sleep Supported	**false**
S2 Sleep Supported	**false**
S3 Sleep Supported	**true**
S4 Sleep Supported	**true**

Platform Power Management Capabilities: Adaptive Display Brightness is supported.

This computer enables Windows to automatically control the brightness of the integrated display.

Platform Power Management Capabilities: Processor Power Management Capabilities

Effective processor power management enables the computer to automatically balance performance and energy consumption.

Group	0
Index	0
Idle (C) State Count	3
Performance (P) State Count	4
Throttle (T) State Count	0

Platform Power Management Capabilities: Processor Power Management Capabilities

Effective processor power management enables the computer to automatically balance performance and energy consumption.

Group	0
Index	1
Idle (C) State Count	3
Performance (P) State Count	4
Throttle (T) State Count	0

Figure 6.10 (*Continued*)   The complete power efficiency diagnostic report.

The first error is due to the display timeout not being set when on battery power, and the second error message is the same when on AC power. Although more important for many laptop and notebook computers than desktops, this should also be set for desktop computers. The third error message indicates that the service has made a request to prevent the system from automatically entering sleep mode. Through the use of different types of availability requests, applications, services, and even drivers can temporarily disable power management features, such as preventing the display from turning off.

The next error message indicates that the processor utilization level is high, which unless you're a power user is probably not necessary for such typical functions as word processing and minor spreadsheet use.

Figure 6.10 shows the complete power efficiency diagnostic report that was run on this author's mini-notebook computer. Note that two of the errors inform us that we may need to update the basic input/output system (BIOS) to alleviate the fifth error, which concerns the definition of the advanced configuration and power interface (ACPI _PSD) object on the computer.

After displaying a series of errors the report continues by displaying a series of warnings. Remember that the report was executed on a mini-notebook computer, so the first warning was expected as this author used AC power to provide power to the computer that had been in his closet after being used on a trip months before. Because it was powered on via AC and being used extensively, the timeout period for the display was considered by Windows to be long. The second warning message concerned the configuration of the wireless LAN adapter, which was set to high for maximum performance whereas the third through eighth warnings indicate that for the type of work performed by this author the utilization level attributed to the processor was considered to be high. Once the warnings are displayed the energy report will show informational messages. Note that the informational messages are truly informational, as they provide a significant amount of information about the power settings on the computer. Although the informational data are self-explanatory, readers should note that the report shown in Figure 6.10 was executed on a computer owned by this author for illustrative purposes and you need to execute the program on the computers in your organization to review their energy efficiency in terms associated with the type of work performed by employees.

Now that we have reviewed the potential utilization of energy reports provided by Windows let's turn our attention to communications, or more specifically what is referred to as Wake-on-LAN technology.

Wake-on-LAN

Wake-on-LAN represents an Ethernet network technology that enables a computer to be turned on or awakened remotely over the network, hence its name. Although this feature is not very valuable for the home hobbyist, it can be an important tool for an organization. This is because it can be used to wake up sleeping machines to apply security patches or software updates at times when employees are out of the office. To activate this capability you first need to enable this capability in BIOS and the network adapter or adapter card. To access BIOS you would boot the computer and press the applicable key displayed to enter the BIOS setup. Once in BIOS you would go to the power management area and look for the Wake-on-LAN setting. Although some computers are shipped with this setting enabled, this is not always the case, thus, you need to verify it is enabled and exit BIOS and then start the computer. Note that there are numerous versions of BIOS and some may not have an option under power management for a Wake-on-LAN setting. Instead, the Wake-on-LAN capability may be in another section so you may need to search through your BIOS options. Once enabled you then have to enable it again in Windows.

Enabling Wake-on-LAN in Windows The manner by which you enable Wake-on-LAN in Windows varies slightly based upon the version of Windows used. If you're using Vista, you would right-click on Computer, whereas under Windows 7 you would right-click on My Computer. For either version of Windows you would select Properties and then click on Device Manager and locate your network card in the list of hardware displayed. You would then perform another right-click operation and click on Properties again. Now you would select the Power Management tab as illustrated in Figure 6.11. By clicking on the entry labeled "Allow this device to wake the computer" you are

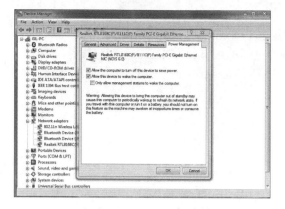

Figure 6.11   Enabling Wake-on-LAN in Windows.

enabling the Wake-on-LAN capability in Windows, however, we are not quite done. First, by clicking on the third entry we can limit the capability of waking the computer to management stations, which in an organization makes sense because you do not want April-fool type actions to occur. Second, we need to consider two options under the Advanced tab for the network adapter. The first option, Wake from Shutdown is shown in Figure 6.12.

Wake-on-LAN Capabilities   The Wake-on-LAN capabilities entry is shown selected in Figure 6.12. There are four possible settings for this option and its selection needs to be set so the computer's network adapter will recognize that it needs to wake up the computer. Normally the network card or adapter will listen for a specific packet referred to as a Magic Packet that will be broadcast on the broadcast address for the LAN or a specific subnet. The listening adapter checks the packet to verify its contents and if valid and it contains the network card's media access control (MAC) address, boots the computer. If you are using a Magic Packet to boot computers you need to ensure that the setting is then Magic Packet. Other options include None, Pattern Match, and Pattern Match and Magic Packet.

The Magic Packet   The Magic Packet is a special type of broadcast frame. Within the payload of the frame is 6 bytes of all ones, which is FF FF FF FF FF FF in hexadecimal notation, followed by 16 repetitions of the target computer's 48-bit MAC layer 2 address. Depending upon the program used to wake computers the Magic Packet may be

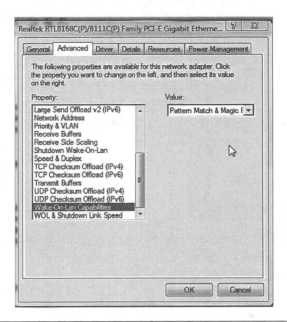

Figure 6.12   Selecting a value for Wake-on LAN capability.

transmitted as a user datagram protocol (UDP) datagram with a destination port of 0, 7, or 9.

Another Option to Consider   A second option that may need adjustment is the one located under the Wake-on-LAN property, WOL & Shutdown Link Speed. Here you want to ensure you have the correct network speed selected.

Limitations   Although Wake-on-LAN has several significant advantages for use in an organization that periodically needs to install security patches and software updates, it also has some limitations. Those limitations concern the inability to perform the operation wirelessly, the lack of delivery confirmation, lack of security, and the fact that the capability is connected to a specific computer.

Wireless Network Use

A Magic Packet or another sequence required to wake a computer can be transmitted over a wireless network, however, a wireless card is powered down when a computer is in a sleep mode of operation. This means that the Magic Packet will be ignored by wireless adapter cards. The only way to successfully transmit a Magic Packet over a wireless network and actually wake a computer is to send it to a conventional Ethernet adapter, which retains enough power to recognize the packet as a signal to wake the computer. Thus, if the Magic Packet flows wirelessly to a wireless hub that has wired connections, such as a wireless bridge, then the Magic Packet becomes capable of being transmitted to a conventional Ethernet port that allows the computer to be awakened.

Delivery Confirmation

Wake-on-LAN can be considered to represent a simplex or one-way transmission method. As such, there is no confirmation that the computer has awakened. Of course, higher-level software can be used to provide an exception list of computers that did not receive an update or security patch, but from a technology standpoint WOL is still a simplex transmission method.

Security Issues

Wake-on-LAN operates at layer 2 in the open system interconnection (OSI) model. This means that it uses media access control addressing that is not secure and which can be easily abused by anyone on the network. In addition, because routers and firewalls typically operate at layer 3 or the Internet Protocol (IP) layer, firewalls and routers may have to be recoded to enable Magic Packets to flow through such devices.

Specific Computer Linkage

Another problem associated with Wake-on-LAN is the need to specify a MAC address for each computer. In the era of the Internet most people, although familiar with IP addressing, have limited knowledge of MAC addressing. Thus, a good program that learns the MAC addresses on a network may alleviate the necessity to either record or become familiar with the MAC addresses on your network.

Although Wake-on-LAN has a number of limitations, there are many programs that allow network managers and the system administrator to use this capability to update computers on a network. In addition, WOL is being supplemented and eventually succeeded by the desktop and mobile architecture for system hardware (DASH). DASH represents a standard suite of specifications from the distributed management task force (DMTF), which provides a standard for secure out-of-band and remote management of both desktop and mobile computers. Under the latest version of DASH, which was version 1.1 at the time this book was prepared, some features include the ability to remotely change BIOS settings as well as the ability to manage network ports that provide a LAN interface for updating software. With this capability to be performed in a standardized manner you can expect to have a number of management programs available to both conserve energy as well as wake up computers to apply security patches and updates.

7

MAKING YOUR DATA CENTER
ENERGY EFFICIENT

In this concluding chapter our focus of attention is upon using information presented in this chapter as well as some information previously presented in the earlier chapters in this book. To do so we concentrate on examining the use of different techniques to reduce energy consumption. Some techniques mentioned may only reduce your energy consumption by a percent or two, however, as many people might note, cumulatively the total savings can become significant. Thus, the old adage about saving a dollar here and a dollar there can result in some serious savings is true.

Techniques to Consider

In this chapter we summarize a variety of techniques you need to check by providing information on numerous techniques that can be used to reduce energy use. Such information can be considered by both owners and renters of offices. Concerning the latter, even if your organization does not own the facility or have the ability to perform building modifications this information can be used to provide building owners with the ability to consider such modifications to keep your organization as a tenant.

Finding Energy Loss

One saying that bears repeating is the fact that the cheapest kilowatt is the one you don't use. With this in mind, when we can locate an area where we are losing energy and take corrective action we can use less energy, in effect obtaining a large number of the cheapest kilowatts because we will be able to lower the number we use.

One of the first things you need to consider to locate areas where energy loss is occurring is to obtain an interior and exterior view of your data center with respect to thermal loss. Doing so will point out areas where you may be able to reduce thermal loss easily through the use of insulation or tightly closing doors and windows that may appear to be closed but in reality are not. Infrared thermography represents a quick and easy method of detecting energy waste. In addition, it can be used to detect moisture and electrical issues in buildings. Through the use of an infrared camera you can easily determine where potential problems are located and take effective action to alleviate problems that are detected. For example, from the outside of the data center you can use a thermal image sensor to determine if there are areas around doors and windows that need weather-stripping or if some areas of an exterior wall show excessive cooling or heating loss that could indicate the areas that insulation didn't cover. Similarly, within a data center you can use a thermal image sensor to determine if there are hot spots where equipment resides that may require either the movement of equipment or air ducts.

One of the leaders in thermal imaging is FLIR, which offers several types of thermal sensors, ranging from handheld point and shoot to more sophisticated devices. Readers are referred to the website www.flir.com or you can enter the term "thermal imaging energy loss" into a search engine to obtain information concerning different thermal imaging products.

Replacing Monitors

Until a few years ago your choice for obtaining monitors was limited to either antiquated cathode-ray tube (CRT) devices or the more modern and sometimes less energy-efficient liquid crystal display (LCD) flat panel monitors, that in addition to being energy hogs had at least the saving grace that their use considerably reduced the footprint of a monitor on an employee's desk. This author remembers the first time an LCD display replaced the large, bulky CRT displays, resulting in workers discovering that they now had a large desk on which to place information that would be visually available for use. What some people fail to realize is the fact that light-emitting devices (LEDs) are now being used in a new class of monitors that offers the potential to reduce power consumption by approximately 40% beyond the energy use associated with LCD displays. For people at call centers and other workers who need their monitors to be on throughout the day, the power savings by themselves may be able to justify the replacement of existing monitors. Thus, soliciting bids or comparing monitor costs and using the financial information presented in the first chapter of this book can be used to determine the payback time where the lower use of power and associated reduced electrical cost begins to exceed the replacement cost of new monitors. Using this information will allow you to make an intelligent, fiscally based decision concerning the practicality of replacing monitors.

Waiting Area Display

One of the more interesting aspects of some data centers is their waiting areas where visitors check in and wait for someone to escort them to the person with whom they have an appointment. Similar to an airport gate, the waiting area typically has a row of chairs or a couch facing a television monitor hanging from the ceiling with the channel invariably set to an all-news broadcast channel, such as CNN. For reasons that remain beyond comprehension, during late 2010 this author was able to note several data center waiting areas that had very large first-generation plasma-based flat screen televisions, either hanging from the ceiling or when extremely large, sitting on a table and facing an area that more often than not was devoid of humanity. Although this author was a bit curious about when those televisions were turned off, after my meetings were over I did not stay around to the end of the day to see if anyone turned them off. However, I did learn that all too often the most energy-efficient data center may not consider its waiting area.

Although you might be tempted to leave well enough alone, today you can considerably reduce energy consumption by simply replacing first-generation plasma-based flat screen televisions with LED backlight flat screen televisions. In fact, for approximately $300 during Christmas 2010 you could purchase a 42-inch LED backlight high definition (HD) television with several high definition multimedia interface (HDMI) ports as well as a coaxial port. Because this type of television uses approximately 130 watts whereas a first-generation plasma television may consume double that amount, over an 8-hour day this can result in a savings of approximately 1 kWh per day. If the data center waiting area leaves the TV on a 24/7 schedule, the savings will exceed 3 kWh per day, or approximately 1,100 kWh per year. Depending upon the cost per kWh in your area, you might recover the cost of a replacement television in approximately two years, a recovery period that normally makes your accountant salivate.

Although the prior illustration concerned the replacement of a first-generation plasma television with an LED backlight television, you can also consider its replacement with a more modern plasma television. In fact, according to ads run by Panasonic in the *Wall Street Journal* during December 2010, their Viera HDTV ultra-slim 42-inch plasma TV is powered by under 99 watts. In addition, if you are concerned about the environment you will also find the facts that the TV is mercury-free, uses lead-free solder, has no lead in its glass, and provides a life span exceeding 100,000 hours to be a very attractive series of additional features. With a life exceeding 100,000 hours and a year containing 8,760 hours you could actually leave the television on 24/7 until the data center closed. This is not recommended, but it does illustrate the fact that purchasing a modern television results in a product life that can easily satisfy most if not all longevity requirements.

Upgrading the Operating System

As strange as it may sound, depending upon the existing operating system used by servers and personal computers significant energy savings may occur when they are upgraded. For example, under both Windows 7 and Windows Server 2008 R2 features were added that can reduce the energy consumption of the hardware. In addition, Windows Server 2000 R2 supports the advanced configuration and power interface (ACPI) processor management features described briefly in Chapter 6 that can be used for controlling the power profile of servers. For Windows 7 personal computers, organizations can write scripts to operate the previously described powercfg.exe program to manage the power settings on client computers. Similarly, if your data center uses Sun, UNIX, or another operating system (OS), you may wish to examine the availability and cost of upgrades as well as the energy-saving features incorporated into those OSs.

Purchase Energy Star Compliant Products

The Energy Star program was launched in 1992 by the U.S. Department of Energy and the U.S. Environmental Protection Agency. Until a few years ago it was a recognized fact that under the prior Energy Star approval process it was not necessary for manufacturers to have their paperwork approved by an independent third party, resulting in a few vendors sort of bending the curve. Today that glitch in the Energy Star approval process has been removed, resulting in test results provided by the vendor having to be first submitted to an accredited laboratory. Thus, when you now purchase Energy Star certified monitors, computers, and even refrigerators and microwave ovens for the break room you know that the product specifications including its use of energy were verified by an independent laboratory. Today energy-rated products are available in over 60 categories. Such rated products provide either the same or better performance in comparison to other products while using less energy.

Although Energy Star products are available in many countries in Europe, European Union (EU) legislatures approved a new method by which EU energy efficiency labels will allow for up to three new energy classes that will enable technological progress in reducing power consumption to be noted. The new method of labeling in effect enables narrower distinctions in the classification of a product's energy use as well as the use of color codes to denote different levels of power efficiency. Under the color-coding scheme the highest energy-efficient products are denoted by a dark green label and the least energy-efficient products have a red label. One of the more interesting aspects of the use of color-coded labels is the fact that the labels will also apply to construction products that do not consume energy but have a significant impact on energy savings, such as door frames, outside doors, and windows.

Consolidation and Virtualization

If you examine the performance of servers in a data center there is a high degree of probability that you will find some servers with a limited level of both utilization and level of performance. In fact, if you have a Windows-based server, one of the built-in tools you can

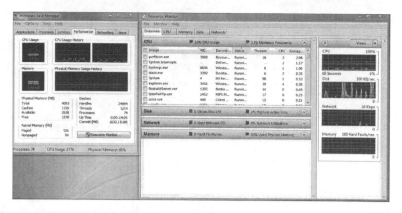

Figure 7.1   Viewing Windows Task Manager and Resource Manager.

easily use is the so-called "three finger salute" to bring up or invoke the Windows Task Manager. From the Windows Task Manager you can instantly view the CPU and memory usage by clicking on the Processor tab as well as view historical data. For example, by clicking on the Applications tab you can determine what applications are being used, whereas other tabs such as Processes, Services, Networking, and Users provide information related to the titles of those tabs. Although the use of the Applications and Performance tabs can be used to determine if the server is a candidate for consolidation, you might want to consider using the Performance tab so you can then select the Resource Monitor button. Figure 7.1 illustrates the result of this action.

In examining Figure 7.1 note that although CPU usage is shown as being 17% in Windows Task Manager, there was a spike due to the use of an image capture program used to capture the portion of the screen shown in the previously referenced figure, with both CPU usage history from the Windows Task Manager and Windows Resource Manager showing a significantly lower level of usage. In fact, if you focus your attention on the right portion of Figure 7.1 that shows the Windows Resource Manager you can note both the current and highest active percentage of use for the CPU, disk, network, and computer memory, with the ability to click on the right arrow to obtain detailed information about computer usage for a specific entity. By examining the usage of a server over time you might be able to determine if it is what is referred to as a ghost server, a server drawing power and extracting a license fee but not performing any useful activity.

In addition to being able to consolidate servers and reduce licensing fees there is another key issue that consolidation achieves: a reduction in the direct and indirect consumption of electricity. A reduction in direct electricity results from the fact that consolidating servers results in less energy being used to power the remaining servers, even if larger capacity servers are required to perform the operations of a large number of smaller servers. Because power consumption generates heat that must be removed from the data center, each watt saved at the server generates between one and two additional watts saved by not having to remove the extra heat, with the exact number of indirect watts saved based upon the location of the data center and the type of cooling employed.

Although no two data centers are the same you can typically expect an energy reduction between 5 and 10% through the use of virtualization. Whether this reduction is cost effective depends upon the cost associated with virtualization software, possibly expanding existing hardware, and the potential reduction in license fees and energy use.

Telework

It is relatively easy to understand how virtualization can save energy, however, it might be a bit harder to understand the benefits of telework and energy efficiency. Because teleworkers work outside the office they do not require the active use of an organizational computer located at the office, nor do they use office space and require heating and cooling. In fact, some airlines have recognized that not only does the use of teleworkers save energy but, in addition, usually obtains a higher level of performance from employees working at home. This author does not believe organizations should consider telework based upon energy savings, but I do believe that it should be considered along with other factors when considering if teleworking should be implemented.

Consider Cloud Computing

Many years ago this author worked in a data center where a large time-sharing system was labeled "son of a batch." Although the original intention of the sign may have had a more sinister meaning, it did indicate the evolution of batch processing to time sharing, where remote terminal devices shared the use of a central processor and could have their jobs returned to them for printing or directed to high-speed printers physically attached to the computer. If we fast-forward about 40 years we now have the term *cloud computing* where vendors are targeting organizations to use remotely located information technology services via the Internet instead of the low-speed telephone-based connections that were used many years ago. Technology has certainly advanced over the past 40 years, however, the use of this technology involves many of the same considerations as 40 years ago, including the cost associated with cloud computing, security issues, and whether your organization has trained personnel required to perform operations within a data center. What is different when we fast-forward from time-sharing to cloud computing is the promotion of the time-to-market capability of cloud computing, which enables an organization to achieve an information processing capability once an Internet connection is obtained that provides the required bandwidth.

When considering cloud computing, organizations need to consider the fact that moving processing to another organization also moves some energy consumption to the other organization. Because processing uses electricity that generates heat, you need to consider both direct and indirect energy benefits flowing into the picture. In addition, if your organization has an excessive amount of processing capability you might consider becoming a cloud computing facility. Although there are numerous aspects you need to consider, in effect your organization will become a retailer, selling excess computer capability to other organizations. Regardless of whether a user or provider of cloud computing, the key to its effective utilization is the ability of an organization to identify capabilities that can be used remotely through a shared services infrastructure. Once identified, a cost comparison needs to be performed, with both direct and indirect energy costs included along with both tangible and intangible costs. Concerning the latter, politics can be an intangible cost that terminates the use of cloud computing due to the resistance of senior management, an area that is beyond the scope of this book.

Consider Desktop and Server Power Management Products

In the previous chapter in this book we noted how we can configure power management under Windows 7 on a single computer. Such information is helpful, but if our organization has hundreds to thousands of desktops and servers we more than likely want a method to automate our power management settings. Fortunately, there are several desktop and server power management software programs you can consider. We do not recommend a particular program as each organization can have different requirements, but we do discuss some features you may wish to consider. For example, if your organization operates a large number of servers you might consider the ability of software to read the utilization level of each server in a common pool and move workloads to a fewer number of servers in the pool when conditions permit. Then, unused servers can be placed into a low power state and awaken to a load-bearing state when conditions warrant. This capability can significantly reduce energy costs when an organization uses hundreds or thousands of servers during prime time after which utilization levels significantly fall. For each server placed into a low energy state for just 10 hours each day savings can easily exceed $100 per year, with an additional $10 to $30 or more of savings achieved by reducing cooling loads that will depend upon the location of the data center.

In addition to saving energy the use of desktop and server power management products can extend the life of equipment while reducing labor costs. Concerning the former, by placing equipment in a low power state heat buildup is reduced, which will normally extend the life of just about all electronic-based equipment. With respect to labor cost, automating the setting of power management features across an organization reduces the time required to individually set each computer. Assuming your staff can do some other function or functions, the use of power management allows those functions to be performed earlier and perhaps without overtime charges.

Consider Processor Efficiency

Most data centers can be characterized by the periodic replacement of personal computers and servers by new equipment. Although there are many aspects involved when considering the replacement of computers, one that needs consideration is the processor efficiency. Unlike the U.S. Department of Transportation fuel efficiency standards for automobiles that are posted on vehicles when you visit an automobile lot, there are no standards that measure the processor efficiency on a nationwide basis. Instead, you can use the Thermal Design Power (TDP) as a proxy for computer power consumption. The TDP represents a value often used in CPU or graphics card reviews and tests and represents the maximum power consumed by a device under normal and regular use that needs to be dissipated. Thus, you can view the TDP as the maximum power a service can use when operating applications. However, it should be noted that the TDP is not the maximum power consumed by a processor. Under some conditions, the device can consume more power than the TDP. For example, in the world of graphics processors there are some applications that can overclock the graphics card.

In some ways you can compare processors to automobiles. For example, a BMW will typically provide higher acceleration but at an additional cost over another brand that this author will not mention but is well known. Similarly, processor manufacturers provide lower voltage versions of their processors that consume fewer watts than their standard processors but charge more for such products. Whether they are worth the additional cost depends upon how you intend to use such products and the cost your organization pays for electricity. For example, without considering the time value cost of money let's assume a low-voltage version of a processor will cost $100 more than the higher voltage version. If you assume this processor will deliver an average savings of 30 watts and will operate 24/7 over a three-year period and electricity costs 10 cents per kWh, the cost savings becomes:

$$30 \text{ watts} \times 24 \text{ hours} \times 365 \text{ days/year} \times 3 \text{ years} \times 10 \text{ cents/kWh}$$
$$\times 1/1{,}000 = \$78.84$$

Thus, if you assume the cost of electricity will remain at 10 cents per kWh for three years and at the end of that period there is no residual value for the computer then it would not be economical to pay extra for low-power processors other than to feel good about doing so or obtain bragging rights for your decision. However, what happens if the cost of electricity rises 1 cent per kWh each year and the life of the servers is extended to four years? Then, the average cost per kWh would be (10 + 11 + 12 + 14)/4 or 11.5 cents and our computation becomes:

30 watts × 24 hours × 365 days/year × 4 years × .115 cents/kWh
   × 1 / 1,000 = \$120.88

In the second example we obtain a completely different financial decision, which illustrates why it is extremely important to consider the life of equipment as well as the price your organization will pay for electricity.

Consider Data Storage Consolidation

Although the processors in servers consume a lot of power, data storage can contribute to making the data center manager flinch when he or she receives the monthly power bill. To economize upon power use you may wish to consolidate data storage from direct attached storage to network attached storage devices.

By changing to network storage you may be able to considerably reduce individual disk requirements as processors would now share disk usage. Whether the movement to network attached storage makes economic sense will depend upon the number of servers currently used and projected to be used and the type of data storage used and projected to be used. In addition, you need to determine the cost of moving to a network attached storage facility as well as the cost to upgrade that facility.

Examine IT Hardware Utilization

On a periodic basis it pays to check the use of equipment within a data center. Often a periodic visit to the communications area will uncover dead, obsolete, or excess equipment that although drawing power performs little if any useful work. This author remembers the use of the world's largest dial-in secure communications network that he at one time was responsible for managing. This network had a 90-position rotary with then state-of-the-art modems and datacryptors connected to each position that were on 24/7 awaiting calls from investigators roaming around the country. The only problem with this setup was the fact that a dial-in network management system showed that the highest position on the rotary ever used was position 37 and that after 8 p.m. Eastern time the highest position used was position 6 on the rotary. Thus, the network management system was in effect telling the organization that their dial-in configuration was drastically overconfigured. However, the agency responsible for funding the investigator network was diametrically opposed to reducing the size of the rotary, possibly because someone might then question the support staff located in another state that probably spent a good portion of the time performing tasks unrelated to supporting the investigators. Your organization may not have a similar problem, however, you need to examine the output of different management systems to determine if your organization is making effective use of equipment, and if not, what equipment should be consolidated, enabling excessive equipment to be powered off. It is hoped that in this era of budgetary responsibility, your organization will be more forthcoming regarding the elimination of unnecessary devices.

Consider Higher Voltage Power Distribution

As many physics and engineering students may know, using higher AC voltages for power distribution will result in reduced energy losses. Although Europe and Asia locations may have AC voltages of 415 V or higher, many U.S. manufacturers of UPS systems are capped at 220 to 240 VAC. Thus, although your organization may have to "shop around" to locate higher power distribution systems by considering the loss associated with lower voltage against the cost for distributing power at higher voltages you can make intelligent decisions that may allow your organization to benefit. In fact, most servers and many other types of IT equipment can operate at 240 VAC and will usually operate at an increased level of efficiency at the higher voltage level. Although delivering a higher level of voltage may only provide an energy savings of 1 to 2%, each minor savings will cumulatively result in a significant overall level of efficiency.

Utilize Wireless Humidity and Temperature Transmitters

One of the problems facing data center and communications managers is the fact that they often react to problems instead of being proactive and able to resolve such problems when they are not in a major situation that requires immediate action. At a time when wire-less devices are being introduced to the market at a furious pace there are several products that should be considered for utilization in the data center. Several such wireless devices are now available that can be used to transmit both relative humidity and temperature at dis-tances up to 120 meters or 400 feet. With a size smaller than a pack of cigarettes and the ability to be placed by an equipment rack or wall mounted, such devices can be used with software that turns a personal computer into a multichannel chart logger or data recorder. By plac-ing these humidity and temperature transmitters at critical areas you obtain the ability to monitor conditions throughout your data center, observe abnormalities, and consider corrective action prior to small problems becoming major ones.

In addition to transmitting relative humidity and temperature at periodic intervals, most humidity and temperature sensors will trans-mit their battery status, allowing you to replace aging batteries prior to losing the ability to record the data they provide. Typically costing under $200, the use of wireless humidity and temperature monitors and their associated base station should be employed within data cen-ters to include rooms used for data communications equipment.

This author does not name manufacturers of wireless humidity and temperature monitors, but briefly discusses how to find such products. Although these products are commonly found in a variety of product catalogues, in the age of the Internet you can use the term "wireless humidity and temperature monitor" in a search engine, such as Bing, Google, or Yahoo!. Doing so will result in a number of products from which you may select. Once you select a few appropriate products you should ascertain their transmission range and software features simi-lar to the manner in which you would select other hardware products that operate with certain types of software. However, there is one caveat this author needs to mention that makes it safe to obtain a loaner prior to purchasing a number of devices. This caveat is based upon the fact that many buildings housing data centers were con-structed using metal studs in their walls. If the building housing your data center includes metal studs in interior walls this can adversely affect the range of wireless transmission. Thus, you may need to per-form an analysis of the places where you plan to install wireless tem-perature and humidity monitors with respect to their ability to have their transmissions received by one or more base stations. For some data centers with walls used to separate different types of equipment this may result in the need to consider the use of LAN-based products or multiple base stations.

Minimize Phantom Energy Loss

As previously discussed earlier in this book, phantom or vampire energy loss is associated with devices that consume power when they are not being used. In an office environment we usually do not have to worry about televisions, DVD players, and cable or satellite boxes that use energy when we think they are turned off as we typically do not have them in the data center. However, many employees bring into the office a variety of products, such as cell phone chargers, stereos, and other types of electronics that may or may not have modern charging capabilities that result in a minimum loss of energy when plugged in but unused. Recognizing the old adage that "If you can't beat 'em, join 'em," you might consider installing smart power strips that today can be found with red-, blue-, and green-colored outlets. The red ones stay on continuously and are for plugging in any device that needs constant power. The blue outlets function as control plugs and the green plugs are sensitive to current flowing through the blue plugs. Thus, you could have employees place chargers as well as printers into green outlets and devices such as monitors and computers could be plugged into blue outlets. In this manner you assume that at the end of the day when the computer and monitor are turned off any charger and printer will also be turned off, resulting in the minimizing of phantom or vampire energy loss.

Although your first inclination concerning the use of power strips is that this author is splitting hairs, in actuality the savings can be considerable. When this author was at Robbins Air Force Base at the end of July, 2010, Building 905 on the base had just installed 20 power strips. They estimated that each power strip would save about seven kWh per week or 364 kWh per year, for a total savings of 364×20 or 7,280 kWh. Thus, simply installing 20 intelligent power strips would save $72.80 if the cost of electricity were only a dime per kWh.

Use Energy-Efficient Motors

If you look beyond the data center into utility rooms and perhaps a separate UPS building you will probably note a number of motors, ranging perhaps from sump pumps and fans to motor generators. What most of those motors have in common is a degree of inefficiency, especially if they are just a few years old. In fact, the recent U.S. motor efficiency of December 19, 2010 almost ensures that the vast majority of motors found in and around a data center could be more efficient.

The recent U.S. motor efficiency compliance deadline resulted in new motors having higher efficiency through the use of additional copper in their windings, which reduces stator losses and the use of higher grade electrical steel that reduces iron-core losses. As a result, lower losses translate into fewer watts required to operate the motor. According to published reports a higher efficiency motor operating just 40 hours per week can reduce yearly operating costs by over $250 when the cost per kWh is a dime. If the motor operates 80 hours per week cost savings can be expected to exceed $800 per year, whereas a continuously operated motor, such as those used by fans to assist airflow can result in savings accelerating to over $2,000 per year. Thus, it may be worthwhile to perform an inventory of electric motors with a view to periodically analyzing their cost of operation and potential replacement by more efficient motors. However, when doing so you need to look beyond the plate efficiency of a motor and examine the application. As an example, a premium efficiency AC induction motor will not save much energy if it is run mostly at a partial load condition or is in an idle state for long periods of time. Thus, common sense needs to prevail when considering motor replacements.

If your organization resides in the European Union a series of minimum degrees of efficiency for three-phase electric motors are scheduled for introduction on June 16, 2011, January 1, 2015, and January 1, 2017. The 2011 switchover date concerns motors with .75 to 375 kW with 2-, 4-, or 6-pole three-phase asynchronous motors. Other switchover dates involve geared motors and motors operated by an inverter, with the January 1, 2015 date for 7.5 to 375 kW devices whereas the January 1, 2017 date lowers the power to 0.75 kW.

Examine Airflow

In Chapter 6 we noted the use of a hot/cold aisle configuration to save on energy use. With applicable temperature and humidity monitors you may be able both to use that configuration as well as adjust environmental conditions to a wider tolerance but still meet vendor specifications. By doing so you will more than likely reduce energy consumption that will translate to the bottom line of the organization.

In the event your data center is located in a northern climate you might also consider using outdoor air for cooling when conditions permit. Earlier in this book this author mentioned how Yahoo! was using outside air at a data center in upstate New York to reduce energy use. Thus, the use of outdoor air as well as cooling towers should also be considered if your data center location experiences a range of temperatures. For example, even in a desert location where the temperature crosses the 100°F point during the day, after sunset some desert locations can experience a rapid decline in temperature that may make the cold night air suitable for use. Thus, although most locations using outside air are located in northern climates, this situation may be practical for other locations, especially if the data center operates 24/7 and has a worldwide presence.

Reduce Air Handler Operations When Not Necessary

One of the major uses of energy are the air handlers in most buildings. You need to ensure they operate 24/7 for the data center that has those hours of operation, but the other areas of a building may not require their use in the evening or on weekends. Thus, the ability to use programmable thermostats that change the temperature in different zones within a building can result in significant energy savings.

Controlling the Power Factor

As explained earlier in this book, the power factor is the ratio of actual power, voltage × current, at the same instant in time, to the apparent power level that is not corrected by time or phase. The power factor is only applicable to AC power systems and most utilities will include a surcharge for large customers based upon the power factor that can increase as energy consumption arises. For a large data center there are two methods that can be used to provide a power factor correction, either from improved power supplies used in servers and personal computers or through the use of large capacitors. The former can be obtained by an appropriate procurement of equipment whereas the latter should be considered in conjunction with the serving utility and representatives of the vendor selling or leasing such devices. Concerning the former, one item that warrants mention is the fact that to meet Energy Star guidelines personal computers with internal power supplies must achieve a power factor greater than 0.9. Thus, this represents another reason for considering PCs that meet Energy Star guidelines.

Use Caulking and Weather-Stripping to Block Air Leaks

Perhaps one of the easiest methods to reduce the cost of energy is to minimize air leakage. Such leakage can include gaps in air ducts where sheet metal is commonly bent to make a duct flow to a desired area as well as by windows and doors, especially those that are on exterior walls of a building. By using caulking and weather-stripping you can close gaps and thus reduce energy loss, in effect helping your bottom line.

Both caulking and weather-stripping products have certain restrictions concerning their use. Typically, they need to be applied to clean dry surfaces that are at or above a certain temperature. By noting the directions on the product prior to its purchase you can alleviate the need for a redo by getting the job done correctly from the beginning. Another area that deserves attention is the location where caulking or weather stripping should be applied. This is actually a bit easy, as most areas that need weather-stripping can be noted by seeing light between a door and its frame or the floor. Gaps and cracks on exterior windows, light fixtures, and other openings such as electric sockets or even hose outlets in the outside wall of a business are good candidates for caulking. In addition, where a window frame meets brick, frame, or stucco you may note prior caulking that has come loose and needs to be recaulked. To do so you need to first remove existing caulk and then apply the new caulk.

Another area that is easily overlooked is the roof of many buildings. Here skylights, chimneys, rooftop vents, plumbing risers, and conduits containing electrical wiring to roof-mounted heat pumps and chillers may have gaps that literally make your energy expenses go through the roof. Again, you need to periodically have any roof gaps located and sealed, using roof caulk to seal gaps.

By periodically having maintenance personnel check your building from the foundation to the roof you can more than likely find areas that can be sealed through the use of caulking and weather-stripping. Doing so is relatively easy and the cost to close gaps may be recovered in days or weeks.

Consider a Chargeback Policy That Includes Energy Cost

Many organizations that have a chargeback policy simply base charge-back on a square foot usage basis. That is, if one department occupies 10,000 square feet and a second department occupies 20,000 square feet, then the first department would pay one-third of the cost of the data center. Although simplistic, this policy ignores the actual usage of the data center, including processing and overhead costs. For example, the first department might be engineering, which although occupying one-third of space might use two-thirds of the processing capability of the data center. There is nothing more efficient than having users pay their fair share of usage including overhead in the form of energy consumption. There are many chargeback models available to consider, however, if you have an organization applicable for using a chargeback scheme you should consider a model that allocates overhead including energy use. In doing so you might actually have customers that might tell you they do not need servers to be operational after hours when they have to pay for the cost associated with keeping the server up. Thus, there is nothing like being billed for service to have people realize that they might prefer to do without a certain service when they are paying for services they do not require.

Consider Increases in Electricity Cost

If you analyze the cost of electricity over the past decade you will note that the cost of electricity only increases, year after year, similar to the Energizer Bunny marching into the sunset. If you go to the following Department of Energy URL, http://www.eia.doe.gov/electricity/

epm/table5_3.html, you can obtain the latest average retail price of electricity for residential, commercial, industrial, and transportation sectors. The set of tables is updated monthly and provides insight into how you might use the past increases to predict future cost increases.

Water Considerations

Until now we have focused our attention upon data center energy reduction techniques that did not consider the water environment. If we are truly interested in reducing costs then we also need to examine the use of water.

Examine Water Heater Settings

When a conventional hot water heater is installed the plumber may ask the person nearest the heater for the temperature to which it should be set. Occasionally the installer might recommend a setting, or simply select a high setting. If the setting is too high not only will you more than likely waste energy but you can create a condition where it's possible that employees can scald themselves if not too careful when washing their hands. By setting your water heater to a maximum of 120°F you can save between $35 and $60 per year per water heater. In addition, if your employees only work one shift you might consider the use of an appropriate timer for electric hot water heaters that turn off the heater at 5 p.m. and restart heating water at 7 a.m. Thus, instead of heating water 24 hours per day you might be able to reduce the time by 14 hours per day. Although more expensive, you might consider the use of programmable digital timers that might enable you to adjust periods where the water heater is turned off to include weekends and holidays. However, in doing so you need to verify that the timer will work with the water heater.

Examine Water Usage

Unfortunately the water bills at most organizations get little scrutiny. Perhaps this is due to the mistaken belief that there is little to be accomplished from minimizing water use. Fortunately, there are at least two things that deserve consideration. First, if you have old-fashioned water closets in bathrooms, simply placing a brick in each tank might reduce water consumption by a quarter gallon per flush. Although not something to get excited about, the flushing adds up over the billing cycle and the reduction in water should have no effect upon the ability of the water closet to perform its function.

A second area that deserves consideration depends upon the degree of landscaping and your organization's need to water shrubbery. Because most water authorities bill for water and sewerage based upon water consumption, when you water shrubbery in effect you are also paying for sewage even though the water does not return into the sewerage system. To alleviate this billing problem many water authorities will install a second water meter, which is used to measure irrigation use. There is no free lunch, thus you need to determine the cost for installing the second water meter and the potential savings that may occur from the ability to be billed only for water use when irrigating.

Now that we discussed potential water savings areas to consider we return our attention to one energy-saving method that has received a considerable amount of attention. That area involves the potential replacement of incandescent lights with either compact fluorescent lighting (CFL) or an LED package. In the next section this author uses the term LED package as LED lighting that involves the use of a group of LEDs that on a singular basis do not produce enough light to replace the use of an incandescent bulb, but when grouped into a package become suitable as a potential replacement.

Replacing Lighting

One of the easiest methods to conserve energy as well as reduce costs is through the replacement of incandescent lighting by compact fluorescent lighting or LED-packaged lighting. In fact, the U.S. Department of Energy has estimated that the projected growth in the use of LED lighting will reduce total U.S. lighting energy use by 25% within 20 years. Although you may think it's nice to think about the future but you would rather begin to save energy by reducing the cost of lighting, it's important to note that CFLs use approximately one-third the energy of the traditional incandescent lightbulbs invented by Edison over 130 years ago and last up to 10 times longer. In the event you want to do even better, you can consider LED-packaged lightbulbs, which although relatively costly are rapidly declining in price and use a fraction of the energy of an incandescent lightbulb. In this section we turn our attention to several lighting measurement metrics as well as compare different types of lighting.

When comparing LEDs to incandescent lighting it's important to note that a direct comparison of the two is not possible. This is because the amount of light emitted from an LED is specified by the measurement at a single point, known as the on-axis luminous intensity value (lv). That measurement of LED luminous intensity is not directly compatible to the light produced by incandescent lightbulbs, with the latter using spherical candlepower as a mechanism to denote the quantity of light emitted by the lightbulb. Thus, to obtain a solid appreciation for the relationship among different types of lighting, let's turn our attention to the manner in which different lighting metrics are related.

Lumens

A lumen represents a unit of light output equal to $1/60 \times$ pi of the light emitted by one square centimeter of an ideal blackbody surface at the melting point of platinum, with pi equal to the constant 2.14159.... Lumens were defined in terms of the 1931 official photopic function that was modified in 1988 and which essentially examines the quantity of light produced at every wavelength that is present. One watt of light at any single wavelength represents a lumen, which is mathematically 681 times the official photopic function of the wavelength.

Watts as a Measurement Tool

To alleviate some potential confusion concerning watt numbers let's differentiate between the watt number used for light output and the unit used for measuring electrical power. When used as a measure of electrical power, watts represent the product of volts and amperes. When the watt number is used to express light output, as previously noted, it is mathematically 681 times the official photopic function of the wavelength. To simplify this, manufacturers use the watt number as a mechanism to compare light output to that of an incandescent lightbulb. For example, a 60-watt light output is then equal to a 60-watt incandescent lightbulb. To further muddy the water, many times two watt numbers are used in a product specification, one for the electrical power consumption and the other used to specify light output. Fortunately, reading the fine print on the package usually alleviates the potential confusion.

Returning our attention to the standard 100-watt lightbulb we can obtain knowledge of several different lighting terms. The standard 100-watt, 120-volt incandescent lightbulb is typically rated for 750 hours and emits 1,710 lumens. The first number represents the longevity of the bulb having power applied or the life of the bulb. In comparison, the lumens rating represents the unit of luminous flux and is equal to the light radiated by a source of one candela intensity radiating equally in all directions. Thus, in some ways we can actually think of a 1,710 lumen incandescent lightbulb as providing the light of 1,710 candles, inasmuch as a candela can be thought of as being loosely equivalent to a burning candle. Lumens are used to measure and compare lightbulbs as stand-alone light sources. You can usually examine the packaging of a lightbulb and obtain its rated life in hours of operation, its wattage, voltage, and amount of light it provides in lumens. Although CFLs are similar to incandescent lightbulbs with respect to having a rated life after which the bulb can be expected to fail, LEDs are quite different. The life of an LED bulb unlike CFL and incandescent bulbs does not suddenly go dark. Instead, the lumens diminish until the life of the LED reaches a point where its light output is considered to represent 70% of its luminous flux value, where luminous flux represents a photometric quantity that defines the total amount of electromagnetic radiation emitted by a source spectrally weighted for sensitivity by the human eye.

Lumens per Watt and Lux

Another pair of terms that warrant our attention are lumens per watt and lux. Lumens per watt provide an indication of the efficiency of a lightbulb including its efficiency in converting electrical energy into light. Currently, commercially available LEDs introduced to the market during late 2010 have a luminous efficacy of 130 lm/w for cool white and 107 lm/w for warm white.

The second term we want to briefly review is luminous flux or lux. Lux is used to measure the light intensity produced by a lighting fixture and is measured in lumens per square meter. Thus, the higher the lux reading the more light the fixture provides over a given area. Note that certain LEDs are specified in units of radiant power (mW) instead of luminous flux. Typically, 450 to 465 nanometer (nm) blue LEDs are commonly used in medical applications in which the spectral sensitivity of the human eye is not relevant. However, because we are literally focused on lighting and not LED medical applications we ignore the radiant power of LEDs.

Determining Watt Dissipation

If you examine the packaging on an LED you can usually find information concerning the number of watts the device will dissipate. If this information is not displayed on the package you can easily compute the watts dissipated by determining the forward voltage (V_f) and millamp (ma) rating of the LEDs. In some cases both V_f and ma are listed on the package, with watts dissipated curiously missing. Thus, let's review how we can compute the watts dissipated by an LED.

Let's assume you plan to use an LED that has a forward voltage rating of 2 volts and a current rating of 20 ma. The wattage is obtained by multiplying voltage by current ($W = I \times V$), then

$$\text{Watts} = 2 \text{ volts} \times .20 \text{ amperes} = .04$$

Because LED lights typically have 10 or more individual LEDs packaged in a bulb, instead of having the watts for each individual LED, more than likely the wattage is for the "bulb," which consists of the individual LEDs. In addition, when you carefully examine certain types of LED packaging you may note that its emission in lumens is also provided. On other LED packages you may find the metric lumens/watt cited, which actually represents the efficiency of the LED. The latter provides a mechanism to compare the output efficiency of different LEDs to one another as well as to various types of other light sources.

If the LED package indicates its efficiency in terms of lumens per watt, you can compute the watts dissipated or use the value from the package and multiply it by the lumens per watt. Doing so will allow you to obtain the LED emission in lumens. Thus, there are several minor computations you can perform to determine the LED's efficiency and heat dissipation if those metrics are not provided on its packaging. Fortunately, most modern LED lighting products include not only lumens and watts but, in addition, whether the LED package is dimmable. Now that we have an appreciation for the fact that most LED-based lights are really a package of two or more LEDs let's become acquainted with three additional lighting-related terms: luminous energy, illuminance, and lighting efficiency.

Luminous Energy

Another term that you may see upon occasion that is often misleading is luminous energy, which many people confuse with luminous intensity. As a refresher, luminous intensity of a light source represents the density of luminous flux emitted in a given direction. In comparison, luminous energy is a term used to denote the perceived energy of light. Because the human eye is limited to seeing light in the visible spectrum, luminous energy will differ considerably from luminous intensity in the infrared spectrum and more than likely differ in value from person to person in the visible spectrum due to differences in the manner by which humans see light. Inasmuch as most people will not be purchasing lighting that operates in the infrared spectrum luminous energy represents a term we rarely encounter.

Illuminance

Illuminance represents the total luminous flux incident on a service and is measured in lumens per square meter (lm/m^2). Because illuminance represents a measure of light at a point in time it is also referred to as brightness. If you watch some of the premium cable channel movies that have a "before the scene" show, it's quite common to see a studio technician use a lux meter to check the illuminance level to adjust video cameras prior to the shout of "action."

Lighting Efficiency

Another term that warrants our attention is luminous efficiency, which we shortly note is also referred to as lighting efficiency. This

Table 7.1   Luminous Efficiency and Efficiency Examples

	OVERALL LUMINOUS EFFICIENCY (LM/W)	OVERALL LUMINOUS EFFICIENCY (%)
INCANDESCENT		
5-watt tungsten	5	0.7
40-watt tungsten	12.6	1.9
100-watt tungsten	17.5	2.6
FLUORESCENT		
5–24-watt compact fluorescent	45–60	6.6–8.8
34-watt tube	50	7.0
HALOGEN		
Glass	16	2.3
Quartz	24	3.5
LED		
White	20–70	3.8–10.2

term provides us with the ability to compare the efficiency of different types of lighting.

Luminous efficiency is measured in lumens/watt (lm/w) and provides a measurement of the efficiency of a light emitter when its output is adjusted to account for the spectral response curve. When expressed as a dimensionless value, the overall luminous efficiency is referred to as the lighting efficiency. Table 7.1 provides examples of the overall luminous efficiency and luminous flux for eight light sources. Note that luminous efficiency represents the ratio of emitted luminous flux to radiant flux whereas overall luminous efficiency indicates efficiency of the conversion of electrical energy to optical power.

Color Temperature

Color temperature provides a measure of the color of a light source that is relative to a blackbody at a particular temperature. That temperature is expressed in degrees kelvin (K), where kelvin represents a thermodynamic temperature scale where the coldest temperature possible is zero kelvin (0K). The kelvin scale and the kelvin are named after the physicist and engineers, William Thomson and Baron Kelvin, who identified the need for an absolute thermometric scale.

Table 7.2 Representative Color Temperatures

LIGHTING	KELVIN
High pressure sodium	2,200
Incandescent (soft white)	2,800
Halogen	3,000
Fluorescent (cool white)	4,000
Daylight	>5,000
LED (cool white)	8,000

Absolute zero (0K) is equivalent to −459.63°F and −273.15°C. Another term related to kelvin that you will occasionally encounter is the mired. The mired represents the color temperature in kelvin divided by one million.

Representative Lighting Color Temperature Incandescent lights have a low color temperature of approximately 2,800 K. In comparison, daylight has a high color temperature at or above 5,000 K. In between the two are popular fluorescent lighting referred to as "cool white" at approximately 4,000 K and "white" or "bright white" at approximately 2,900 to 3,100 kelvin. Table 7.2 provides a summary of different lighting and their color temperatures or temperature range in kelvin.

In general, lighting with a low color temperature at approximately 2,200 kelvin has a red-orange tone. At 2,800 kelvin they have a red-yellowish tone and are typically referred to as being "warm white" or "soft white." Daylight has a relatively high color temperature at and above 5,000 kelvin and appears bluish. In between, a halogen lamp at 3,000 kelvin generates a yellowish light whereas the most popular fluorescent light, which is rated at approximately 4,000 kelvin, is referred to as "cool white." At the high end of the color temperature an LED "cool white" occurs at a color temperature of 8,000 kelvin.

Comparing Lighting

Now that we have a basic appreciation for some essential lighting-related terms we compare the three main types of lighting we normally consider: incandescent, CFL, and LED lights. In doing so this author uses information taken by examining lights available at several big box hardware stores in late 2010 to include packaging data and their retail prices.

In late 2010 a package of six 75-watt incandescent lightbulbs were being sold for $3.25 plus tax, which we do not consider in our computations. Each bulb provided 1,085 lumens of light and was rated for 1,500 hours, which explains why they were referred to as "double-life lightbulbs." On a cost per bulb basis we can compute that the cost is slightly more than 54 cents, again excluding tax. Although the cost per bulb is nominal, we need to compute the cost over a period of time including energy cost. In doing so let's assume the lightbulb is located in an area where it is on 8 hours per day, 5 days per week or 40 hours per week, which represents the typical workweek for many people.

At 40 hours per week and 52 weeks per year the lightbulb will be on 2,080 hours per year or 6,240 hours over a three-year period. The reason this author uses a three-year period for his initial computations is due to the fact that many technology-driven products have a useful life of three years and LEDs can be considered to represent an evolving technology.

The life of the incandescent lightbulb is 1,500 hours, which means that we will use at least 4 lightbulbs over the three-year period. At 54 cents per bulb, the bulb cost is $2.16 not including the time required to replace the bulb four times. As we soon note, the energy cost associated with the use of incandescent lighting far exceeds the cost of the lightbulbs. That is, a 75-watt bulb turned on for 6,240 hours results in $75 \times 6,240/1,000$ or 468 kWh of energy being used. At just a dime per kWh, that 75-watt incandescent lightbulb will result in the use of $46.80 of electricity. Thus, the three-year operating cost of a 75-watt incandescent lightbulb is $2.16 for four bulbs and $46.80 for electricity, or a total of $48.96. As a matter of digression, the incandescent lightbulb converts to heat approximately 80 to 90% of the energy used, which explains why it is not efficient unless used where you can utilize the heat generated by the bulbs.

Although originally CFL bulbs were limited to spiral devices that were unsightly unless plugged into a socket under a lampshade or behind a glass partition that hid the bulb from view, today they are manufactured within white globes so they appear to resemble incandescent lightbulbs. Because this author is attempting to provide a realistic comparison of products, he used both a CFL white globe

14-watt (60 equivalent watts) device that provides 800 lumens of light and a 23-watt spiral CFL (100 equivalent watts) that provides 1,600 lumens of light, with both the white globe and spiral CFL bulb rated for 8,000 hours of use. At the time this chapter was written the CFL white globe bulb was being sold as a 2-pack for $9.97 whereas the 23-watt spiral CFL was being sold in a 12-pack for $110.

For the use of either bulb only one would be required for use over the three-year period. Concerning energy usage, the 14-watt CFL white globe turned on for 6,240 hours results in 14 × 6,240/1,000 or 87.36 kWh of energy being used. Again, at just a dime per kWh, that 14-watt CFL lightbulb will result in the use of $8.73 of electricity. Thus, the three-year operating cost of a 14-watt CFL lightbulb is $4.98 for one lightbulb and $8.73 for electricity, or a total of $13.71. However, remember that this 14-watt CFL bulb provides 800 lumens of light whereas the incandescent lightbulb provides 1,085 lumens of light or approximately 30% more light. Inasmuch as we are trying to compare products this author also used a 23-watt spiral CFL bulb, which provides more light at 1,600 lumens than the incandescent lightbulb because I could not locate an exact duplicate replacement. Thus, we bracket the light output of the incandescent lightbulb. Continuing our comparison, using a 23-watt spiral CFL lightbulb turned on for 6,240 hours results in 23 × 6,240/1,000 or 143.52 kWh of energy being used. Again, at just a dime per kWh, that 23-watt CFL lightbulb will result in the use of $14.35 of electricity. Thus, the three-year operating cost of a 23-watt CFL lightbulb is $9.16 for one lightbulb and $14.35 for electricity, or a total of $23.51.

For our final comparison of lighting we use a 950-lumen 18-watt, dimmable LED package. At the end of 2010 the cost of this package was $44.75 and the rated life was in excess of 30,000 hours. Although the lumens were less than that obtainable by the use of the previously mentioned 75-watt incandescent lightbulb, on the packaging it was noted that the LED was "equivalent" to a 75-watt bulb. Once again doing our three-year cost comparison we note that the LED bulb package requires only one bulb, however, its cost is exceedingly high at $44.75. The 18-watt LED lightbulb package will be turned on for 6,240 hours resulting in 18 × 6,240/1,000 or 112.32 kWh of energy being used. Again, at just a dime per kWh, that 18-watt LED lightbulb package will result in the use of $11.32 of electricity. Thus,

Table 7.3   Comparing Use of 8-Hour/Day Lighting over a 3-Year Period

TYPE OF LIGHTING	WATTS	LUMENS	BULB COST	ENERGY COST	TOTAL COST
Incandescent	75	1085	2.16	46.80	48.96
CFL white globe	14	800	4.98	8.73	13.71
CFL spiral	23	1600	9.16	14.35	23.51
LED package	18	950	44.75	11.32	56.07

the three-year operating cost of an 18-watt LED lightbulb package is $44.75 for one lightbulb and $11.32 for electricity, or a total of $56.07. Table 7.3 compares the results from our four computations.

When examining the comparison of lighting shown in Table 7.3 we can note two rather interesting pieces of information. First, over a three-year period the cost of LED lighting is not economical when a bulb is used eight hours per day and the cost per kWh is a dime. The use of LEDs may make you feel better as they do not contain mercury as CFLs do, but they are not presently economical for periodic use due to the high cost of the bulb. In comparison, both the use of white globe and spiral CFL bulbs provide significant cost savings in comparison to the use of incandescent bulbs. Second, although the cost of replacing bulbs was not considered, they usually represent what is referred to as "sunk costs" that would occur even if a bulb were not replaced. Thus, if maintenance personnel were not replacing lightbulbs they might be either doing something else or sitting at their desks, still drawing their weekly salary. Thus, although you might be tempted to include the cost of labor in replacing bulbs, unless they are located where they are difficult to change and require a bucket lift or another device to access you can probably exclude labor costs from consideration.

Now let's assume the lights will be on 24/7 and let's recompute the costs associated with each type of light. If the lights are on continuously this means that each type of lightbulb will be on 8,760 hours per year or 26,280 hours over a three-year period.

Because the life of the incandescent lightbulb is 1,500 hours, this means that we will use approximately 18 lightbulbs over the three-year period. At 54 cents per bulb, the bulb cost is $9.72 not including the time required to replace the bulb, which per our previous discussion we ignore. As we soon note, the energy cost associated with the use of incandescent lighting far exceeds the cost of the lightbulbs. That is, a 75-watt bulb turned on for 26,280 hours results in 75 ×

26,280/1,000 or 1,892 kWh of energy being used. At just a dime per kWh, that 75-watt incandescent lightbulb will now result in the use of $189.20 of electricity. Thus, the three-year operating cost of a 75-watt incandescent lightbulb that burns 24/7 is $9.72 for 18 bulbs and $189.20 for electricity, or a total of $198.92.

Now let's turn our attention to the two CFL lights that will also operate 24/7 and have a life of 8,000 hours. The 14-watt CFL white globe turned on for 26,280 hours results in 14 × 26,280/1,000 or 367.92 kWh of energy being used. Again, at just a dime per kWh, that 14-watt CFL lightbulb will result in the use of $36.79 of electricity. Thus, the three-year operating cost of a 14-watt CFL lightbulb is $4.98 × 4 or $19.92 for four lightbulbs (that will last 32,000 hours) and $36.79 for electricity, or a total of $56.71. However, remember that this 14-watt CFL bulb provides 800 lumens of light whereas the incandescent lightbulb provides 1,085 lumens of light or approximately 30% more light. Because we are trying to compare products and he could not locate an exact duplicate replacement, this author once again used a 23-watt spiral CFL bulb that provides more light at 1,600 lumens than the incandescent lightbulb. Thus, like an artillery specialist, we bracket the light output of the incandescent lightbulb. Continuing our comparison, using a 23-watt spiral CFL lightbulb turned on for 26,280 hours results in 23 × 26,280/1,000 or 604.44 kWh of energy being used. Again, at just a dime per kWh, that 23-watt CFL lightbulb will result in the use of $60.44 of electricity. Thus, the three-year operating cost of a 23-watt CFL lightbulb operating 24/7 is $9.16 per lightbulb or $27.48 for three bulbs and $60.44 for electricity, or a total of $87.92.

Again, for our final comparison of lighting we use a 950-lumen 18-watt, dimmable LED package. The cost of this package was $44.75 and the rated life was in excess of 30,000 hours; we therefore only require one LED package, which when we conduct a new comparison will tell us a lot about the viability of LEDs when operated near continuously. Although the lumens were less than those obtainable by the use of the previously mentioned 75-watt incandescent lightbulb, on the packaging it was noted that the LED was "equivalent" to a 75-watt bulb. The 18-watt LED lightbulb package will be turned on for 26,280 hours resulting in 18 × 26,280/1,000 or 473.04 kWh of energy being used. Again, at just a dime per kWh, that 18-watt LED

Table 7.4   Comparing Use of 24/7 Lighting over a 3-Year Period

TYPE OF LIGHTING	WATTS	LUMENS	BULB COST	ENERGY COST	TOTAL COST
Incandescent	75	1085	9.72	189.20	198.92
CFL white globe	14	800	19.92	36.79	56.71
CFL spiral	23	1600	27.48	60.44	87.92
LED package	18	950	44.75	47.30	92.05

lightbulb package will result in the use of $47.30 worth of electricity. Thus, the three-year operating cost of an 18-watt LED lightbulb package is $44.75 for one lightbulb and $47.30 for electricity, or a total of $92.05. Table 7.4 compares the results from our four computations when the bulbs are assumed to be on 24/7 over a three-year period.

If we now perform another comparison of the four lightbulbs we can see how continuous or near-continuous lighting can have both a dramatic effect upon the use of electricity as well as provide a justification for the use of CFL and LED lighting. Turning our attention to Table 7.4, note that for an incandescent light the energy cost has now escalated to $189.20 whereas the CFL and LED energy costs are a fraction of the incandescent light's energy cost. If you then examine the bulb cost you will note that although the cost for CFL and LED bulbs is higher than the cost of incandescent bulbs for continuous use, because they have significantly lower operating cost with respect to the consumption of energy their total cost ranges from approximately a quarter of the cost of an incandescent bulb for a white globe CFL to one-half the cost for an LED package. Thus, the longer a bulb is on the greater the potential for its economical replacement by either CFL or LED bulbs.

In performing the cost comparisons we assumed the costs of bulb replacements were sunk costs which for some locations, such as two-story ceilings in a lobby may not be exactly true. In one situation this author remembers that once every few years the local fire department had to be called to change lightbulbs, requiring a donation to the firemen's fund. Thus, there may be some locations within a building where the use of long-lasting LED bulb packages may pay for themselves many times over, not only from a lower energy cost but, in addition, by not having to replace them every 1,500 hours as with an incandescent lightbulb or 8,000 hours for most CFL lightbulbs. When comparing lightbulbs you should at a minimum consider their longevity. For example, if an LED is rated for 30,000 hours of operation and a double-life incandescent is rated for 1,500 hours, then simply dividing 30,000 by 1,500 informs you that over the life of the LED lighting package you would need 20 double-life incandescent lightbulbs. Similarly, if you divide 30,000 by 8,000, then the LED light package is equivalent to 3.75 CFL lights.

If the lighting you are considering replacing is in difficult-to-access areas you might then consider factoring in some labor costs, especially if the bulb replacement takes a considerable amount of time. When you consider the fact that most LED packages have a rating of at least 30,000 hours of use, this is where their additional cost over incandescent and CFL bulbs can be offset. In addition to using less energy than incandescent bulbs and having a similar energy use to CFLs, the additional life of LEDs means that for extended use of over three years they can become more economical than other forms of lighting. Thus, when you perform lighting computations you need to consider the time period that the lighting will be used, the ease of lighting replacement, and the cost of energy per kWh over the period the lighting computations will occur. Because energy costs can be counted on to increase on an annual basis, you need to consider how often the utility serving your organization has increased rates and the likelihood of future rate increases.

Building Management Areas to Consider

Lighting replacement can be a building management responsibility therefore we conclude this chapter with three building-related areas and an "outside the building" area that requires an overhang or dock as well as an outlet for charging. The first three areas we discuss are adding insulation to walls, floors, and ceilings; changing the color of the roof of the building; and periodically changing filters. We conclude this chapter by discussing a type of electric vehicle that you may wish to consider if your data center requires a vehicle that makes frequent pickups and deliveries.

Consider Adding Insulation

It is a well-known fact that for most buildings, general heating and cooling can account for between 50 and 70% of the energy used, although the proportion of energy used for heating and cooling a building with a data center is less due to the amount of energy consumed by equipment and the direct use of cooling to dissipate heat from the building. Thus, a data center may not benefit directly from the use of insulation, but it can be used to reduce heating and cooling costs that may have an effect on the overall consumption of energy. In addition, through the use of insulation, walls, ceilings, and floors within a building can be made to retain a desired temperature with a minimum of heat loss.

How Insulation Works Heat flows naturally from a warm location to a cooler location. In the winter heat moves from heated working areas to the outdoors, whereas during the summer heat moves from the outdoors to the interior of a building. To maintain comfort the heat lost during the winter is replaced by a heating system and heat gained during the summer is removed by an air-conditioning system. By insulating ceilings, walls, and floors you can decrease the number of heating and cooling systems.

Types of Insulation There are numerous types of insulation available for consideration, ranging from foam and air to batts, blankets of fiberglass, cellulose, and even polystyrene. Still air is an effective insulator because it eliminates convection and has a low level of conduction. In fact, this author used a pair of Plexiglas inserts inside a corner window to create an air gap that significantly reduced his heating and cooling bills. Concerning foam insulation, some foams including polyurethane and extruded polystyrene, are filled with special types of gases that provide additional resistance to heat flow. In addition to the previously mentioned insulation you can also consider the use of reflective insulation. Such insulation works by reducing the amount of energy that travels in the form of radiation. You are probably familiar with reflective insulation if you drove through a development of houses being built and noticed shiny panels put up on the outside of homes prior to bricks, stone, or wood being placed on exterior walls. Note that some types of reflective insulation also divide a space up into small regions to reduce air movement, or convection.

If on a cold winter day you place your hand on the outlet on an exterior wall you may be able to judge the level of insulation in a building. Many older buildings were constructed using cellulose batts of fiberglass in walls where the electrician would cut to install outlets easily. Although this made it easy for the electrician, it typically resulted in a gap in the insulation that your hand will feel. If you have several outlets in exterior walls you may wish to consider hiring an insulation firm and consider the use of spray foam insulation behind each outlet. To accomplish this the installer will typically remove the outlet covers, unscrew the outlets and then spray the foam into the wall. If you have competent maintenance personnel they may be able to purchase foam insulation in cans and spray the foam themselves. For either situation the use of foam insulation can be used to close air gaps that in turn will reduce heating and cooling costs.

Rating Insulation   Insulation is rated in terms of thermal resistance, which is commonly referred to as the R-value, which indicates the resistance of an insulating material to heat flow. As you might expect, the higher the R value the greater the effectiveness of insulation.

The R-value of an insulation product depends on the type of material, its thickness, and its density. In calculating the R-value of a multilayered installation, the R-values of the individual layers are added. Thus, if you add a roll of batt insulation rated as R-12 to an existing ceiling rated at R-18, the result would be an insulation value of R-30 in the ceiling. Note that the actual effectiveness of an insulated wall, ceiling, or floor depends on how and where the insulation is installed. For example, insulation that is dense and added over light insulation will result in the first type of insulation becoming compressed. That insulation will not give you its full rated R-value and typically occurs in an attic or ceiling where dense insulation is placed on top of a lighter type of insulation. This situation can also occur when batts rated for one thickness are squeezed into a thinner cavity, such as placing insulation rated for a 6-inch ceiling cavity into a 5-1/2-inch wall cavity.

Changing the Building Roof Color

According to a 1999 study performed by the Lawrence Berkeley National Laboratory's Heat Island Group, if your building is located in a relatively sunny location, a building with a white roof requires up to 40% less energy for cooling than those with black roofs. This study reinforces common sense as white reflects sunlight and a dark color, such as a black roof, absorbs sunlight. After living in the southern United States for over 30 years, the number of dark roofs I notice on both residential and commercial buildings in middle Georgia still amazes me. Although it may not be beneficial financially to change a residential roof after only a few years of use, the study pointing the economy of light roofs is over 20 years old. Thus, it is always a bit puzzeling to this author as to why buildings that are fairly modern have dark roofs.

If you own your building and it has a dark roof, you should consider the use of a white elastomeric coating that can be used on certain types of roofs. This blend of polymers is durable, flexible, and waterproof so often it can be used to extend the life of some roofs. Because it is easy to apply by using heavy-duty paint rollers, the cost of its application may result in a payback period of a few months through lower cooling costs. When in doubt, consider a reputable roofer to determine if your dark roof is suitable for an elastometric coating.

Use Reusable Filters

Maintenance over a period of time can be costly. Similarly, the replacement of filters on a periodic basis can add up. One method to reduce costs, especially when in-house personnel perform maintenance is to use more expensive reusable filters that can be cleaned by water or the use of a solvent. By periodically cleaning filters at least according to the manufacturer's recommended frequency you cannot only extend the life of equipment but also reduce your power consumption by ensuring that motors are literally not working overtime to pump air through clogged filters.

Consider Electric Vehicles

In concluding this chapter we go out of the data center and discuss a topic that is mostly encountered in magazines and trade journals but requires the attention of the data center manager: the use of electric vehicles, especially trucks that may provide a larger payback than electric automobiles. This is because a data center may have a backup site to which backup data are transferred frequently, typically on a daily basis. In addition, the data center manager may have one or more employees who typically visit office supply stores to obtain forms and other products that do not fit conveniently in an electric automobile. Recognizing the fact that a small electric truck may be more practical than an electric automobile for short defined routes, the use of electric trucks, although typically much more expensive than diesel trucks, will significantly reduce maintenance costs as an electric motor rarely needs anywhere near the maintence of a diesel. In addition, because electric trucks use regenerative braking in which some of the force associated with stopping is returned to the batteries in the form of electricity, the brakes will last much longer in an electric truck. When you factor in fuel costs the potential payback period may be under 4 years. The expected life of a truck may be between 8 and 10 years, therefore this means that for some data centers the next light truck used by the organization might be an electric vehicle. Of course, you need to consider the cost of recharging the vehicle and whether an outlet can be placed where the truck can be recharged overnight without exposure to the elements.

Index

24/7 operation, xv, 165
   lighting comparisons, 243
   waiting area TVs, 216
90-position rotary, 223
120-volt current, 60
240-volt current, 60
   operating IT equipment at, 224

A

Absolute zero, 238
Absorption chillers, 111–112
Absorption heat pumps, 88
AC connectors, 73
AC measurements, 51
   ground, 54–57
   power factor (PF), 53–54
   root mean square (RMS), 51
ACPI specification, 185
Acquisition costs, *vs.* operating
   costs, 39
Active state power management
   (ASPM) policy, 189

Advanced Configuration and
   Power Interface (ACPI)
   specification, 185
Air conditioners. *See also* Central air
   conditioners
   managing via EnergyWise
   technology, 170
   optimizing computer room
   location, 173
Air Conditioning Contractors of
   America (ACCA), 105
Air filters, examining for chillers,
   114–115
Air gaps, 245
Air handler operations, reducing,
   228
Air leaks
   blocking with caulking and
   weather-stripping,
   229–230
   minimizing in raised floor
   systems, 172–173
Air-source heat pumps, 88, 92

Airflow mixing, positioning supply and returns to minimize, 172

Airflow optimization, 172, 228

Alternating current (AC), 39, 46–48
  converting to VAC, 48
  economic advantages, 46
  measurements, 51–57

Always on chargers, 152

Ambient temperature, and fan speed, 171

American National Standards Institute (ANSI), C12.20 electric meter standard, 133

American Power Conversion (APC), 175

Ammeters, 51

Amperage, 42
  measuring, 51

Ampere (A), 39

Amps (I), 42

Analog telephones, DC power, 47

Annual fuel utilization efficiency (AFUE), 83

Annual percentage rate (APR), 25

Annuities, 19
  future value, ordinary annuity, 20–22
  IRR computation, 31–33
  monthly cash flows, 23–25
  payment frequency, 20
  present value, 22–23
  types, 20

Annuity due, 20, 25
  discounted cash flow and, 27
  Excel use for computing, 33–36
  internal rate of return, 30–31
  mathematical notations, 26
  payback period, 26–27
  weighted average cost of capital (WACC), 27–30

Apparent power, 53

Atlanta Gas Light Company, 138

Atoms, 40

Automated meter reading (AMR) capability, 140

Automatic delay, 106

Automatic switching, 170

Automatic transfer switch, in standby generators, 77

Average consumption per employee, 138

Away Mode, 191

AXRS4 electric meter, 127, 128

B

Barrels of oil, 5
  refinery components, 6

Baseboard heaters, 96–97
  installation, 97

Basic input/output system (BIOS), 207
  updating, 206

Batteries, 46, 47

Battery chargers, 151. *See also* Chargers

Battery status, wireless transmission, 225

Bidirectional heat pumps, 85

Bill estimation, natural gas, 141–143

Billing inaccuracies, 135
  causes in smart meters, 134–135, 137

Blade servers, xiii

Blowers, 82
  two-speed variable, 93

Boiler horsepower, 4

Boilers, 83
  acquisition and maintenance guidelines, 116
  rating and capacity, 83–84

Bonding conductors, 55

Brake life, in electric vehicles, 248

Branch circuits, 70

Breaker service panels, 65, 66, 67

British thermal units (BTUs), 2, 3–4
boiler ratings, 84
content of common energy units, 5
Broadband over power lines (BPL), 129
Brownout provisions, 126
BTU per hour (BTU/h), 3
Building managers, xiii
Building service panels, 68–69
Bus rates, 164

C

California, smart meter implementation, 120
California Public Utilities Commission, 135
Capacitors, 54
Carbon dioxide emissions. *See also* Greenhouse gases
promotion by telecom equipment, 165
Cash flows, 12, 37
discounted, 27
hypothetical, 32
at irregular intervals, 34, 35, 36
monthly, 23–25
at regular intervals, 34, 35
in ROI analysis, 12
Cash inflows, for RAID system, 13
Cash outflows, for RAID system, 13
Caulking, 229–230
Ceiling height, energy consumption considerations, 173–174
Cell phone chargers, 226
phantom power load, 151
power loads, 153
ratings, 154–155
Cell phone manufacturers, USB charging agreement, 154–155
Cell phones, as DC devices, 48

CenterPoint Energy, smart meter billing problems, 132
Central air conditioners, 103–104
acquisition and maintenance guidelines, 117
automatic delay feature, 106
cost comparison, 105–106
factors to consider, 106
fan-only switches, 106
sizing, 105
types, 104–105
Centralized return system, 82
Centrifugal compression chillers, 111
Chargeback policies, 230
Chargers, 48
always on *vs.* partially on, 152
five-star rating, 154
phantom power generation, 151
universal, 155
Chicken coop data center, 113
Chillers, 107–108
absorption type, 111–112
acquisition and maintenance guidelines, 117
air filter examination, 114–115
centrifugal, 111
classification, 110
compressor type, 109
condenser type, 109
controls for, 110
cooling towers, 109–110
ductwork examination, 114
evaporator type, 109
expansion valve type, 109
frictionless centrifugal, 111
mechanical compression type, 108
operating multiple, 112
optimizing in cold weather, 113–114
rapid restart capability, 112
reciprocating, 110

refrigerant line examination, 113

rotary screw type, 110–111

selection considerations, 112–113

types, 108

use in air conditioning, 108

Circuit breakers, 55, 64, 65

as protection devices, 70

Circuit isolation, 66

Circuit measurements, 42–43

Circuits, 39, 43–44, 69–70

general-purpose, 70

individual, 71

schematic diagram, 43

small-appliance, 70–71

types, 70

Cisco 3750 series, 167–168

Cisco Catalyst 3750 series switch models, 167

Cisco EnergyWise Technology, 168, 169–170

Cisco StackPower, 168–169

Climate control systems, 79, 80–81

three components, 80

ventilation, 81–82

Closed circuits, 69, 70

Closed-loop geothermal heat pumps, 93

Closely coupled cooling, 176

Cloud computing, energy benefits, 219–220

Coaxial cables, meter transmission via, 130

Coiled water heaters, 101

Cold-air return systems, 82

Cold aisle configuration, 174–175, 228

Cold weather

optimizing chillers during, 113–114

unsuitability of heat pumps for, 85–86

Color coding

of electrical wires, 63

in smart power strips, 226

Color temperature, 237–238

comparisons, 238

Command prompt use, 180, 192–193

Powercfg command line options, 194–200

Commercial customers

monthly price of natural gas, 8, 9

natural gas costs, 9

Communications equipment, 151

Cisco 3750 series, 167–168

cost computations, 165–167

Compact fluorescent (CFL) bulbs, 38

8-hour/day use, 241

24/7 use, 243

energy use, 232

life cycle, 239–240, 242

luminous efficiency, 237

present value equation, 24

regulation of disposal, 31

Compound value interest factor (CVIF), 1

Compressor chillers, 109

Compressors, 104, 107

Computer memory

cost computation, 163–164

low-voltage, 162–163, 164

Computer power efficiency, 192

TDP as proxy for, 222

Computer room air conditioners, location optimization, 173

Computers

energy consumption relative to monitors, 179

power load in sleep mode, 153

remote turn-on, 207

turning off, 156–157

Condensation problems, 114

Condenser chillers, 109

Condensers, 104
  in heat pumps, 85
Condensing coils, 107
Conductors, 40
Conservation, promotion by water
      company billing, 149
Consolidation, for energy efficiency,
      217–219
Consumption, 45
Control outlets, 154
Control panel, Windows 7, 181
Controllers for chiller systems, 110
Cooling computation, 105
Cooling systems, 79–80, 103
  acquisition and maintenance
      guidelines, 116–117
  central air conditioners,
      103–106
  checklist, 115
  chillers, 107–115
  heat pump cooling, 107
  long-term considerations, 115
Cooling towers, 109–110
Corporate tax rate, 29
Cost comparisons, central air
      conditioners, 105–106
Cost computations, 158–159
  Cisco Stackpower, 168–169
  communications equipment,
      165–171
  device consumption, 159–161
  EnergyWise Technology,
      169–170
  rack pack considerations, 165
  servers, 162–165
  varying cost per kWh, 161–162
Cost of equity (COE), 38
  equation, 29
CPU states, 185–186
CPU use percentage, 218
CRT monitors
  energy consumption, 155–156
  replacing, 214

Crude oil, 5
  distillates, 6
  separation into different fuels, 6
Cubic feet, 143, 145
Current
  physiological effects, 56
  waste, 53
Current flow, 40
Cycles per second (CPS), 46, 50

D

Data center energy efficiency, xiv,
      213
  air leak blockage, 229–230
  airflow considerations, 228
  building management areas to
      consider, 244–248
  chargeback policies, 230
  cloud computing, 219–220
  consolidation and virtualization,
      217–231
  data storage consolidation, 223
  electric vehicles, 247–248
  electricity cost increases, 230–231
  energy-efficient motors, 227
  energy loss detection, 213–214
  high-voltage power distribution,
      224
  insulation additions, 244–246
  IT hardware utilization, 223–224
  lighting replacement, 232–244
  minimizing phantom energy loss,
      226
  monitor replacement, 214–215
  operating system upgrades, 216
  power factor control, 228–229
  power management products,
      220–221
  processor efficiency, 221–223
  reducing air handler operations,
      228
  reusable filters, 247

roof color and, 246–247
techniques to consider, 213–217
telework benefits, 219
waiting area displays, 215–216
water considerations, 231–232
wireless humidity/temperature
transmitters, 224–226
Data center equipment energy
consumption, 151–152
commonsense items, 154–158
cost computations, 158–176
general cost computations,
158–176
operational modes to consider,
152–153
power loads, 152–153
smart power strips, 154
Data centers
electricity costs, 137
water bill extract, 148
Data recording, by electric meters,
127–129
Data storage consolidation, 223
Data transfer rates, 163, 164
Daylight color temperature, 238
DDR2 memory, 164
DDR3 memory, 162, 164
Debt
market value, 29
repayment of, 30
Debt financing, 28
tax deductibility, 28
Dehumidification, 104
Demand quantities, 127
Demand water heaters, 101
Department of Energy, 230
Depreciation, 12
Desktop and mobile architecture for
system hardware (DASH),
211
Device consumption, 159–161
Diesel fuel, 6
Diffusers, 172

Digital smart meters, 128–129. *See also* Smart meters
Direct current (DC), 39, 46–48
Directional grills, 103
Discount rate, 30
Discounted cash flow, 10, 27, 37, 38
Discounted cash flow rate of return,
30
Disk Operating System (DOS), 180
Distributed management task force
(DMTF), 211
DOS commands, 192, 194–200
Dual fuel heat pumps, 86, 88, 89,
90–91
cost considerations, 92
Lennox programmable
thermostat for, 91
thermostat for, 92
Dual in-line memory modules
(DIMMs), 162
Dual-phase AC, 62, 63
Dual power supplies, 165
Ductwork
examining for chillers, 114
ventilation considerations, 81
Ductwork leaks, 114
Dumb meters, 119, 120
DVD players, power loads, 153
Dynamic random access memory
(DRAM), 165

E

Earth-coupled heat pumps, 92
Earth temperature, as exchange
medium, 93
Earthing conductors, 54, 55
Eco-friendly data centers, 113
Edison, Thomas, 47
Effective interest rate, 30
Electric baseboard heaters, 96–97
Electric bills, estimating, 125
Electric furnaces, 96

Electric meters, 119
 analog type, 119
 author's home-based, 121
 AXRS4, 127, 128
 categories, 119–120
 dial rotation, 124
 digital smart meters, 128–129
 dumb, 119–120
 examining, 120–124
 inaccuracy due to age/
  maintenance, 134
 load meters, 126–127
 loss of accuracy with age, 124
 manual reading, 123
 operation, 128
 reading and understanding, 119,
  125–129
 recording data in, 127–129
 smart meters, 119–120, 129–138
 solid-state, 133
Electric motors, power factor, 54
Electric resistance heating, 95
 acquisition and maintenance
  guidelines, 116
 electric baseboard heaters, 96–97
 electric furnaces, 96
 hot water heaters, 99–103
 hot water radiators, 98–99
 radiators, 97
 steam heating, 97–98
 types of heaters, 95
Electric trucks, 247–248
Electric vehicles, 247–248
Electrical conductors, 40
Electrical current. See Current
Electrical insulators, 49
Electrical outlet adapters, 72
Electrical power, 44–46
 alternating current, 46–48
 direct current, 46–48
Electrical rating, 158
Electrical terms, 39–40
 AC measurements, 51–57

atoms, 40
 circuit measurements, 42–43
 circuits, 43–44
 electrical power, 44–48
 electricity distribution, 57–78
 electrons, 40
 ground, 54–57
 meters to consider, 51
 power rating, 50
 power supply, 48–50
 turbines, 42
 understanding electricity, 40–44
Electricity
 atoms and electrons in, 40
 circuit measurements, 42–43
 circuits and, 43–44
 electric generators, 40–42
 life-cycle cost, 39
 and magnetism, 41
 source, 43
 turbines and, 42
 understanding, 40
Electricity costs, xv, 5–6, 8, 9–10
 for data center, 137
 increases, 230–231
 natural gas and, 9
 per employee, 138
Electricity distribution, 57
 plugs and sockets, 71–74
 power plant, 57
 service panel, 64–65
 single-phase, 62–64
 standby generators, 76–78
 three-phase, 62–64
 transformers and, 57–64
 uninterruptible power supplies,
  74–76
Electricity rates, importance of,
  137–138
Electromechanical meters, 122
Electronic equipment, preventing
  loops/transients in, 55
Electrons, 40, 41

Emerson Network Power, 175
Employee rules, 154
   cell phone charger ratings,
      154–155
   Energy Star equipment, 157–158
   monitor turnoff, 155–156
   rarely used devices, 155
   screen savers, 181
   smart power strips, 154
   standby mode, 156–157
Employees, teleworking
   performance, 219
Energy, etymology, 2
Energy comparison, 5
   oil, gas, and electric costs, 5–6, 8
Energy conservation, xiv, 37
   annuities and, 19–25
   annuity due, 25–37
   energy comparisons and, 5–10
   energy costs and, 2–4
   financial metrics, 10–19
   rationale and financial
      implications, 1
Energy consumption
   airflow optimization, 172
   available calculators, 176–177
   ceiling height and, 173–174
   cold aisle zone arrangement,
      174–175
   command prompt use, 192–193
   computer power efficiency, 192
   costs per 22-day month, 161
   costs per 30-day month, 160
   data center equipment,
      151–152 (*See also* Data
      center equipment energy
      consumption)
   DDR3 memory, 162
   device computations, 159–161
   diffusers, 172
   energy reports, 200–201,
      206–207
   fan speed considerations, 171
   hot aisle zone arrangement,
      174–175
   insulation role, 173
   minimizing, 179
   miscellaneous techniques for
      reducing, 171–176
   optimizing computer room air
      conditioner placement, 173
   power efficiency diagnostic
      reports, 201–205
   processor power management,
      189–191
   rack placement and cooling
      considerations, 171
   raised floor system air leaks,
      172–173
   return plenum, 173
   sleep mode considerations,
      170–191
   supplemental cooling, 175–176
   supply and return positioning,
      172
Energy costs, 2
   2007 costs, 7
   BTUs and horsepower, 3–4
   electricity costs, 9–10
   energy and power, 2
   natural gas, 8–9
   units of power, 2–3
Energy efficiency, data center, 213
Energy-efficiency reports, 192
   viewing as HTML, 201
Energy-efficient motors, 227
Energy loss detection, 213–214
   phantom energy, 226
Energy reports, 200–201, 206–207
Energy Star ratings, 180
   favoring equipment with high,
      157–158
   and power factor, 229
   purchasing guidelines, 217
Energy Star website, 157, 159
Energy units, BTU content, 5

Environmental Compliance Cost Recovery fees, 132

Equations
annuity due, 25
cost of equity (COE), 29
electrical power, 44
future value of ordinary annuities, 21–22
internal rate of return, 32
lightbulb present value, 24
payback period, 26
power, 2
present value of annuities, 22, 23
simple ROI, 13
WACC, 29

Equipment cost sheet, 177, 178
Equipment leasing, 1
Equipment life, extending via energy conservation, 1
Equipment purchase, 1
Equity
cost of, 29
market value, 29
Equity financing, 28
Europe
BPL metering transmission, 129
CPS rate, 46, 50
energy efficiency classes, 217
motor efficiency regulations, 227
Evaporator coils, 107
Evaporators, 85, 109
Excel. *See* Microsoft Excel
Excess kVA charges, 132
Expansion valve chillers, 107, 109
Explanation of charges, 142

F

Fan-only switches, 106
Fan speed, and ambient temperature, 171
Faraday's law, 58
Fast-acting fuses, 66

Fault current protection, 55
Financial metrics, 10, 37
future value interest factors (FVIFs), 16–17
present value basics, 17–18
return on investment (ROI), 10–14
time value of money, 14–16
Financing methods, 28
FLIR thermal sensors, 214
Fluorescent lighting. *See also* Compact fluorescent (CFL) bulbs
color temperature, 238
Forced-air heating systems, 82–83
Franchise fees, 132
Frequency shift keying (FSK), 129
Frictionless centrifugal compression chillers, 111
Fuel cells, 46, 47
Fuel Cost Recovery fees, 132
Furnace sizing, 83
Furnaces, in packaged single-device air conditioners, 104
Fuseboxes, 64
as protection devices, 70
Fused service panels, 65
Fuses, industrial uses, 65
Future cash flows, 28
discounting, 28
Future value, 14–16, 15, 16
annuity due, 25
ordinary annuities, 20–22
Future value interest factors (FVIFs), 16–17

G

Gadgets, power draw from, xv
Gas. *See* Natural gas
Gas bill extract, 142
Gas meters
reading and understanding, 119
rotary type, 139

Gas-solid interactions, 111
Gas South, business rate plans, 141
General-purpose circuits, 70
 schematic diagram, 71
Generators, 40–42. *See also* Standby
 generators
 selection criteria, 78
GeoExchange heat pumps, 92
Georgia Power Company
 electric meter, 120, 121
 Power and large light schedule
  PLL-5 electric service
  tariff, 130, 131
Geothermal heat pumps, 88,
  92–93
 closed-loop systems, 93
 horizontal closed-loop systems,
  94
 open-loop systems, 95
 types, 93–95
 vertical systems, 94
 water-based systems, 94–95
Glass-enclosed cabinets, 174
Green energy projects, 90, 103
Greenhouse gases, 170
Grills
 directional, 104
 in return ducts, 103
Ground, 54–57
Ground-source heat pumps, 81, 92
Ground wire, 68
 in electric meters, 121
Grounding electrode conductor
  (GEC), 55, 56
Grounding pins, 72

H

Halogen lighting
 color temperature, 238
 luminous efficiency, 237
Hard drives, sleep mode options,
  187–188

Heat dissipation, 166
 reducing, 37
 reduction with tankless water
  heaters, 101
 with tank-based hot water
  heaters, 101
Heat flow, 245
Heat generation, by electronic
  devices, 152
Heat pump cooling systems, 107
 acquisition and maintenance
  guidelines, 116
 ground-source, 81
Heat pump heating systems, 85–86
 absorption type, 88
 air-source, 88, 92
 dual fuel, 88, 90–91
 geothermal, 88, 92–93
 hybrid, 88, 89
 SEER and HPSF ratings, 86–87
 solar-assisted, 89–90
 types, 87–95
Heat pump hot water heaters, 102
Heating computation, 105
Heating oil, 6
Heating seasonal performance factor
  (HSPF), 86. *See also* HSPF
  ratings
Heating systems, 79–80, 82
 acquisition and maintenance
  guidelines, 116–117
 boilers, 83–84
 checklist, 115
 electric resistance heating, 95–97
 forced-air systems, 82–83
 heat pumps, 85–86
 long-term considerations, 115
 radiant heating, 84–85
 SEER and HSPF ratings, 86–87
Hedging commodities, 8
Hertz, Heinrich, 46
High ceilings, energy inefficiency,
  173

High performance power plan, 183
High voltage DC (HVDC), 47
High-voltage power distribution,
        energy savings, 224
Home telephone wire transmission,
        130
HomePlug transmission, 130
Horizontal closed-loop geothermal
        systems, 94
Horsepower, 2, 3–4
    boiler ratings, 83–84
Hot aisle configuration, 174–175,
        228
Hot bus bars, 68
Hot outlets, 154
Hot spots, 175, 176
Hot water heaters, 79, 99
    acquisition and maintenance
        guidelines, 116–117
    indirect type, 102–103
    tank storage type, 100–101
    tankless, 101–102
    types, 99
Hot water radiators, 98–99
    acquisition and maintenance
        guidelines, 116
Hot wires, 60, 68
    in breaker service panels, 66
    in electric meters, 121
Hours of operating use, 158
HSPF ratings, 86–87, 116
Hubbell, Harvey, 72
Hubbell adapters, 72
Humidifiers, 98
Hybrid heat pumps, 88, 89
Hydroelectric generation, 45
Hydroelectricity, 9

I

IBM Tivoli, 170
IEC 60309 receptacle, 73, 74
IEC 60320 receptacle, 73, 74

IEC 61036 standard, 133
IEEE 802.11 WiFi standard, 129
Illuminance, 236
Imperial horsepower, 4
Incandescent bulbs
    8-hour/day use, 241
    24/7 use, 243
    color temperature, 238
    life cycle, 239, 241
    luminous efficiency, 237
    present value equation, 24
Indirect water heaters, 102–103
Indirect watts saved, 219
Individual circuits, 71
Indoor coils, 85
Inductors, 54
Inflows, 12
Infrared thermography, in energy
        waste detection, 214
In-ground radiant heating, 85
Insulation
    adding extra, 244–245
    for hot water heaters, 99
    for indirect water heaters, 102
    mechanism of operation, 245
    minimizing energy consumption
        using, 173
    R-value, 246
    rating system, 246
    for steam heating systems, 98
    still air, 245
    types, 245–246
Intangible benefits, 38
Interest, 1
    as tax-deductible expense, 30
Interest on interest, 1
Interest rates, 14
    trial-and-error method, 31
Internal rate of return (IRR), 1, 10,
        11, 30–31, 36–37
    computation, 31–33
    equation, 32
    Excel function, 36

as financial investment decision
    tool, 36
management misuse, 36
as roots of NPV function, 35
International Electrical Commission
    (IEC), AC interconnection
    standards, 73, 74
International Electrotechnical
    Commission (IEC), 133
International Telecommunications
    Union, 155
IP devices, reducing energy
    consumption, 169
Irrigation, 232
IT hardware utilization, 223–224

J

Joule, James Prescott, 122
Joules, 2, 122

K

Kelvin temperature, 237
Kilowatt hours (KWh), 3, 45

L

LAN switches, 166, 167, 169
    stackable, 167
Landis & Gyr, electric meter with
    data recording, 127
Landscaping irrigation, 232
Laser temperature sensors, 114
LCD displays, energy consumption,
    156
LCD monitors, 214
Lease vs. purchase, 1
LED backlit flat screen televisions,
    215
LED lighting
    8-hour/day use, 241
    24/7 use, 243
    color temperature, 238

life cycle, 234, 240–241
    luminous efficiency, 237
    projected growth, 232
LED monitors, 214
Lennox programmable thermostat,
    90
    for dual fuel system, 91, 92
Lennox XP14 heat pump, 86, 87
Lennox XP15 heat pump, 86
Licensing fees, reducing through
    server consolidation, 219
Life-cycle cost, 39
Life expectancy, 12
Lightbulbs
    cost comparisons, 238–244
    electrical consumption, 45
    longevity, 243–244
    replacing, 232–233
Light emitting diode (LED) bulbs,
    24
    electrical savings, 23
    present value equation, 24
Lighting comparisons, 238–244
    8-hour/day use, 241
    24/7 use, 243
Lighting efficiency, 236–237
Linear power supplies, 48
Load, 43, 44
Load matching, 112
Load meters, electric, 126–127
Local group policy editor, 180
Locks, 57
Long-term contracts, 141
    utility cost advantages, 142
Loop prevention, 55
Lumens, 233
Lumens per watt, 234–235
Luminous efficiency, comparisons,
    237
Luminous energy, 236
Luminous flux, 234, 236
Luminous intensity, 236
Lux, 234–235

M

Macon Water Authority, 147
  residential and nonresidential
    water and sewerage base
    rates, 146
Magic Packet, 208–209
Magnetic field, 41
Magnetism, 40
  relationship to electricity, 41
Mains electricity, 54, 69
Manual J, 105
Manual meter reading, 123
Market value
  of debt, 29
  of equity, 29
Mathematical notations, for
    annuities, 26
Maximum processor state, 189
Mechanical compression chillers,
    108, 110
Mechanical energy, converting to
    electrical energy, 40
Mechanical horsepower, 4
Megawatt-hours (MWh), 45
Memory. *See* Computer memory
Metal studs, issues with wireless
    temperature sensors, 225
Metals, as electrical conductors,
    40
Meter base fees, 145
Meter readers, elimination through
    smart meters, 124, 132
Meter reading
  on alternate months, 140
  natural gas meters, 139–141
  reduction in cost of, 124
  smart meters, 130, 132
  wireless transmission, 124, 129
Meters, 51
  in overhead power lines, 64
Microprocessors, in smart meters,
    128

Microsoft Excel, 33–34
  built-in functions, 34
  IRR functions in, 36
  NPV functions in, 34–35
  ROI functions in, 35–36
Microwaves, power loads, 153
Mineral buildup, in radiant heating
    systems, 84–85
Minibreakers, 68
Minimum processor state, 189
MMBTU, 4
Monitors
  automatic turn-off, 184
  energy consumption relative to
    computers, 179
  as energy hogs, 182
  replacing with energy-efficient
    equivalents, 214–215
  sleep mode settings, 191
  turning off, 155–156
Motor efficiency, 227
Motors, energy-efficient, 227
Multicore products, incorporating
    into servers, 162–163
Multimedia settings, sleep mode,
    191
Mutually exclusive projects, rating
    using IRR, 36

N

National Electrical Manufacturer's
    Association (NEMA), 97
Natural gas
  as cleanest-burning fuel, 8
  costs, 5–6, 8–9
  growth in demand, 8
  increased reserves, 9
  long-term contracts costs, 141,
    142
  monthly U.S. price to commercial
    customers, 9
Natural gas bills, 142

Natural gas meters, 119, 138
  with flow measuring diaphragm,
    138, 139
  and gas bill estimation, 141–143
  gas bill extract, 142
  meter reading, 139–141
  meter types, 138–139
Neptune water meter, 144, 145
Net present value (NPV), 10, 37
  Excel functions, 34–35
Networking devices, energy
    consumption, 179
Neutral wire, 56, 60, 63
  in electric meters, 121
Night setback systems, 97
Nonresidential customers, Macon
    Water Authority rates, 146
North America
  CPS rate, 46, 50
  single-phase AC in, 63
Number of periods, 23
Number of years, 23

radiant heating systems, 84
sample equipment cost sheet, 178
space heaters, 81–82
vs. acquisition costs, 39
Operating system upgrades, energy
    efficiency and, 216
Operational modes, 152–153
Opteron multicore products,
    162–163
Ordinary annuities, 20
  future value, 20–22
  future value equation, 21–22
  present value equation, 22
Oscillation, 44
  and phase shifts, 49–50
Outdoor air, using for cooling, 228
Outdoor coils, 85
Outflows, 12
Overflow pan, 104
Overhead costs, chargeback policies,
    230
Overhead power lines, 60, 64

O

Off-peak consumption, 120, 134
Ohm, 39, 42
Ohmmeter, 51
Ohm's law, 43
Oil
  costs of, 5–6, 8
  variable pricing, 6
On-axis luminous intensity value
    (lv), 233
One-way transmission, 210
Open circuits, 69, 70
Open-loop geothermal systems, 95
Open system interconnection (OSI)
    model, 210
Operating costs
  computing for individual device
    types, 158
  energy efficiency and, 166

P

Pacific Gas & Electric
  smart meter billing problems, 132
  time-of-use service rate schedule,
    135
  time periods for small general
    time-of-use service, 136
Packaged single-device air
    conditioners, 104
Panasonic Viera HDTV models, 216
Partial-peak periods, 134
Partially on chargers, 152
Passwords
  for power settings, 186
  for sleep mode, 187
Payback period, 1, 10–11, 26–27, 38
  failure to consider time value, 26
Payments, at end of each period, 21
PCI express option (PCIe), 189

Peak consumption, 120
Peak load clauses, 126
Peak periods, 126, 134
Perforated server doors, 174
Personal computers, connectors for, 73
Petrawatt-hour (pWh), 3
Phantom load, xv, 48, 152
   minimizing energy loss due to, 226
   production by chargers, 151
Phase angle, 50, 53
Phase converters, 69
Phase shifts, 49–50
Pickens, T. Boone, 9
Pin counts, 73
Plasma-based flat screen televisions, replacing, 215
Plexiglas insulation, 245
Plugs, 71–72
   office-based, 72–74
Polarity, 41
Pole-mounted transformers, 61
Politics, as barrier to coherent financial decision making, 31
Potential cash flows, 38
Potential savings, projecting with annuities, 19
Power
   equation, 2
   etymology, 2
   units of, 2–3
   in watts, 123
Power buttons, 188–189
Power efficiency diagnostic reports, 201, 202–205
Power factor (PF), 53
   controlling, 228–229
   electric motors, 54
   importance, 53–54
   penalties, 53
   utility surcharges based on, 228

Power factor correction, 229
Power factor monitor, 54
Power line, 64
Power loads, 152–153
Power management, xv, 182, 221
   desktop- and server-based, 220–221
Power options
   advanced settings, 186–187, 190
   CPU states, 185–186
   in Microsoft Windows, 180
   monitors, 191
   multimedia settings, 191
   power plan selection, 182
   Wake-on-LAN, 207–209
Power Options dialog box, 190
Power plans, 180
   balanced, 182
   default settings, 184
   editing, 183–185
   selecting, 182
Power plants, 57
Power rating, 50
Power strips, energy consumption, 153
Power supply, 48
   operation, 49
   phase, 49–50
   types, 48–49
Powercfg command line options, 194–200
Prepayment meters, 120
Present value, 17–19
   of annuities, 22–23
   annuity due, 25
   of energy consumption, 24
Present value interest factor (PVIF), 1
   comparison to FVIFs, 18
   tables, 19
Primary voltage, 58
Primary windings, 59
Printers, power loads, 153

Processor efficiency, 221–223
  comparison to automobiles, 222
Processor power management,
    189–191
Proper Planning Prevents Problems,
    73

R

R-value, 246
Rack pack, energy cost computation,
    165
Rack placement, cooling
    considerations, 171
Radiant heating systems, 84–85
  acquisition and maintenance
    guidelines, 116
Radiators, 97
RAID system, 12–13
  cash inflows and outflows, 13
  life expectancy, 12, 28
Raised floor systems, minimizing air
    leaks in, 172–173
Random access memory (RAM),
    163
Rapid restart, in chillers, 112
Ratio, 11
Real power, 53
Receptacle types, 74
Reciprocating compression chillers,
    110
Redundancy, 169
  powering off, 224
Reflective insulation, 245
Refrigerant line examination, 113
Refrigerators, electrical
    consumption, 46
Registry Editor, 180
Regulatory compliance, open-loop
    geothermal system issues,
    95
Residential customer rates, Macon
    Water Authority, 146

Resistance, 42
  in transformer circuits, 59
Return air temperature, 172
Return ducts, 82
  grill problems, 103
Return on investment (ROI), xiii, 1,
    10–11, 26–27
  analysis, 12–14
  energy consumption calculators
    for, 176
  equation, 13
  Excel functions, 35–36
  failure to consider risks, 11
  limitations, 11
  SEER ratings and, 105
Return plenum, sizing
    considerations, 173
Reusable filters, 247
Right-hand law, 41
Risks, ROI failure to consider, 11
ROI analysis, 12–14
ROI calculators, 176–177
Roof color, and energy efficiency,
    246–247
Roof gaps, 229–230
Room heaters, 95
Root mean square (RMS), 51–52
Rotary screw compression chillers,
    110–111
Rule of Ps, 73

S

Screen brightness, reducing energy
    consumption via, 183
Screen savers
  enforcing non-use by employees,
    181
  management walk-through to
    determine use, 156
  obsolescence, 156
  settings in Windows, 181
  Windows 7 settings, 183

Screw-in sockets, 71
SeaMicro 10U system, 165
Seasonal energy efficiency ratio (SEER), 69, 86. *See also* SEER ratings
Secondary voltage, 58
Secondary windings, 59
Security issues, Wake-on-LAN, 210
SEER ratings, 86–87, 116
   Lennox XP14 heat pump, 87
   minimum, 105, 106
   for new air conditioners, 105
Series circuits, 43
Server consolidation, 177
Server utilization software, 221
Servers
   consolidating and virtualizing, 217–219
   cost computation, 162–163
   memory cost computation, 163–164
   minimizing energy consumption, 179
   perforated doors for, 174
   rack pack considerations, 165
Service panels, 64–65
   inner workings, 68
   operation, 66–68
   with overhead power lines, 64
   types, 65–66
Sewerage
   base rates, 146
   cost for data center, 148
Shock prevention, 54
Short circuits, 55, 70
Short-term interest rates, 14
Silica gel, 112
Simplex transmission, 210
Sine waves, 50
Single-phase AC, 62–64
   electric meters using, 120
   in homes, 68
Single-pipe hot water radiators, 98

Six Sigma compliance, 133
Sleep mode, 153, 179
   accessing power options, 180–183
   advanced settings, 186–187
   CPU states, 185–186
   defining period of, 188
   display options, 191
   editing power plans, 183–185
   energy consumption in, 152, 156
   hard drive, 187–188
   multimedia settings, 191
   PCI express, 189
   power buttons and lid, 188–189
   power options, 180
   USB setting, 188
   wireless adapters, 188
Sleep states, 185
Small-appliance circuits, 70–71
Smart grid, 120, 129–130
   goal, 129
Smart meter display, reading, 130, 132
Smart meters, xiv, 119, 120, 129–130
   accuracy rates, 135
   billing advantages to utility company, 149
   causes of billing inaccuracies, 134–135, 137
   customer migration to, 134
   defective rates, 133
   digital, 128–129
   display reading, 130, 132
   elimination of meter readers by, 124
   one-way transmission, 128
   problems, 132–133
   rate issues, 137–138
   standards governing, 133–134
   two-way transmission, 128
Smart power strips, 154, 226
Smart water meters, 149
   rationale, 149

Sockets, 71–72
   office-based, 72–74
Solar-assisted heat pumps, 89–90
Solar calculator, 89
Solar hot water heaters, 102
Solar panels, 46, 47
   mating with heat pumps, 89–90
Solid-state electric meters, 133
Space heaters, operating cost
     considerations, 81–82
Split-system air conditioners, 104
Spreadsheet programs, 33
   using to calculate operating costs,
     176
Stackable LAN switches, 167
StackPower, 168–170
Standby generators, 76–78
Standby mode, placing computers
    in, 156–157
Steam heating, 97–98
Steam turbines, 42
Step-down transformers, 60
Still air insulation, 245
Substations, 59
Sump pumps, 227
Supplemental cooling, 171, 175–176
Switch-mode power supplies, 48, 49
Switched outlets, 154
Switches
   Cisco Catalyst 3750 series, 167
   electricity operating costs, 166
Synchronous dynamic random
     access memory (SDRAM),
     163
System cooling policy, 189, 190
System grounding, 55

T

Tablet computers, energy
    consumption, 157
Tank storage water heaters, 100–101
Tankless water heaters, 101–102

Televisions, power loads, 153
Telework, energy efficiency benefits,
   219
Tesla, Nikola, 47, 63
Texas, smart meter implementation,
   120
Therm, 4
Thermal demand, 128
Thermal Design Power (TDP), 222
Thermal image sensors, 214
Thermal loss, 214. *See also* Energy
   loss detection
Thermal resistance, 246
Third-party management systems,
   170
Three finger salute, 218
Three-phase AC, 62–64, 63
   advantages, 69
   circuit breakers for, 66
   electric meters using, 120
Three-prong sockets, 72
Tiered cost structure, 146
Time delay fuses, 65
Time-of-service rate schedules,
    PG&E, 135
Time-of-use service, PG&E time
    periods, 136
Time sharing, 219
Time value of money, 1, 14, 222
   future value basics, 14–16
Transfer switch failure, 77–78
Transformers, 46, 57–60
   enclosure for underground power
     lines, 62
   energy consumption, 158–159
   schematic diagram, 58
   service methods, 60, 62
   types of, 60
   utility pole-mounted, 61
   wiring, 60
Transients, preventing in electronic
    equipment, 55
Travel adapters, 72

Turbine generators, 42
Turbines, 42, 57
Two-pin electrical plugs and sockets, 71
Two-pipe hot water radiator systems, 98
Two-way communication
    natural gas meters, 140
    via smart meters, 129

U

Underground power lines, 60, 64
    transformer housing for, 62
Underwriter's Laboratories (UL), 97
Uninterruptible power supply
        (UPS), 39, 74–76
    battery changes, 76
    schematic diagram, 75
    with standby generator, 76
Units of power, 2–3
    BTU contents, 5
Unity, PF of, 53
Universal chargers, 155
Unplugging devices, rarely used, 155
USB cables, lack of standardization, 155
USB ports
    cell phone charging via, 155
    sleep mode settings, 188
Utility savings, as future cash flows, 27

V

Vampire load, xv, 48, 152, 226
Variable rates, 120
Variable-speed fans, 171
Ventilation, in climate control
        systems, 81–82
Vertical closed-loop geothermal
        systems, 94

Virtualization, for energy efficiency, 217–219
VMware Orchestrator, 170
Volt (V), 39
Voltage, 42
Voltmeter, 51
Volts alternating current (VAC), 48

W

Waiting area displays, 215–216
Wake-on-LAN, 207
    capabilities, 208
    enabling in Windows, 207–208
    lack of delivery confirmation, 210
    limitations, 209
    Magic Packet, 208–209
    security issues, 210
    selecting capability values, 209
    specific computer linkage
        limitations, 210–211
    wireless network limitations, 209–210
Wake-up passwords, 187
Wall sockets, 72
Wasted current, 53
Water-based geothermal systems, 94–95
Water bills, 145–147
    abnormalities, 147–149
    base fees, 147
    considering in budgeting, 147
    data center extract, 148
    leaks affecting, 149
    pricing complexity, 146
    rate structure abnormalities, 147
    seasonal variances, 147
    tiered cost structure, 146
    variances, 145
Water closets
    age of, 148
    upgrading for water efficiency, 232

Water filters, installing in radiant
    heating systems, 85
Water heater settings, 231
Water meters, 119, 143
    bill abnormalities, 147–149
    dials, 143
    locating, 143, 145
    Neptune brand example, 144
    reading and understanding, 119
    smart, 149
    water bills and, 145–147
Water-powered turbines, 42
Water sensor switch, 104
Water-side economizers, 113
Water usage, 231–232
Watt (W), 39
    light output *vs.* electrical power
        measurements, 233
    as measurement tool, 233–234
    vs. lumens, 233
Watt dissipation, 235–236
Watt-hours (Wh), 45
    common multiples, 3
Watt second (Ws), 123
Watts (W), 2
    horsepower conversion to, 4
Weather-stripping, 229–230
Weatherhead, 64
Weighted average cost of capital
        (WACC), 27–30
    equation, 29
    as minimum return, 30
White elastomeric coatings, 247
Windows 7
    default power plan settings, 184
    editing power plans in, 183–185

enabling Wake-on-LAN in,
    207–208
energy costs through upgrading,
    216
screen saver settings dialog box,
    183
Windows 7 control panel, 181
Windows Resource Manager, 218
Windows Server 2000 R2, 216
Windows Task Manager, 218
Wire color-coding, 63
Wireless adapters, sleep mode, 188
Wireless humidity/temperature
        transmitters, 224–226
Wireless networks, Wake-on-LAN
        limitations, 209–210
Wireless transmission, 137, 149
    of meter readings, 129
    with natural gas meters, 140
Wiring systems, pin counts and
        applications, 73
Wye (Y) configuration, 63

X

Xeon multicore products, 162–163

Y

Yahoo!, eco-friendly data center,
    113

Z

ZigBee, 129
Zonal heaters, 96